Charlotte
Perkins
Gilman·

Nonfic
Reade

Charlotte Perkins Gilman: A Nonfiction Reader

. . . . .

Edited by

Larry Ceplair

Columbia University Press

New York

Columbia University Press
New York   Oxford
Copyright © 1991 Columbia University Press
All rights reserved

Library of Congress Cataloging-in-Publication Data

Gilman, Charlotte Perkins, 1860–1935.
  Charlotte Perkins Gilman : a nonfiction reader / edited by
Larry Ceplair.
    p.   cm.
  Includes bibliographical references and index.
  ISBN 0-231-07616-9 (CL.).—ISBN 0-231-07617-7 (PA)
  1. Gilman, Charlotte Perkins, 1860–1935.   2. Feminists—United
States—Biography.   I. Ceplair, Larry.   II. Title.
HQ1413.G54A3   1991
305.42'092—dc20
[B]   91-13669
                                                          CIP

c 10 9 8 7 6 5 4 3 2 1

p 10 9 8 7 6 5 4 3 2

To Steven Englund,
for *agape, amor intellectualis,*
and *ma prose.*

Contents

Preface

THIRTY-FIVE years ago, Professor Carl N. Degler wrote that Charlotte Perkins Gilman (1860-1935) had "suffered a neglect in American intellectual history difficult to explain."[1] Although women's historians have long since awarded Gilman her rightful place as one of the most significant feminist thinkers and writers of the early part of this century, she still has not been accorded the more universal consideration Degler rightfully judged she merited.

Nor has she been adequately rooted in her intellectual milieu. Arguably one of the most radical, and certainly one of the most original, thinkers of her era, she is missing from virtually every general intellectual history.

And yet she was the first social thinker who tried to understand social conditions and social consciousness from the perspective of human evolution, economic change, and women's conditions. Whatever else may seem dated in the framework of analysis she crafted, the bedrock of gender consciousness remains uneroded, informing her perspective on a vast range of topics.

Positive Darwinism, the social gospel, social welfare, feminism (including its purity, temperance, and suffrage streams), socialism (Bellamy Nationalism and Fabianism), populism, progressivism, all these and more merged in her. There is no other corpus of fin-de-siècle theorizing in the United States in which so many concepts intertwine. And no other body of feminist thinking had the broad theoretical base or the wide aim of Charlotte's: to demonstrate, in the face of the scientific consensus, that women were fully human and capable beings, meriting full independence and equal treatment. To an even more strongly entrenched public opinion, Charlotte insisted that sexual disfunctions blocked political, social, and economic progress.

Though her stream of thought was fed by the main intellectual (mostly male) currents of the late-nineteenth century, she was an original radical feminist thinker, using her own experience and thought processes to mark the course of her ideas. But her gender consciousness did not lead her to value women's perceptions over men's or to follow closely the studies in gender that began to flow from women graduate students at the beginning of the twentieth century.

Charlotte spoke and wrote widely about her social philosophy, but most students only know her through her fiction, as the author of "The Yellow Wallpaper" and *Herland*. Some may know her through her most important nonfiction book, *Women and Economics*, or her autobiography (*The Living of Charlotte Perkins Gilman*). But those are a mere sampling of her intellectual labors. She published five other full-length nonfiction books and hundreds of articles for numerous magazines and newspapers, composed hundreds of lectures, and, for seven years, wrote every article for a magazine she edited and published, *The Forerunner*.

In terms of the central themes advanced—that the complete liberation of women was the *sine qua non* of the complete liberation of humanity—there is no divide between Charlotte's nonfiction and fiction. However, and this is the reason for this book, almost all of her currently in-print work is her fiction, and there existed no convenient mode to introduce students and scholars to the breadth of her nonfiction.

The range of her interests made her nonfiction difficult to categorize. In terms of what she was trying to do—explain human behavior—there are no logical breakpoints. Years might pass between her introduction to a topic and her development of it. She wrote so much on so many different topics that occasionally the corpus of her work seems diffuse and eclectic. Nevertheless, the leitmotifs of evolution, gender, social consciousness, and human freedom thread through all her work, and though she did not believe she had woven them all together into a satisfactory synthesis, these threads, like Ariadne's, lead the editor and reader to an understanding of her purpose. Therefore, after attempting various types of organization, I decided that a chronological approach offered the clearest perspective.

Within that chronology, some general trends are evident: her early articles and lectures concerned women breaking free from the binds of the traditional home and the bonds of cultural conventions; her first four books deepened her critical examination of the institutions and traditions confining humans; and in the *The Forerunner* she explored the relationship between social consciousness, human culture, and social change.

I have not attempted to represent every topic of her nonfiction writing; rather I have selected material that demonstrates the development of key themes and concepts and omitted work that is simply interesting or evocative.

Finally, although I usually avoid using first names to refer to historical subjects, believing that it implies a false intimacy or familiarity, it seemed to me to be the least awkward and artificial means of dealing with a subject known by three names—Charlotte Anna Perkins, Charlotte Perkins Stetson, and Charlotte Perkins Gilman. Again to avoid confusion, I refer to her first husband, Charles Walter Stetson, as Walter, her second husband, George Houghton Gilman, as Houghton, and her close friend, Grace Ellery Channing Stetson, as Grace.

I owe a large debt of gratitude to Kate Wittenberg, my editor at Columbia University Press. The exceptionally helpful and congenial people at the Arthur and Elizabeth Schlesinger Library on the History of Women in America, located at Radcliffe College, made it a wonderful place to work. I am also grateful to the director for permission to reprint material from the collection.

The Huntington Library in San Marino, California, also provided an amenable workplace and permission to quote from several documents.

I received encouragement and assistance from Walter Chamberlin, Charlotte's grandson, and help in tracking down annotations from Tom Andrews (History Society of Southern California), Caroline Strickler (*Los Angeles Times* History Center), Virginia L. Haycock (Montclair Historical Society), Maureen Taylor (The Rhode Island Historical Society), Wilma R. Slaight (Margaret Clapp Library, Wellesley College), Sally Colby (California History Center, Rosemead branch of the Los Angeles County Library), and the research librarians at the University Research Library (U.C.L.A.).

Charlotte
Perkins
Gilman:
A
Nonfiction
Reader

Introduction

SEISMIC demographic and economic forces shook the post-Civil War decades, fracturing traditions, customs, and confidence. The war and Reconstruction disrupted the work and outlook of many reform movements, and new ideas, particularly those associated with the writings of Charles Darwin (1809–1882), upset many of the ideologies, philosophies, and perspectives of reformist thinkers.

Most postbellum reformers agreed on the need to break through the impersonality of the new, huge corporations and municipalities, to design buffers between large enterprises and individuals, to redefine individualism into individual responsibility for community improvement, and most accepted the notion that Darwin's theory of evolution carried a message of progress. They believed in the perfectibility of human society and the transformative power of the well-directed individual will.

As prewar reform leaders and the younger generation of postwar activists regenerated and reshaped the movement to meet the recent developments, sexual issues divided and racial attitudes tainted fin-de-siècle reformism. But whereas racial elitism pervaded the ranks of reform organizations, and most reformers proved insensitive to racial and ethnic issues, sexual elitism did not go unchallenged. A small group of female and male feminists viewed sexual oppression as one of the major social evils and believed that if the barriers separating sexual roles could be toppled women would be freed from their isolation to intro-

duce new and needed values that would blunt the male interests—
aggression and competition—destroying their communities. Calling for
cooperation and harmony, they tried to humanize all aspects of life
within the community and the community itself.[1]

Among those who spoke and wrote for female liberation, Charlotte
Perkins Gilman was acknowledged, for two decades (1896–1916), as the
most influential spokesperson for human freedom and perfection through
the liberation of women.

Charlotte Perkins Gilman

As Her Contemporaries Saw Her

Carrie Chapman Catt (1859–1947), who presided over the National
American Woman Suffrage Association from 1900–1904 and 1916–1920,
and who was one of its strongest personalities and successful organizers,
ranked Charlotte first on her list of the twelve greatest American
women, "because there was a period in the woman's movement when
she brought out first one book and then another . . . which were
scientifically done and widely read by all classes of people. And I credit
those books with utterly revolutionizing the attitude of mind in the
entire country, indeed of other countries, as to woman's place."[2] The
longtime editor of Woman's Journal, Alice Stone Blackwell (1857–1950),
called her "one of the great sources of mental stimulus and ethical
inspiration."[3] Amy Wellington (1873?-1948), who devoted a chapter of
her book on "the feminist tradition" to Gilman, called her "one of our
few creative thinkers, with an extraordinary power of social analysis."[4]
Edith Houghton Hooker (1878–1948), national chairperson of the National Woman's Party and editor of its journal, Equal Rights, claimed that
Gilman "probably made more Feminists among the generation now
around 40 years old [born in 1895] than any other person," and extolled
"the clarity and keenness of her vision."[5] And the writer Rebecca West
(1892–1983) said, in 1924, that Charlotte was "the greatest woman in
the world today."[6]

Men were equally complimentary. The sociologist Edward A. Ross
(1866–1951) wrote: "She was the most brilliant woman I have known."[7]

The editor of *The Land of Sunshine,* Charles F. Lummis (1859–1928), wrote to her: "You are as straight as a bullet and as logical. . . . [Y]ou are enough to wake up anybody's mind. I am glad that there are not any other women like you. But I am also glad that there is one."[8] William Dean Howells (1837–1920) and Floyd Dell (1887–1969) hailed the brilliance of her satirical verse, and the Socialist writer, Upton Sinclair (1878–1968), called her "America's most brilliant woman poet and critic."[9] And the feminist playwright George Middleton (1880–1967) thought that she was "one of the brainiest and most stimulating of nationally known leaders."[10]

Her friends particularly admired her strength of will. Harriet Howe (1865?-1948), who met her shortly after she had moved to Pasadena and then boarded with her in Oakland, worshipped Gilman's intellectual courage and clarity: "Nothing daunted her, nothing could daunt her."[11] Alexander Black (1859–1940), a writer and close friend during the twenties, described her as "an incorrigible current. Her tide seems to have no ebb. She is the poorest compromiser I know. She is never pugnacious. No one could have less interest in conflict for its own sake. . . . She wanted to move as she thought—straight through."[12] And Zona Gale (1874–1938), in her foreword to Gilman's autobiography, agreed that she could be "direct, abrupt, blunt, devastating, as the need arises, and oblivious." Gale also marveled at her mental energy, which she described as "super-natural."[13]

As Historians See Her

Between her death, in 1935, and the mid-1950s, Charlotte Perkins Gilman's name and reputation virtually disappeared. Carl N. Degler, in his 1956 article recalling her to the attention of the scholarly world, credited her with writing "truly thought-provoking analyses of woman's position in a man's world—in remarkable anticipation of modern writers on the subject."[14]

Scholars, however, responded slowly. Eleanor Flexner, in her history of the woman's movement (1959), barely mentioned Charlotte, simply noting that she was one of several well-known public figures associated with the suffrage movement and "one of the most widely-read women of her day."[15]

William T. Doyle, in the first extensive treatment of her—his 1960 doctoral dissertation—acknowledged her influence, but did not provide an in-depth analysis of her writing and portrayed her as a frustrated woman and mother, completely dependent on others for her ideas.[16]

Although she continued to receive approving mention, and portions of her work appeared in anthologies,[17] it required the growth of the women's movement and feminist scholarship, the sale of her papers to the Arthur and Elizabeth Schlesinger Library on the History of Women in America (in 1971), and reprints of her major work, to open the path to more profound and sensitive treatments of her.[18]

Though Patricia Meyer Spacks and Carol Ruth Berkin offered interesting psychological sketches,[19] the first full-scale, archival-based study, by Mary A. Hill, did not appear until 1980. The first volume of her projected two-volume study carried Charlotte's life to 1896, and her article provided a critical overview of her feminism. Hill's analyses are detailed and thoughtful, though she chose not to use psychological categories.[20]

Ann J. Lane, meanwhile, had edited the reprint of Charlotte's important utopian novel, *Herland,* and a select anthology of her other fiction.[21] Lane's one-volume comprehensive biography, published in 1990, focused on the personal elements and relations, providing plausible analyses of Charlotte's personal life and artistic and intellectual work.[22]

Perhaps the single most indispensable contribution to the study of Charlotte Perkins Gilman was Gary Scharnhorst's bibliography, published in 1985, along with a book analyzing her written work and an article detailing her California years.[23]

More specialized approaches to Charlotte's work began to appear at the end of the 1980s, focusing on her urban and home design work.[24]

In sum, though Charlotte is receiving her due from women's studies, the broader fields of cultural and intellectual history have still failed to alter their categories and concepts to include the thinking of Charlotte and the dozens of other worthy pre-World War I women social theorists.

As I See Her: An Overview

The most convenient approach to an understanding of Charlotte Perkins Stetson Gilman begins with her autobiography, *The Living of Charlotte Perkins Gilman*. It stands in stark contrast to her other writing: desultory and superficial, rather than energetic and incisive. Much of it is dreary travelogue, and it only becomes compelling when she describes her nervous breakdown. She makes little effort to bring to life the people who deeply affected her; they are shadowy figures, for the most part. The man she loved best, to whom she would address thousands of pages of letters, with whom she would live for over thirty years—her second husband, George Houghton Gilman (1867–1934)—has only the vaguest outline. Part of the problem may be that she regarded writing the autobiography as a chore, a poor substitute for the ideas that were no longer in demand. She wrote Edward A. Ross, on July 6, 1925: "I have started in a feeble way on my Autobiography, but it does not interest me as much as it ought to. My real interest is in ideas." [25]

She did not use the autobiography as a vehicle to examine her ideas or herself. She basically recounts the details of her life, presenting herself as a sufferer from the effects of "nerve bankruptcy," leading "a crippled life," a "life of limitation and wretchedness," and possessing a "weakness of mind," "a mind like a piece of boiled spinach." [26] Relentlessly, she blames herself for this "weakness," finding no fault with her environment, her parents, or her first husband.

And yet, this "weakened" person lectured and wrote prodigiously, by splitting, in her mind, her emotional needs and career desires and enforcing the separation by strength of will. To Charlotte, mind power meant force of will and self-control—the ability to renounce emotional needs, such as intimacy and dependency, no matter how avidly one desired them. As she would write Houghton:

> You see all my life I haven't had what I wanted in the way of being loved. . . .
>
> The whole way is lined with—not all gravestones, but some and some kind of trap-door stones that keep things down. When the will-strength, or brain-strength, or whatever it is that keeps me happy and steady and brave, gives out, up hop all these buried things, dead and alive.

I want every thing I haven't had—all at once.

I have never had—save in the one girl friend [Martha (Luther) Lane (b. 1862)]—a satisfied love.

The others have all gone wrong somehow—like a stopped sneeze!

It is not clear grief—one of the easiest things to bear—but a choked, thwarted, fiercely unreconciled feeling —an accumulated revolt—both mental and physical. And they all pile up together—I want them all— from Child to Mother —Sister—Brother—Father—Lover—Husband —Friend.[27]

When this "accumulated revolt" broke out, leading her to "grab" someone or something, she became "unsteady," and "with a morbid sensitiveness, and an intermittent consciousness" of what the other person must be thinking, attempted "to break out."[28] Thus, to maintain her equilibrium, she could "not afford to be fond of anybody," "to want things."[29]

During the periods when her mind power was strong, she found that lecturing was "a perfectly natural expression of as natural clear thinking," and "writing similarly is easy and swift expression."[30] But, inevitably, not feeling well meant not writing well. "Feeling well I write —write easily, swiftly, clearly, forcibly, interestingly. Presently I don't feel so well. Never mind, say I, work you must! And I continue to write —with conscious effort and cumulative exhaustion. And then the stuff written is not good! That's the finality of it. It's not good and I can't make it good. . . . So I have learned to drift—to wait—not to waste energy and delay improvement by trying when I can't."[31]

Even at "full strength," she could write only three hours a day and read three hours a day. She estimated that the permanent "weakness" engendered by her breakdown cost her "twenty-seven years, a little lifetime in itself. . . . Twenty-seven adult years, in which with my original strength of mind, the output of work could have been almost trebled. Moreover, this lifetime lost has not been spent in resting. It was always a time of extreme distress, shame, discouragement, misery."[32]

She wrote quickly and did not rewrite or revise extensively. She did not read widely or deeply in the fields that most interested her, and, though she kept abreast of some developments in the natural and social sciences, she did not study them in depth and did not necessarily alter her thinking to fit new empirical evidence. Certain ideas and insights, once gained, stuck, and there is a scatter-shot quality to her reading. Finally, she did not achieve the synthesis she sought nor a praxis, combining theory and activity.

And yet, her will, her faith in its power, and the quality of her intellect enabled her to pass through her episodic psychic deserts, gain success as a lecturer and writer, support herself, her daughter (for five years), and her dying mother, resolve her ambivalence about a permanent love relationship with a man by happily remarrying in 1900, and end her own life.

Not so admirable, however, is her racism. Partly she reflected the era in which she lived: the fin-de-siècle period was deeply stained by its lack of concern for the often violent circumstances faced by people of color in the United States—blacks, Native Americans, Latinos, and Asians—and the stark condescension visited on immigrants from eastern and southern Europe. But part of her racism was a self-conscious accretion. She admits in her autobiography that living in New York City, alongside various ethnic groups, convinced her of their inferiority and the threat they posed to her vision of human progress. She also allowed herself to develop a conspicuous hostility toward the Germans during World War I.

Though she was not a conscious or virulent "racist"—Edward A. Ross, for example, was far more strident and blatant than she in this regard[33]—the epithets she casually used in her articles and the attitudes informing her 1908 article on blacks cannot be explained away or rationalized. Nor can her failure to address any of the issues pertinent to the economic and social conditions of black women, or the racial policies of the largest women's organizations—the Women's Christian Temperance Union, the General Federation of Women's Clubs, and the National American Woman Suffrage Association.

As She Saw Herself

"I have nothing to offer the world but what I *think*—not what I have read," she wrote Houghton.[34] "I think that the thing I am here to do is a big thing—the truth. I see deep basic truths; and that I have been given unusual powers of expression. I truly hope that my life will count for much good to the world." [35] "I am not a poet," she wrote Caroline Hill (1866–1951), editor of *The World's Great Religious Poetry* (1923), "I'm only a preacher, whether on the platform or in print." [36]

Mainly, she preached to and about women. "I know women best, and care more for them. I have an intense and endless love for women —partly in reverence for their high estate, partly in pity for their blind feebleness, their long ages of suffering." [37] But, she unequivocally told her close friend, Grace Channing Stetson (1862–1937), near the end of her life, "I abominate being called a feminist." [38] She preferred to be thought of as a humanist, and she saw herself as a "transition woman," who had met her share of difficulties. "A few generations more and it will be easier. And I know I've helped a little. Every little counts." [39]

Chapter One
. . . . .
The Early Years,
1860–1889

CHARLOTTE ANNA PERKINS was the youngest child and only daughter of the marriage of Frederick B. Perkins* (1828–1899) and Mary Ann Fitch Westcott (1829–1893). They had married in 1857, conceived three children in three years (a Thomas, who died within one month, another Thomas, 1859–1938, and Charlotte, born July 3, 1860), conceived another girl, who lived only eight months in 1866, permanently separated in 1869, and divorced in 1873.

Charlotte associated her father's departure with frustrated sex: "The doctor said that if my mother had another baby she would die. Presently my father left home. Whether the doctor's dictum was the reason or merely a reason I do not know. What I do know is that my childhood had no father."[1]

From the evidence, Frederick Perkins was a dilettante, a scholar manqué, charming but rootless. He attended Yale College but was never graduated, studied law but never practiced, was graduated from Connecticut Normal School (1852), and spent the rest of his life as an editor, librarian, and writer. He was a genteel reformer, believing in the restoration of the pre-industrial family and a family-centered nation. He sympathized with the poor but was opposed to organized forms of

---

* Frederick was the grandson of Lyman Beecher (1775–1863), an influential religious reformer in the early decades of the nineteenth century. Three of Beecher's daughters, Catharine (1800–1878), Harriet (1811–1896), and Isabella (1822–1907), won renown as writers and reformers; Frederick was the son of the fourth daughter, Mary, and Thomas C. Perkins.

protests; he believed women should have interests outside the home before they married but when married should "find perfect gratification in their own homes, in their families."[2] He was not a source of love or affection for his children, but he was "a sender of books, catalogues of books, lists of books to read."[3]

He could not earn a sufficient income to support his family, frequently moving them from relatives' house to relatives' house, and increasingly absenting himself altogether. He moved to San Francisco, in 1880, to direct the public library there. On his death, Charlotte wrote her cousin and future husband, George Houghton Gilman: "What a sad dark life the poor man led." "So able a man—and so little to show for it. Poor father!"[4]

Mary Fitch Westcott had grown up in an undemanding and highly protected environment. Before she married Frederick, she had made and broken several engagements.[5] Now she was alone, with two children, no money, and no marketable skills. The material existence of the family and the psychological state of Mary Perkins were precarious. In one of the more poignant passages of her autobiography, Charlotte wrote:

> my mother's life was one of the most painfully thwarted I have ever known. After her idolized youth, she was left neglected. After her flood of lovers, she became a deserted wife. The most passionately domestic of home-worshipping housewives, she was forced to move nineteen times in eighteen years, fourteen of them from one city to another. After a long and thorough musical education, developing unusual talent, she sold her piano when I was two, to pay the butcher's bill, and never owned another. She hated debt, and debts accumulated about her, driving her to these everlasting moves. Absolutely loyal, as loving as a spaniel which no ill treatment can alienate, she made no complaint, but picked up her children and her dwindling furniture and traveled to the next place. She lived with her husband's parents, with her own parents, with his aunts, in various houses here and there when he so installed her, fleeing again on account of debt.[6]

From Charlotte's vantage point, these material strains produced a mother unable to express tenderness toward her daughter. As in most of her characterizations of those close to her, she strives to understand, to make allowances, but the reproof always shines through the covering fabric. "If unswerving love, tireless service, intense and efficient care, and the concentrated devotion of a lifetime that knew no other purpose make a good mother, mine was one of the best." But "she heroically determined that her baby daughter should not so suffer if she could help it. Her method was to deny the child all expression of affection as far as possible, so that she should not be used to it or long for it. . . . Mother loved us desperately, but her tireless devotion was not the same thing as petting, her caresses were not given unless we were asleep, or she thought us so." [7]

Since Charlotte and her brother did not develop a warm and loving relationship either, she sought solace within herself, imagining the happiness and affection lacking in her actual existence and writing, when she was ten or eleven, a series of fairy stories.[8] But her mother, discovering this world, ordered her "to give it up," and Charlotte obeyed.[9] The world of imaginative recreation was replaced by a rigorous regime of self-perfection. Poetry was the only concession, and Charlotte "learned it by heart, miles of it, from early childhood." [10]

To cope with this emotional uncertainty, Charlotte sought order and method and became a passionate devotee of what she called "physical culture" (exercise) and "Natural Philosophy" (physics). The former offered a daily regime and the latter "Law, at last; not authority, not records of questionable truth or solemn tradition, but laws that could be counted on and *Proved*. That was my delight, to know surely." [11] When she entered the Rhode Island School of Design, in October 1878, she wrote in her diary: "This school teaches me just what I need: some system, some method beyond my eye." [12]

When she was fifteen, her mother slapped her for refusing an order, and Charlotte made a crucial discovery: "She might do what she would, it could not alter my decision. I was realizing with an immense illumination that neither she, nor anyone, could *make* me do anything. One could suffer, one could die if it came to that, but one could not be coerced. I was born." [13] She would obey her mother until she was twenty-one, "and then stop." Meanwhile, Charlotte would mark "out a line of work . . . to help humanity." [14] To prepare herself, she asked her father for a reading list weighted with accounts of human and historical development. He recommended: William Boyd Dawkins, *Cave Hunting* . . . (1874); James Fergusson, *Rude Stone Monuments in All Countries* . . . (1872); William E. H. Lecky, *History of European Morals: From Augustus to*

Charlemagne (1859); John Lubbock, *Prehistoric Times as Illustrated by Ancient Remains . . .* (1865) and *The Origin of Civilisation and the Primitive Condition of Man* (1870); George Rawlinson, *The Five Great Monarchies of the Ancient Eastern World* (1862–1867), *The Sixth Great Oriental Monarchy* (1872), and *The Seventh Great Oriental Monarchy* (1875); Edward Tylor, *Researches into the Early History of Mankind and the Development of Civilisation* (1865) and *Primitive Culture . . .* (1871); Andrew White, *The Warfare of Science* (1876); and *Popular Science Monthly*.

She began to "read connectedly, learning the things I most wanted to know, in due order and sequence, none of them exhaustively but all in due relation . . . . Humanity was always the main interest, the sciences held useful as they showed our origin, our lines of development, the hope and method of further progress."[15] She also joined "The Society for the Encouragement of Studies at Home," taking courses in Ancient History (focusing mainly on the Hebrews and Egyptians). From these studies, she derived "a clear, connected general outline of the story of life on earth, and of our own nature and progress."[16]

She also began to examine the nature and necessity of religion, perceiving both the errors of received religion and the brain's need "for a basic theory of life, for a conscious and repeated connection with the Central Power, and for 'sailing orders,' a recognized scale of duties. I perceived that in human character there must be 'principles,' something to be depended on when immediate conditions did not tend to produce right conduct." She decided to construct her own religion, "based on knowledge." "God was Real," she concluded, "under and in and around everything, lifting, lifting. We, conscious of that limitless power, were to find our places, our special work in the world, and when found, do it at all costs."[17]

She became as well a devotee of physical fitness. Her "bible" was William Blaikie's *How to Get Strong and How to Stay So* (1879), in which the author prescribed exercise as a solemn, determined, and regular activity, designed to overcome general physical weakness.

Although she claimed her mother limited the invitations she could accept, Charlotte became friends with the children, and regularly visited the homes, of some of the most intellectually stimulating families in the area, including those of Eli Whitney Blake (1795–1886, professor of physics at Brown), Jeremiah Lewis Diman (1831–1881, professor of history at Brown), William F. Channing (1820–1901, scientist and inventor), Rowland Hazard (1801–1888, scientist and writer), Edward Everett Hale,* and her Stowe cousins, the daughters of Harriet Beecher and Calvin.[18]

She found among these families what she called "a larger outlook," "broad free-thinking, scientific talk, earnest promotion of great causes —life." She began to reflect on the world around her and discovered that it "seemed to be suffering from many needless evils, evils for which some remedies seemed clear to me even then. I was deeply impressed with the injustices under which women suffered, and still more with the ill effects upon all mankind of this injustice." But she was not in close touch with the suffrage movement and rejected the temperance movement, because she "was not at all at home in that atmosphere of orthodox religion and strong emotion."[19] She subscribed to *The Advocate & Family Guardian,* a moral reform journal, but did not "admire it much."[20]

Her diary entries reflect a person in perpetual motion, constantly lamenting her "laziness," and obsessed with will power and self-control. In March 1879, following a month of nursing both her mother and Thomas, she wrote: "must really abolish all desire for comfort or any sort of happiness if I expect to have any peace."[21]

When she achieved her majority, she felt a "triumphant sense of freedom and power"; she was her "own mistress at last" and "looked ahead to a steady lifetime of social study and service, with no reward whatever, on the theory that one should face life giving all and asking nothing."[22] She was feeling economically self-sufficient, tutoring, teaching, and serving as a governess for ten weeks.

That year she also experienced her first intense emotional connection—with a female friend, Martha Luther. Charlotte and Martha had been friends for several years, but in the spring of 1881, they entered what Charlotte called a "compact of mutual understanding," "to be utterly frank with each in word and deed, never to pretend anything

---

* Edward Everett Hale (1822–1909) was her uncle; he had married Emily Perkins, Frederick's sister. A Unitarian minister and prolific and popular writer and speaker, he harbored a strong cooperative vision, wrote two utopian novels, and helped found the Nationalist movement and the Cooperative Union of America.

we did not fully feel. . . . This was my first deep personal happiness."[23]
When Martha left Providence for the summer holidays, Charlotte wrote
her virtually daily. In a letter of July 24, Charlotte wrote:

> I am really getting glad not to marry. For the mother side of me is strong
> enough to make an interminable war between plain duties and inexpres-
> sible instincts, I should rage as I do now at confinement and steady work,
> and spend all my force in pushing two ways without getting anywhere.
> . . . Whereas if I let that business alone, and go on in my own way; what
> I gain in individual strength and development of personal power of
> character, *myself as self,* you know, not merely as a woman, or that useful
> animal a wife and mother, will I think make up, and more than make up
> in usefulness and effect, for the other happiness that part of me would so
> enjoy.[24]

Part of the reason Charlotte felt capable of relinquishing intimacy
with men was her love for Martha, a love she openly expressed on
August 15:

> I think it highly probable (ahem!) that you love me however I squirm,
> love the steady care around which I so variously revolve, love me and will
> love me—why in the name of heaven have we so confounded love with
> passion that it sounds to our century-tutored ears either wicked or absurd
> to name it between women? It is no longer friendship between us, it is
> love.[25]

But that autumn, Martha became engaged to Charles A. Lane, and
in her diary entry of December 31, Charlotte wrote: "A year in which I
knew the sweetness of perfect friendship and have lost it forever."[26]
Reflecting, in her autobiography, Charlotte wrote: "This was love, but
not sex. . . . With Martha I knew perfect happiness. . . . Four years of
satisfying happiness with Martha, then she married and moved away.
. . . [A]nd I had no one else."[27]*

She resolved to bury her pain in work. On the leaf of her diary for
1882, she wrote: "My watchword at 21—1882 WORK! *Once and for all;*

---

* The friendship endured, and whenever Charlotte was in New England, she would visit the
Lanes at Hingham, Massachusetts. In 1890, following her separation from her first husband,
Charlotte would write Martha: "But this I will say of my love for you. Through the first year
or two of my marriage, in every depth of pain and loss and loneliness, *yours* was the name my
heart cried—not his. I loved you better than any one, in those days when I had a heart to love
and ache." Mary A. Hill, *Charlotte Perkins Gilman: The Making of a Radical Feminist, 1860–1896*
(Philadelphia: Temple University Press, 1980), p. 161.

to Love and personal happiness—so called—NO!"[28] But a few days after writing that she met Charles Walter Stetson, and a tormented courtship and marriage followed.

Charles Walter Stetson (1858–1911) was born in Tiverton Four Corners, Rhode Island. His family moved to Providence in 1869, and Stetson decided, when he was eighteen, to be a painter, and began to pursue it earnestly in 1878. Self-taught, he struggled for many years to sell enough paintings to support himself and his families. He emphasized mood and personal feeling, typifying the subjectivist mode of late-nineteenth-century United States painting. He would enjoy a short spurt of posthumous fame, but then disappear in the rush toward modernism.[29]

"He was," wrote Charlotte, "quite the greatest man, near my own age, that I had ever known. . . . In courage, in aspiration, in ideals, in bitter loneliness, we were enough alike to be drawn together." He asked her to marry him; she declined, reconsidered, and told him that "if he so desired he might come to see me for a year and we would find out—which he was very willing to do." She found in his company "the pleasure of association with a noble soul, . . . the natural force of sex-attraction between two lonely young people, . . . [and] on my part, periods of bitter revulsion, of desperate efforts to regain the dispassionate poise, the balanced judgment I was used to." The question of marriage threatened the divide she had established between work and love. "On the one hand I knew it was normal and right in general, and held that a woman should be able to have marriage and motherhood, and do her work in the world also. On the other, I felt strongly that for me it was not right, that the nature of the life before me forbade it, that I ought to forego the more intimate personal happiness for complete devotion to my work."[30]

Perhaps had Charlotte known precisely what her "work" was, she would have stood on firmer ground and been more capable of balancing her wants and her needs. But she did not have "work," she had activities and a vague purpose; she lived at home; she had just suffered the "loss" of Martha; and she felt a strong physical attraction to the very handsome Walter. She began to suffer descents into black, depressive moods.

He was obsessed with her. He wrote, in his first diary entry devoted to her: "She is an original: eccentric because unconventional, and well versed in almost everything, I guess! She is an athlete—strong, vivacious, with plenty of bounding blood. She is an indefatigable worker." Twelve days, later, on January 26, he wrote: "She is a poetess: a philosopher, and no mean one, and more of a mystic than she guesses. A warm soft, sensuous nature, held in check and overcome by a strong will, a sound intellect & a good moral nature."[31]

But though he was attracted to her strength and intellect, and seemed to admire her independence and nonconformity of spirit, it is clear that he was a conventional man, harboring conventional ideals, and that he, at least in his diary, patronized her worldly ambition and agonized over it. Fourteen months after they had met, he wrote:

> She had one of those spasms of wanting to make a name for herself in the world by doing good work: wanting to have people know her as Charlotte Perkins, not as the wife of me. She drew back with her old time feeling of independence from the prospect of sinking herself in our community. . . .
>
> Every one knows that I believe in the utmost freedom for women but that freedom is false which makes them rebel against the ties of love and home. She thinks much of her irregularity comes from her father. It may be: but more comes from ill-digested reading of philosophical works mixed with her imagination & the tradition of what she *ought* to inherit from her parents.[32]

Despite her doubts and depressions, Charlotte kept busy in 1883, and began to write for publication, sending articles to the *Providence Journal* and poems to *The Century,* the *Christian Register, Alpha,* and *Woman's Journal.* Her first nonfiction article, "The Providence Ladies Gymnasium," appeared in the *Providence Journal* (May 23, 1883). But two months before the wedding, Charlotte wrote Grace Ellery Channing:*

> The whole thing [marriage] seems to me far different from what it is to most women. Instead of being a goal—a duty, a hope, a long-expected fate, a bewildering delight; it is a concession, a digression, a thing good and necessary perhaps, as matters stand, but still a means, not an end. I look through it, beyond it, over it. It is a happiness no doubt, a duty no

* Grace Ellery Channing, daughter of William F. Channing and granddaughter of the Unitarian minister and writer, William Ellery Channing (1780–1842), was a girlhood friend who had moved to Pasadena, California for health reasons. She too was a writer.

doubt; but a happiness to result in new strength for other things; a duty only one of others.

It fills my mind much; but plans for teaching and writing, for studying, *living* and helping, are more prominent and active.[33]

Charlotte and Walter married on May 2, 1884. In August she learned she was pregnant. Her diary records for these months indicates that she was feeling "numb—helpless," sick, and sad that Walter seemed to find her overly affectionate.[34]

Walter's diary indicates that except for a few days in September, he thought the marriage and pregnancy were doing well. On September 15, he wrote: "Truly, I think she is becoming better fitted for usefulness. She has learned some lessons of humility and self-sacrifice and patience."[35]

At the beginning of the new year, 1885, Charlotte noted that in the past year she had "done little, read little, written little, felt and thought ————————— little to what I should have. I am a happy wife. I bear a child. Ambition sleeps. I make no motion but just live."[36] She did, however, write her second published nonfiction article, "The Sin of Sickness" (*Buffalo Christian Advocate*, February 5, 1885).

On March 23, 1885, she gave birth to a daughter; they named her Katharine. But feelings of "nervous exhaustion" immediately descended upon her, and she became a "mental wreck." Her mother was summoned in early May, but Charlotte's misery continued to plummet: "Here was a charming home; a loving and devoted husband; an exquisite baby, healthy, intelligent and good; a highly competent mother to run things; a wholly satisfactory servant—and I lay all day on the lounge and cried."[37]

Chapter VIII of *The Living*, "The Breakdown," is a harrowing account of how she felt during those four years before she and Walter decided to separate. A key factor in her downward spiral was her relentless self-blame:

Prominent among the tumbling suggestions of a suffering brain was the thought, "You did it yourself! You did it yourself! You had health and strength and hope and glorious work before you—and you threw it all away. You were called to serve humanity, and you cannot serve yourself. No good as a wife, no good as a mother, no good at anything. And you did it yourself!"[38]

On August 5, 1885, she rallied slightly, hoping she could now "pick up the broken threads again and make out some kind of a career after all."[39] But Walter, feeling sorry that he had married, chafing at the burdens of housework, debt, and Charlotte's criticism of his efforts, erupted (in his diary) when she resumed her writing (her third nonfiction article, "On Advertising for Marriage," was published in *Alpha* on September 1) and told him of her plans to commence lecturing on human reform.

> My darling wife thinks now that she shall some day preach—sermons about health, morality and the like—from the pulpit on what you will. Ah well, my dearest love, if you have anything to say that will help us, and real solution to offer for moral problems and the destruction of moral miasma, for God's sake preach! And may you have power beyond all the preachers of all time! Leave me—Leave mother—Leave child —leave all and preach! We need some one to tell us what of all these "truths" *is* truth. Go. God help you![40]

They began to quarrel heatedly and regularly. In early October, Grace invited Charlotte to come to Pasadena, and it was decided that she would leave Providence for an indefinite stay in the West, visiting her brother in Ogden, Utah and her father in San Francisco. She left on October 22. She felt better immediately and remained in the West until the end of March 1886. Just before returning, she wrote Martha: "I look forward with both joy and dread [to going home]. Joy to see my darlings again, and dread of further illness under family cares."[41]

Within one week of her return, she descended into a long, deep, tearful melancholy.[42] During the summer she again rallied and recommenced writing, painting and drawing, and exercising at a gymnasium. One of the poems, "The Answer," appeared in the *Woman's Journal*. It was a sarcastic assessment of marriage.[43]

The *Journal*'s editor, Alice Stone Blackwell, encouraged Charlotte, awarding her a prize for "The Answer," giving her a year's free subscription to the newspaper, and accepting an article, "Why Women Do Not Reform Their Dress."[44] In early October, Charlotte attended the American Woman Suffrage Association's* convention.

---

* Elizabeth Cady Stanton 1815–1902) and Susan B. Anthony (1820–1906) founded the National Woman Suffrage Association in May 1869. Six months later, Lucy Stone (1818–1893) and her husband Henry Blackwell (1825–1909) founded the American Woman Suffrage Association, an

She began the new year, 1886, with a new library card and a new reading program—women. She checked out several books, among them Margaret Fuller's *Woman in the Nineteenth Century* (1845), Julia Kavanagh's, *Woman in France During the Eighteenth Century* (1850), and Madame [Jenny P.] D'Hericourt's *A Woman's Philosophy of Woman* (translated from the French in 1864). She wrote poems, began an article on the destruction of the sexes, and sent two letters to the *Woman's Journal:* the first, "A Protest Against Petticoats," contained the nucleus of her lifelong philosophy—"as long as half a race is imperfect, the other half must remain so"; the second, "Pungent Paragraphs," commented sarcastically on men's reactions to women's complaints about their conditions.[45] She wrote six articles for the *People,* a weekly Providence newspaper sponsored by the Rhode Island Knights of Labor,* discussing women caught between families and careers and the need for women to have work as well as love. She did not, however, participate in the campaign for a statewide referendum on votes for women, scheduled for April 6. "[F]orty women are ready to go to the polls Wed. to distribute ballots and influence voters. I don't see my way clear to do that," she wrote in her diary.[46] (The referendum was defeated.)

She collapsed utterly in April 1886, moved into her mother's house, and then, with the financial assistance of friends, went to Philadelphia to be treated by Dr. S. Weir Mitchell.† Mitchell told Charlotte that she suffered from hysteria, not dementia. He prescribed his "rest cure" while she was in Philadelphia, and a life of enforced passivity when she

---

organization more conservative in tone and method. The two groups merged in February 1890. Among Charlotte's three reformer great aunts, Catharine never seriously supported suffrage; Harriet Beecher Stowe did, but in a qualified manner; while Isabella Beecher Hooker, staunchly supported the NWSA.

* The Noble and Holy Order of the Knights of Labor was founded, as a secret fraternal order, in Philadelphia, in 1869. Ten years later it became an open organization, aggressively organizing all who "toiled," including women and blacks. Advocating a broad program of immediate and utopian reforms, it reached its peak membership in 1885 (over 700,000). By the early 1890s, it had disintegrated.

† Silas Weir Mitchell (1829–1914) was educated at the University of Pennsylvania and the Jefferson Medical College. Highly experimental, he concentrated on neurology during the 1870s and wrote over thirty studies. Between 1873 and 1878, he developed the course of treatment for "nervous" women that would make his office a mecca for them: a disciplined course of enforced rest, rich foods, and massage. Though the medical profession divided over this treatment, most of his women patients adored him. He also wrote poetry and published several novels.

returned home: " 'Live as domestic a life as possible. Have your child with you all the time. Lie down an hour after each meal. Have but two hours' intellectual life a day. And never touch pen, brush or pencil as long as you live.' "[47]

"I went home," she wrote, "followed those directions rigidly for months, and came perilously near to losing my mind." Walter, at first, reported that she appeared "very much better; is loving and brave and trying to follow the directions of complete recovery. I have never seen her so well." But nine days later, on June 30, he wrote: "Charlotte was in the depths of melancholia again, with talk of pistols and chloroform." Grace began to urge Charlotte to insist on a complete separation, to come to Pasadena with Katharine.[48]

Charlotte agreed, but it was decided that financial problems required that the move be postponed for a year. Meanwhile, Charlotte decided "to cast off Dr. Mitchell bodily, and do exactly as I pleased." She decided she would be more sociable, join a whist club, learn to play chess, and give up "trying to assimilate with Walter."[49] And so Charlotte and Walter endured another year together. It was not a productive writing time for Charlotte: none of her poems or articles appeared in print between mid-April 1887 and July 1889.

Grace came East in June 1888, and she and Charlotte and Katharine spent the summer in a rented cottage in Bristol, Rhode Island. Four days after they arrived, Charlotte wrote Walter: "The fogs and mists are rolling away; I begin to feel alive and self-respecting. Oh the difference! You are very dear to me my love; but there is no disguising the fact that my health and work lie not with you but away from you."[50]

It was decided that Charlotte and Katharine would return with Grace to Pasadena and that Walter would follow several months later to try and resolve their marriage. Charlotte sold property she had inherited in Hartford, and, on October 8, she and her daughter traveled West.

Writings

"On Advertising for Marriage" *

Why not? Why not take every means in one's power to discover so important a person as one's husband or wife? What is the prejudice that exists against it?

To say that such advertisements are used for improper purposes is saying nothing against using them properly. To say that "marriages are made in heaven;" that it is "tempting Povidence" to speak of mysterious laws which bring people together, needs only for answer, Look at the majority of marriages now existing! If they are made in heaven let us try some earth-made ones. *The Alpha* and all common sense teaches that we should use reason and discrimination in a selection like this; and if one is desirous to marry and fails to find a fit mate in one's neighborhood or acquaintance, what reason is there that he or she should not look farther?

They have no surety that fate will bring them the desired one without effort on their part, for behold! many of their friends are unmarried and many more mismarried. What certainty have they of a better lot?

I do believe that if we obeyed all the laws of our life as the birds do, we should find mates as they do; but we do not.

One reasonable argument may be adduced against me, namely, that people brought together from different parts of the country would be dissimilar in their tastes and habits, and so suffer when united; also that *one* must be separated from home and friends.

To the latter I reply that in the case of true marriage it would be a small evil, that under ordinary circumstances the separation need not be complete, and that it frequently happens under the present method.

To the former, that people whose local tastes and habits were

* *The Alpha*, 11 (September 1, 1885), p. 7.

stronger than their individualities, who shared the feelings of the neighborhood to such an extent that change would be painful, would not be likely to miss mating, for they would be satisfied with local character.

Conversely, those who found no mate in the home influence and were so constituted as to demand something different would find full compensation in what they gained for all they lost.

It may be said that if the match proved unhappy they would bitterly regret having meddled with fate, and wish they had waited patiently; but in like cases those who meet by chance, or are thrown together in the natural course of events, as bitterly curse fortune, or their own folly, and wish the same.

Errors of judgment need be no more frequent than now, and even in case of mistaking, surely it is better to look back on an earnest attempt to choose wisely than the usual much-extolled drifting.

Surely *The Alpha* teaches that marriage should result not from the will and judgment led by passion, but the opposite. If a man sees a fair woman before he knows her; feels the charm of her presence before he begins to understand her character; if first aroused to the necessity of judging by his strong inclination; surely he stands less chance of a cool and safe decision than one who begins knowingly, learns a character from earnest letters, loves the mind before he does the body. And that first love would improve and be more to him yearly, growing ever richer, stronger, and more lovely with advancing age.

The other does not. I see in writing still another consideration.

It would if it became a general custom, teach both sexes to cultivate the mind and the power of expression in writing more than the beauty of the body and its sexual attraction.

Also when marriage was seen to depend more upon *real* value and worth coolly inquired into than upon feminine charms and snares and masculine force and persistence, that would be a huge power enlisted on the side of good. Young women would take more interest in the affairs of the world if they knew the chance of happy marriage might depend on such knowledge; that they might be written to by such a man as they would love and honor, and expected to sympathize with his ideas, appreciate his work, understand and help him; and man might condescend to think a woman's nature worth studying a little if their hopes rested also on genuine sympathy and appreciation.

(Not her sexual nature! Heaven defend us! They have studied that long and well, but the *rest* of her, the "ninety-nine parts human!")

Will some one explain what harm would result from Advertising for Marriage?

"Why Women Do Not Reform Their Dress" *

It would seem at first sight that there was but one answer to this question, namely, that women are fools.

When you can plainly prove to a woman that her dress is unhealthful, unbeautiful, immoral, and yet she persists in wearing it, there seems no possible reason but the above. But there is a very simple explanation. A physician complained to me that women came to her actually wearing mechanical appliances to counteract diseases which were caused and fostered by the mechanical weight and pressure of their dress. She could see no reason why a woman should deliberately choose pain and weakness. Here is the reason.

Let us take an average woman, with a home, family, and social circle. Like every living organism, she is capable of receiving pain and pleasure. As a human being, she receives these sensations both through mind and body. Now this woman, apart from what she considers duty, will pursue always that course of action which seems to her to bring the most pleasure, or the least pain. This is a law of life, as right and natural as for a plant to grow towards the light. This woman's life as a human being is far more mental than physical; the pleasures and pains of the heart and mind are far more important to her than those of the body. Therefore, if a thing give [sic] pain to her body but pleasure to her heart and mind, she will certainly choose it. Let us see now how this question of dress affects, mind, heart, and body.

The present style of dress means, with varying limits, back-

* *Woman's Journal,* October 23, 1886, p. 338.

ache, sideache, headache, and many another ache; corns, lame, tender, or swollen feet, weak clumsy, and useless compared to what they should be; a crowd of diseases, heavy and light; a general condition of feebleness and awkwardness and total inferiority as an animal organism; with a thousand attendant inconveniences and restrictions and unnatural distortions amounting to hideousness.

But it also means the satisfaction of the social conscience; gratification of pride, legitimate and illegitimate; approbation of those loved and admiration of those unknown; satisfaction of a sense of beauty, however false; and a general ease and peace of mind.

The true and reasonable dress means perfect ease and health and beauty of body, with the freedom of motion and increase of power and skill resultant therefrom. But it also means long combat with one's own miseducated sense of beauty, and fitness, and with all one's friends' constant disapprobation; ridicule, opposition, an uneasy sense of isolation and disagreeable noticeability, loss of social position, constant mortification and shame.

Now, to the average woman, these pains and penalties of the home and social life are infinitely more to be dreaded than the physical ones; and the physical comfort and strength infinitely less to be desired than the mental satisfaction and peace. Physical suffering has been so long considered an integral part of woman's nature, and is still so generally borne, that a little more or less is no great matter. But to offend and grieve instead of pleasing, to meet opposition and contempt instead of praise and flattery, to change pride for shame,—this is suffering which no woman will accept unless it is proved her duty.

And this is why women do not reform their dress.

Chapter Two

• • • • •

The Club and Lecture Years, 1889–1898

On her own, for the first time, and responsible for a small child, Charlotte had to secure a livelihood. Clearly, she would write, and write critically. Already she had a secure theoretical foundation in her progressive evolutionary view of history and an abundance of empirical information concerning the social and economic conditions constricting women and their aspirations. During the 1890s she would strengthen her evolutionary concepts, adopt socialism and utopian reform, and find in various woman's organizations and causes receptive audiences for her ideas.

Evolution

Morton White has called the last two decades of the nineteenth century "a period of ignition in American thought."[1] Though the sparks emanated from a wide variety of sources, the British influence— notably Charles Darwin and Herbert Spencer (1820–1903)—was particularly strong.

Although Darwin's ideas ultimately had a major impact on American thinking, very few Americans of the late nineteenth century could be considered Darwinists. Instead, Herbert Spencer, refracting Darwinian evolution, had a more immediate impact on social and political thinking in the United States. He had the largest following of any

European thinker, and, according to Richard Hofstadter, "It was impossible to be active in any field of intellectual work in the three decades after the Civil War without mastering Spencer."[2] Charlotte, during her first years of motherhood, read Spencer and remembered that from him "I learned wisdom and applied it."[3]

Spencer's most prominent intellectual convert in the United States was William Graham Sumner (1840–1910), who rigidified Spencer's social thought, melded it with classical economic theory and the Protestant ethic, and produced a highly conservative, pessimistic appraisal of social progress. In fact, Sumner's thinking so perfectly symbolized everything that seemed bleak and static in the United States' intellectual tradition, that those who argued that social assistance would not block progress had to level Sumner's belief structure first.

A counterattack against conservative Darwinism began in the early 1870s.[4] Foremost among those who refused to accept the "social Darwinism" of Spencer and Sumner, and who returned to Darwin in order to blaze a new trail of social thinking—a "reform Darwinism"—was Lester Frank Ward (1841–1913).[5] He distinguished natural evolution ("genesis")—the random, often wasteful, processes of biological selection—from social evolution ("telesis")—the conscious alteration of the environment through the operation of human intellect, arguing that both were natural processes, which functioned according to coordinated but essentially different laws.[6]

Ward, an autodidact, probably did as much as anyone in the United States to establish sociology as a recognized discipline. Elected president of the Institut International de Sociologie in 1900, and first president of the American Sociological Society in 1905, he had to wait until 1906 to receive a university appointment, at Brown. He had researched and written his major works, *Dynamic Sociology* (1883), *The Psychic Factors of Civilization* (1893), *Pure Sociology* (1903), and *Applied Sociology* (1906), while employed by the United States Geological Survey as a geologist and then paleontologist.

He believed that human minds armed with knowledge could control the course and direction of evolution. His main goal was social reform, and the body of his work attested to his belief that a scientifically modeled social science would educate people for intelligent social action. In direct antithesis to Sumner, he would argue that social reform plans were as much a part of normal evolutionary development as all other social phenomena.[7]

Although he and Charlotte Perkins Stetson had several factors in common—their connections with the Beecher and Everett families, their abiding faith in education and will power, their rational religion, their utopianism, their friendship with Edward A. Ross—it was Ward's "gynaecocentric" theory that welded the link between them. Proportionately a minuscule portion of Ward's writing, and an area of his work ignored by those who deal with his ideas, it meshed perfectly with Charlotte's developing philosophy, giving her a key element: woman as race-type.

Ward was by no means the first social analyst in the United States to declare that females were superior to males, but he was the first to clothe it in a seemingly rigorous scientific form.* In his first major work, *Dynamic Sociology*, Ward, although he did not use the term gynaecocentric, noted that there are "natural" facts which argue against male superiority. "Indeed, it is a fundamental biological truth that, so far as the mere 'purposes of Nature' are concerned, the fertile sex is by far the greater importance."[8] The gynaecocentric theory, per se, began as a talk Ward delivered to the Six O'Clock Club, in Washington, D.C., on April 26, 1888. It became the basis of the article that most influenced Charlotte: "Our Better Halves."[9] It was not a long article (ten pages), and the evidence was suggestive rather than definitive, but the concluding paragraphs contained a rarely voiced, putatively scientific declaration:

> ... Accepting evolution as we must, recognizing heredity as the distinctive attribute of the female sex, it becomes clear that it must be from the steady advance of woman rather than from the uncertain fluctuations of man that the sure and solid progress of the future is to come. . . . Woman is the unchanging trunk of the great genealogic tree . . . . Woman *is* the race, and the race can be raised up only as she is raised up. . . . True science teaches that the elevation of woman is the only sure road to the evolution of man.[10]

* Among his predecessors were Stephen Pearl Andrews (1812–1886), Henry C. Wright (1797–1870), Ezra Heywood (1829–1893) Eliza Farnham (1815–1864), and Antoinette Brown Blackwell (1825–1891).

Ward's argument appealed to the more radical elements within feminism. The sex reformer Elizabeth ("Elmina") Drake Slenker (1827–1909) used Ward's theory to buttress her arguments that appeared in *Lucifer* in the early 1890s; Josephine Conger-Kaneko, editor of the *Socialist Journal, Appeal To Reason,* and *The Progressive Woman,* included both *Dynamic Sociology* and *Pure Sociology* on her recommended reading list; and most Socialist women's committees studied his works.[11] But woman's suffrage leaders did not respond to his theories,[12] and there is no indication that he was the subject of woman's literary club programs or reading lists. Among American male radicals, the Socialists Eugene V. Debs (1855–1926) and Daniel De Leon (1852–1914) regarded him highly.

Charlotte lavished public praise on his theory, repeating in many venues over the course of two decades that "nothing so important to the woman's movement has ever come into the world."[13] On the other hand, she did not read most of what he wrote, did not agree fully with his analysis of the process by which males came to dominate females, did not think she owed her evolutionary philosophy to him, and rather resented his failure to appreciate the original quality of her thought.[14] (Although Ward did praise her work, he did not do so lavishly, and his private compliments were always qualified.)[15]

Though Ward's statements and his standing buttressed the arguments of radical feminists, Charlotte and her predecessors had independently assessed the value for the feminist cause of Darwin, evolutionary theory, and the scientific method. Antoinette Brown Blackwell, Dr. Clemence Lozier (1813–1888), dean of the New York Medical College for Women, Mary Putnam Jacobi (1842–1906), and Abba Goold Woolson (1838–1921), among others, had been writing and speaking on these topics since the 1860s; *Woman's Journal* and *Woodhull and Claflin's Weekly* regularly printed articles on Darwin; and the new women's colleges (Vassar, Bryn Mawr, Wellesley, and Barnard) emphasized the study of the sciences. The Iowa State Agriculture College at Ames, where Carrie Chapman Catt received her education, had a faculty of dedicated evolutionists. It was not, however, a subject favored by most woman's literary clubs.[16]

Some women reformers, Elizabeth Cady Stanton, for example, preferred the positive sociology of Auguste Comte (1798–1857) to

Darwin, while others, such as Florence Kelley (1859–1932), turned to Lewis Henry Morgan (1818–1881) and Friedrich Engels (1820–1895).[17]

There is no indication that Charlotte read Comte, Morgan or Engels, although she may have learned of the content of their works from Kelley, whom she met in Chicago in the mid-nineties. In effect, then, from her adolescent reading program and general observations, supplemented by Ward, Charlotte wove her evolutionary theory of human history and development. The goals she sought for human progress, however, derived from her involvement with the Nationalist Club movement and socialism.

Nationalism and Socialism

Charlotte Perkins Stetson came to consider herself a socialist, but she steered well clear of the German, Marxist orientation, represented by the Socialist Labor Party. Instead, she was drawn to a variant of native radicalism, combining Protestant morality as the goad, a collectivistic utopia as the end, and reason and good will as the means—that is, to the vision outlined in the best-selling novel written by Edward Bellamy (1850–1898), *Looking Backward* (1888), the Nationalist movement inspired by the book, and, finally, British Fabian social philosophy.

Bellamy's was the third in a series of four socioeconomic critiques that appeared at the end of the century and attracted a popular following; the others were Henry George's (1839–1897) *Progress and Poverty* (1880), Laurence Gronlund's (1846–1899) *The Cooperative Commonwealth* (1884), and Henry Demarest Lloyd's (1847–1903) *Wealth Against Commonwealth* (1894).

Charlotte read them all, rejecting George's "single tax," appreciating Gronlund's popularization of collectivism, and hailing Lloyd's exposés of corporate evils.[18] *Looking Backward* aroused a mixed response. Publicly she said: "The success of 'Looking Backward' was an instance of the triumph of truth over inadequate form. As the great thought of a great mind, as voicing what the whole world ached for, it took the world by storm, and will live always as an epoch-making book." But she would later write Houghton: "I don't imagine you will care for Bellamy anyway; but his books are exceedingly important none the less. I don't like 'em, personally. I don't need that kind. I like a few salient and relevant facts—and then far seeing generalization. Safe but swift and light in touch," but his "kind of laborious detailed explanation of exactly how things are going to be appeals to the mass of American minds." [19]

Appeal it did—*Looking Backward,* Bellamy's fourth book, sold over 500,000 copies within three years. Its popularity stemmed from the simplicity and clarity of its critique of contemporary economic and social arrangements and its reliance on many of the major strands of pre-Progressive era reformist thinking. It rested on the key premises of progressive Darwinism: that people are rational and social; that environment determines character; that societies evolve in a progressive direction; that violent revolution is not necessary. It reflected the sentiment that big business needed to be harnessed. And it contained neither a brief for the wisdom of the working class nor a formula of change relying on it. Bellamy envisioned a peaceful, conscious evolution from private profit-oriented industry to public-owned and -controlled industry.

Believing that a hierarchic bureaucracy was necessary to organize production and distribution in the new society, Bellamy organized it on military lines, as an industrial army, with no grass-roots control over decision making. (This reliance on a central state apparatus was not uncommon among reform Darwinists. Both George and Gronlund had centered their visions around a strong, central administration, and Lester Ward envisioned a "sociocracy.")

Women found Bellamy's book appealing, because it allowed them more freedom than any previous vision. Housework was eliminated, and women were to have as free play of their instincts as men, provided that they did not aim at domination or exploitation. Women were organized into their own, allied industrial force, with its own command structure. They left it only for maternal duties and returned as soon as they were able. No one was to be dependent for material support on another, not even children on parents. Dependence of that sort, said Dr. Leete, the explicator of the Nationalist State, "would be shocking to the moral sense as well as indefensible on any rational social theory." [20]

A Nationalist Club movement sprung up, enrolling, within a few years, over 5,000 members in over 150 clubs from coast to coast.

Although Nationalism's original appeal was to the middle class, and the leaders did not intend to build a popular movement, Bellamy, in 1892, urged his followers to support the newly formed People's Party. Though it was dominated by the National Farmers' Alliance and Industrial Union, Bellamy saw enough delegates from other reform groups at St. Louis, where the party's platform was adopted, to convince him that the new party could transcend its social-class orientation. He also approved of the nationalization planks in the St. Louis platform.[21]

Most women attracted, in the early 1890s, to a collectivist reform vision of the future found Bellamy's socialism more attractive than that espoused by the Marxists, who stipulated that women would gain emancipation as a result of their efforts on behalf of the working class and who rejected separate, gender-based activity. Charlotte, for her part, repeatedly said that she could not read Marx at all, but she also told Houghton that she found "a good deal" in *Woman in the Past, Present and Future* (originally published in 1879), by the German Marxist August Bebel (1840–1913).[22]

Women's Organizations

Women's organizations enrolled the vast majority of women who joined movements in the latter part of the nineteenth century. Families were shrinking in size, divorce rates were increasing, and more women were seeking a higher education and employment as professionals. These "new woman"[23] preferred gender-oriented organizations and activities to mixed, general-purpose political groupings. The Women's Christian Temperance Union (1873) would have 160,000 members by 1890; the General Federation of Women's Clubs (1892) would have one million members by 1912; and the National American Woman Suffrage Association (product of the merger of the National and American Associations in 1890) would have two million by 1917. In addition, settlement houses, employing mostly women, would multiply from two to over 400 between 1889 and 1910. These groups and the churches which supported the Social Gospel or Social Purity endeavors formed a nationwide network, which both provided a haven for women moving beyond the confines of domesticity and a forum for those women who could deliver interesting lectures and talks.

Women in all parts of the country sought enlightenment on a wide range of subjects. And, though the number of co-ed or single-sex institutions of higher learning opening their doors to women increased markedly between 1870 and 1890, men and male-run institutions in society were not receptive to the educated, literary, or professional woman, and, if an occupation or study, such as social science, attracted the attention of a significant number of women, it was soon designated a "woman's field." [24]

Women's isolation and fragmentation goaded Jane Cunningham Croly (1829–1901) and Carolina Maria Seymour Severance (1820–1914) to found what would be the nuclei of the woman's club movement. A highly respected journalist, Croly spurred the foundation of Sorosis, in New York City in March 1868, "a club composed of women only, that should manage its own affairs, represent as far as possible the active interests of women, and create a bond of fellowship between them." [25] Beginning as a club dedicated to ideas and thinking, it moved, under Croly's prodding to reform activity.

The other prototype club, the New England Woman's Club, formed by Severance, in Boston in February 1868, was more reform- than literary-oriented and it admitted men, though not as full members. The objective was "to organize the social forces of the women of New England, now working in small circles and in solitary ways." [26]

In the following decades, woman's clubs sprung up everywhere, mostly stressing personal growth and development by means of intellectual improvement, whereas Sorosis and the New England Woman's Club sought to deepen the reform impulse and widen the reform network. In October 1873, a congress convened by Sorosis created the Association for the Advancement of Women. Four years later, in Boston, the Women's Educational and Industrial Union was founded. And, in 1890, again catalyzed by Sorosis, women established the General Federation of Women's Clubs. Charlotte thought that no part of "the crystallization of thought and feeling among the best women of our country . . . was more important than this union of women in the clubs and the union of clubs in these widespread federations." [27]

In sum, as increasing numbers of women were looking at themselves and their non-home world and determining that they should be doing something to improve both, many, Charlotte Perkins Stetson among them, were also agonizing about the relationship between their public aspirations and their domestic conditioning. Although role models existed for the wife and mother as volunteer or activist, few examples of the single career reformer existed. Only a tiny number of the century's best-known female reformers had not married: e.g., Sarah Grimké (1792–1873), Catharine Beecher, Susan B. Anthony, and Frances Willard (1839–1898). And Charlotte knew nothing about their struggles to overcome insecure socioeconomic conditions or unstable emotional situations. Thus, without a model, Charlotte proceeded to build her own base of support.

Pasadena, 1889–1891

Pasadena, one of the loveliest communities in Southern California, was in the midst of a real-estate boom and population explosion, when Charlotte arrived. Though there was some civic, cultural, and religious activity there,[28] Los Angeles was the focal point of politics. In May 1889, Los Angeles Nationalist Club No. 1 had been formed by two socialist women and several labor organizers. By the following summer, there were seven Nationalist clubs in the Los Angeles area, enrolling over 1,000 members. Statewide, there were over sixty clubs and 3,000 active members, with 1,000 in the San Francisco area, and they would form the California Nationalist Party, in San Francisco, in April 1890.[29]

Not yet having read Bellamy, still not sure of what her life's work would be, Charlotte's main concerns, at the end of 1889, were to earn a living, keep house, and raise her daughter. She felt deep pain at the failure of her marriage, but "the loss of health was worse, the weakness, the dark, feeble mind. . . . When able to think clearly I faced the situation thus: 'Thirty years old. Made a wrong marriage—lots of people do. Am heavily damaged, but not dead. May live a long time. It is intellectually conceivable that I may recover strength enough to do some part of my work. I will assume this to be true, and act on it.' "[30]

A few months before leaving Providence, in August, she had written that social problems would not be solved by charity or "mere scholarship," but by an examination of "those causes which *make* men ignorant and poor" and by thinking. "Facts of any kind, whether in literature, business, or society, bad without thought, inference, comparison, judgment, use."[31]

Walter arrived in Pasadena in December and stayed for a little more than a year, but the only result was that he and Grace Channing became increasingly close, with Charlotte's blessing, and it was agreed that Charlotte and Walter would divorce, a process that dragged out for years. She wrote Martha after he departed: "Now I guess I will shut the door of my heart again; and hang on it '*Positively* no Admittance except on Business!' "[32]

Writing was her main activity. "In that first year of freedom I wrote some thirty-three short articles, and twenty-three poems, besides ten more child-verses."[33] (As of the end of 1890, sixteen of her poems and stories and eleven of her nonfiction articles had been published.) She and Grace wrote plays together and became involved in amateur productions.

At some point, in 1889 or early 1890, she read *Looking Backward* and became a convert to Nationalism. She saw in Nationalism a philosophy that would give "human nature a chance to develope [sic] itself normally," a blueprint for society that encourages and develops "our natural impulse to love each other" and promote the unity of the race.[34] It would, she said, change the way people thought about themselves and their relations to the economy; they would begin to "Work according to ability; receive according to necessity."[35] Whether or not she subscribed to the Nationalist state is unclear. There are scattered approving refences to an "industrial army" in her writings, but she also termed the Nationalist state "a vast stockholding company in which we are all shareholders."[36]

She wrote Martha that Nationalism had hit a deep tap root in its strike at the business system, but it had missed a "possibly deeper" root —"the struggle between man and woman."[37] In fact, Bellamy had not confronted the subject of sexuality, and many of her lectures for Nationalism would focus on the nature of love and sexuality and the need for equality in each.

She received her most important literary lift in April 1890, when *The Nationalist* published her poem, "Similar Cases," a satirical commentary on those who believed evolutionary progress or change could occur only if "human nature" was altered.[38] William Dean Howells wrote her a letter praising it, it was widely hailed in Nationalist circles, and national and state Nationalist publications (Bellamy's *The New Nation,* the *California Nationalist,* and the *Weekly Nationalist*) started to print her articles.

She delivered her first Nationalist lecture, "Human Nature," to the Pasadena Nationalist Club on June 15, 1890. Her theme, based on "Similar Cases," that humans and the world can be changed, achieved "great success," and she was invited to present two more: "Causes and Cures" and "Nationalism and the Virtues." "Human Nature" proved so popular that it was rewritten for publication in the *Weekly Nationalist* and for distribution as a Nationalist tract. In December she was invited by Harriet Howe to lecture at the First Nationalist Club in Los Angeles. Charlotte again judged it a "great success," and she was asked to give three more.[39] She had, wrote Howe, "a voice, clear, compelling, yet conversational, easily reaching to the farthest end of the hall, entirely devoid of effort." The women in the audience, she continued, "had never heard such plain statements of clear facts, and they had never heard anything of the kind from any woman."[40]

Howe and some of her friends, tired of the "usual condescension with which men treat women in all matters supposed to be over women's heads [even in the Nationalist Clubs]," formed a woman's club and invited Charlotte to lecture in January and February. Charlotte's "object," wrote Howe, "was to persuade women to think for themselves instead of accepting what they were told to think. . . . It was magic. It was an EVENT."[41]

Charlotte also lectured at the Socialist Society, the Social Purity Society, the Women's Christian Temperance Union,* and the Friday Morning Club. The main themes were the human and social costs of sex-distinction and the need for women to work.

She also wrote her finest piece of fiction, "The Yellow Wallpaper,"

---

* The Social Purity movement was a loosely organized coalition of moral reformers, attempting to suppress prostitution and impure literature, confine sex to marriage, and generally moderate the sexual activity of husbands and wives. Charlotte helped form a Social Purity Society in Pasadena, contributed to two periodicals that supported it *(Alpha* and *The Arena),* and supported the Social Hygiene movement that formed in 1905 around the American Society for Sanitary and Moral Prophylaxis. Though she had earlier criticized the means and ends of the WCTU, Charlotte came to realize the radical potential of the social reforms it advocated under the presidency of Frances Willard.

a deeply textured, richly symbolic account of a young wife's nervous breakdown in the face of a smothering environment. Some twenty-four years later, she explained that her experience with Dr. Mitchell had motivated her to write the story. His advice to live passively had nearly destroyed her mentally, and she only recovered her mental power when she "cast the noted specialist's advice to the winds and went to work again—work, the normal life of every human being . . . without which one is a pauper and a parasite."[42]

Although Charlotte would judge 1890 "a year of great growth and gain" and the foundation for her "whole literary reputation," she also called it a "very hard year. Cruelly hard since Grace went [first to Providence, then Europe]."[43] Charlotte had written her:

> Do you know I think I suffer more in giving you up than in Walter—for you were all joy to me. And it was not till things were well underway that that side of the arrangement dawned on me. . . .
>
> It is awful to be a man inside and not able to marry the woman you love!
>
> When Martha married it cracked my heart a good deal—your loss will finish it.
>
> I think of Walter with some pain, more pleasure, and a glorious sense of rightness—escape triumph.
>
> I think of you with a great howling selfish heartache. *I* want you—*I* love you—*I* need you *myself!*

It is clear from the letter that Grace and Walter were well advanced in their courtship.[44]

In almost every way 1891 would be more rewarding for Charlotte. She discovered Olive Schreiner, inaugurated a love affair with Adeline Knapp, and scored a great success lecturing in San Francisco. Charlotte began reading *Dreams* on March 4, and in her diary entry of March 6 wrote: "Read Olive Schreiner's 'Heaven' and cry like a child."[45]*

---

* Olive Schreiner (1855–1920) was a South African feminist. A much more eloquent prose stylist than Charlotte, Schreiner was equally didactic. The stories in *Dreams* (1891) depict a woman completely alone and free, especially of the complications of sexuality. Gilman later wrote: "There were two years in which my domicile was a trunk; all immediate personal belongings limited to its contents. Among these necessities were two books—just two. . . . The two were the poetry of [Walt] Whitman [1819–1892] and Olive Schreiner's 'Dreams.' Having them, I had with me mountains and sunlight." *The Forerunner,* 2 (July 1911), p. 197.

Charlotte read and commented favorably on all of Schreiner's writing (see *ibid.,* pp. 197–198), but Joyce Avrech Berkman, who has done extensive work on Schreiner, has found no evidence that Schreiner ever read or knew of Charlotte (personal communication).

The San Francisco trip arrived courtesy of Mrs. Emily Tracy (Swett) Parkhurst (1863–1892), who had organized, in September 1890, the Pacific Coast Women's Press Association. Its object was "to promote acquaintance and good-fellowship among writers and journalists; to elevate the work and workers; and to forward by concerted action through the Press, such good objects in literary, social, industrial, philanthropic and reformatory lines as may, from time to time, present themselves." Within a few months of its formation, it had enrolled 125 active members, begun a library, and taken an interest in public improvement projects and kindergartens.[46]

Mrs. Parkhurst invited Charlotte to join the Association and speak at the upcoming convention; Parkhurst also sent the railroad fare and invited Charlotte to stay with her. Charlotte spent three months in the Bay Area (March 14–June 8). She read a paper and several poems at the convention, and spoke to Nationalist Clubs, literary societies, the WCTU, and working woman's clubs. "Her lectures were," it was reported, "witty and very entertaining."[47]

On May 11, Charlotte was introduced to Adeline E. Knapp (1860–1909), a member of the PCWPA and a writer for the *San Francisco Call*.* They saw each other virtually every day thereafter. On May 21 Charlotte wrote in her diary, "I love her." They began to spend nights together, and on June 7 Charlotte wrote, "we are very happy together." They decided that Charlotte would initiate divorce proceedings and move to Oakland.[48]

In September 1891, Charlotte and Katharine moved north, where, Charlotte thought, "there was a better opening for my work." She could live with Delle and be in a better position to take care of her mother, who had been living with Thomas since Charlotte had left Providence.[49] The four women, Charlotte, Delle, Mrs. Perkins, and Katharine, shared two rooms in a boarding house in Oakland.

Oakland and San Francisco

Politically, the Bay Area was in the midst of a period of intense political activity, led by labor militants. The San Francisco Nationalist Club was one of the few in the nation to recruit workers actively. A

* Knapp is referred to as "Delle" or "Delight" in the diaries and "Dora" in the autobiography.

California Farmers' Alliance had been formed in 1890, and a San Francisco People's Party in 1892.[50]

Bay area women were very active in trade union activity; they had formed a Social League and Labor Lyceum, a section of the Knights of Labor (San Francisco Ladies Assembly 5855) composed entirely of women, a Woman's Educational and Industrial Union, a Woman's Co-Operative Educational Club, joined the San Francisco Typographical Union, and tried and failed to organize a Working Girls' Protective Association.

Middle-class women had founded two newspapers, formed cooperative and kindergarten movements, a state suffrage society (in 1870), and, in the 1893 municipal elections, a woman ran for city attorney and twelve others for the school board.[51]

Charlotte jumped into the thick of this political activity. She still considered herself a Nationalist and was beginning to identify herself as a socialist, "of the early humanitarian kind."[52] She converted Knapp to Nationalism and the two of them reorganized the Oakland Nationalist Club (renaming it "The New Nation Club"); Charlotte attended Farmers' Alliance and People's Party meetings, challenged their assumption that women had circumscribed roles to play, and was asked to run for a school board position; spoke regularly to Socialist groups; worked on behalf of suffrage; joined the Oakland Labor Federation and worked on its committee on unemployed women; actively supported the Pullman strike of 1894;* and participated in efforts to challenge the monopoly powers of the Southern Pacific railroad. On Labor Day, September 5, 1892, Charlotte received a gold medal from the Alameda County Federation of Trades for an essay on the labor movement.

She lectured frequently and widely, on civic reform, morality and ethics, political and economic matters, and women. Within a month of arriving in Oakland, she announced "Twelve Lectures for Ladies":

> The world today calls for help from women. . . . Intelligent and conscientious women feel this responsibility, but are unable to reconcile it with

---

* When the managers of the Pullman Company laid off workers, cut wages, and refused to reduce rents and prices in the company town, the employees struck in May 1894. The company's refusal to negotiate with Debs' American Railway Union led to a walkout of 120,000 workers, paralyzing the western roads. Injunctions, federal troops, the national guard, and arrests broke the strike and destroyed the ARU.

their duties to the family. With time and strength more than exhausted in home duties—how can women do more than they are now doing? The purpose of these lectures is to point to a solution of this problem. The purpose is to stimulate among women original thought on the vital questions of the day.[53]

Charlotte devoted much of her time to organizing women, especially through the vehicle of the PCWPA and the Woman's Congress Association. She served on the PCWPA's Executive Board, as president (1893–1894), and as editor of its journal. She helped organize a San Francisco Council of Women and a State Council, and worked with the Women's Alliance,* the WCTU, and on behalf of woman's suffrage.

She also joined several woman's clubs, beginning what would be a lifelong allegiance to a movement she would call "one of the most important sociological phenomena of the century,—indeed, of all centuries,—marking as it does the first timid steps toward social organization of these so long unsocialized members of our race."[54] She belonged to the Ebell Society (individual research papers), the Ethical Society (improving human conduct through scientific study), the Economic Club, and the Parents Association.

Her writing career continued to blossom. Dozens of poems, short stories, essays, and articles of varying length were submitted to a wide variety of newspapers and magazines. Between 1891 and September 1893, when she began to devote her full attention to *The Impress,* twenty-two pieces of her fiction and seventy-three pieces of nonfiction were published. Her poems were collected and published under the title *In This Our World,* by two Socialist friends. A collection of seventy-five of her poems, it "brought small returns in cash but much in reputation."[55]

She met most of the literary and intellectual notables who lived in or visited the Bay Area, and established a close friendship with some of them. Harriet Howe, who moved to Oakland in August 1892, recalled that Charlotte began, in 1893, having " 'at home' evenings which developed into a sort of salon, but really more of a forum, where various psychological, philosophical, economic, biological, and ethical

---

* Women did not hold prominent positions in the People's Party and the party did not endorse suffrage or temperance, but women actively participated at the local level, and rural women formed a National Women's Alliance that endorsed suffrage and demanded that women be admitted as equals to all political organizations.

questions were discussed."[56] In March 1894, she met David Starr Jordan (1851–1931), the President of Stanford University, who invited her to lecture there.[57]

Emotionally, those years in the Bay Area resembled a roller-coaster ride. Her mother was dying, she and Knapp were fighting, Katharine suffered from the usual childhood diseases, and Charlotte had assumed control of the boarding house. She wrote at the end of 1891: "It has been a year of great and constantly increasing trouble. Poverty, illness, heartache, household irritation amounting to agony."[58]

But even though "I have well nigh gone mad" from weakness, poverty, and domestic irritants, she wrote Grace, there has been "through it all a steady rising of the spirit. . . . I am winning quiet—but increasing acknowledgement as a writer and speaker of power. . . . I am getting better known and better liked by more people constantly; especially 'the people'—which rejoices me. . . . The working men of these two cities know me and love me. That is well."[59]

She was already thinking of freeing herself or being freed from domestic encumbrances. Her letter to Grace indicated that she expected Walter and Grace, when they married, to take Katharine for a few years; her mother died in early March; and Delle left the boarding house in July. Harriet Howe provided her usual staunch emotional and domestic support, and Charlotte met a woman who would provide a different type of emotional support and be a worthy intellectual companion.

Helen Stuart Campbell (1839–1918), twenty-one years older than Charlotte, had been a successful writer of childrens' and adult fiction until the late 1870s, when she became active in the emerging home economics movement as a teacher and writer. In the early 1880s she began what would be a lifetime commitment to investigating and exposing the conditions of the poor, particularly poor women. She was an original member of the First Nationalist Club of Boston, had been influenced by many of the same authors as Charlotte, knew Ward, and had, the year before meeting Charlotte, studied under Richard Ely (1854–1943) at the University of Wisconsin. Charlotte had read and loved Campbell's children's stories before they first met at a PCWPA convention. Campbell would dedicate her *Household Economics: A Course of Lectures in the School of Economics of the University of Wisconsin* (1896) to

Charlotte, and Charlotte spoke of her as "my real mother 'after the spirit.' "[60]

Charlotte began 1894 feeling "wretched," and her doctor administered "some electricity and pills."[61] But the sales and reviews of *In This Our World* temporarily buoyed her spirits, until, that is, the *San Francisco Examiner* learned about her divorce and the "Charlotte-Walter-Grace" triangle, and treated it as a scandal. The divorce decree was granted in April, Katharine was sent to Walter and Grace in May (they married in June), and Charlotte decided to take over *The Impress,* the journal of the PCWPA she had been editing, and move to San Francisco to live with Helen Campbell and Paul Tyner (d. 1925), who would assist her with the journal. "I am about to give up my home," she wrote, "send Kate to her father, and begin anew; being now a free woman, legally and actually."[62] The *Examiner* again attacked her for sending her daughter away.

Charlotte devoted an enormous amount of time and energy writing for and editing the journal of the PCWPA, and she read and reviewed a vast number of books and periodicals for it. She hoped it would fulfill "the legitimate functions of a newspaper . . . to speak the truth."[63] She wrote most of the commentaries, reviews, verses, and announcements; Campbell contributed a two-page feature entitled "The Art of Living"; and Tyner served as business manager and wrote political news stories, theatrical notes and a series on "The Spiritual Life." It was, she thought, an "excellent paper. . . . It was not propagandist in any line, not exclusively feminist in tone, but varied and interesting."[64]

Charlotte felt "loved and cared for" by Campbell and Tyner and saw "nothing to hinder building up" her health and strength."[65] But in February 1895, *The Impress* folded, leaving Charlotte with a several-thousand dollar debt, and Campbell and Tyner decided to return to the East. All the ties that had once bound Charlotte to the Bay Area had dissolved, and she was free of personal obligation. She felt, she wrote Grace, "happier now, freer, stronger, braver, wiser, *gladder* than in twelve long years. Open sea is before me—the great wide sea, storms and calms and danger of the deep no doubt, but no more danger of the shallow."[66]

She received a letter from Campbell, carrying fond regards from Jane Addams (1860–1935), whom Charlotte had met earlier that year in

San Francisco, and inviting Charlotte to spend three months at Hull House, the settlement house Addams had founded, "and do some work with Chicago as a base."[67] This proposal appealed to her: "As far as I can judge my work lies mainly in public speaking, in writing for a purpose and organizing. In the world's life of today I stand greatly gifted, nobly trained, most strangely led, stepping forward now swiftly into the full light of large usefulness."[68]

In Chicago, she and Campbell worked together on a Home Economics Commission, and they planned to establish a settlement house, but in March 1896, she felt the "beginning of melancholia"; it was "a return of the intense nervous weakness and depression enough to make me feel that I cannot live so for any length of time."[69] She decided to leave Chicago, as soon as she and Campbell finished drafting the prospectus and constitution for the Chicago Household Economic Society. It established training classes for household servants, householders' alliances to employ the graduates, and a central office to register employees, employers, speakers, and teachers. They also advocated the establishment of people's kitchens in every poor quarter of the city.[70]

Charlotte left Chicago on April 18. Two weeks later she wrote Grace: "Health comes at once as I take the field again. I shall always have to keep moving I fancy." And one month later, she seemed elated with the life of an itinerant lecturer: "it seems almost a dream. To be travelling as wide—doing the things I love so well—so kindly received and honored—it is a beautiful dream indeed. May I be strong to bear the other side if it should come again!"[71]

For the next five years, Charlotte would call no place home. These were her true revolutionary years. She cut all the ties that bound her to home or domesticity as then understood, severed all dependency relationships, and provided herself the space to develop freely her thinking and writing. She lectured in a variety of denominational churches (Presbyterian, Baptist, Congregational, Methodist, Unitarian, and Universalist), settlement houses, colleges, at suffrage meetings, before woman's clubs, social reform clubs, Single-Tax clubs, and liberal clubs, and testified before various state legislative committees. She spoke mainly about her "social philosophy"—"my organic theory of social economics. . . ; the theory of the economic independence and specialization of women as essential to the improvement of marriage, motherhood, domestic industry, and racial improvement." Though she supported suffrage activity, she did not think it was "as important as some of its protagonists held."[72]

Lecture writing and an extended trip to England consumed most of her energies during the remainder of 1895 and all of 1896, and only two pieces of her nonfiction were published during that time.

For reasons not clear (and not documented), when Charlotte departed Chicago, she also left behind her working-class activity. Very little of what she would speak or write thereafter was addressed to workers. Perhaps the defeats the radical movement had suffered since 1894—the disintegration of the Nationalist Clubs, the Pullman strike, the presidential election—discouraged her. Perhaps she decided that the message of social consciousness she was in the process of developing and delivering could only be understood and implemented by the educated middle class. She may also have begun to wonder whether working-class people could rise above their terrible conditions and immediate needs and accept her long-term goals for social reconstruction. In any event, among the hundreds of articles she later wrote, fewer than one-half dozen focused on workers and working conditions, and most of those concerned middle-class working women.[73]

She kept her distance from trade unions and the Socialist Party of America, which would be established by Eugene V. Debs in 1900, and she did not consider herself a Progressive; she thought Progressives overemphasized academic expertise and organization.

In July 1896 Charlotte traveled to London to attend the International Socialist and Labor Congress (not as a Socialist, she emphasized in her autobiography, but as a delegate from the Alameda County Federation of Trades),[74] and she stayed in the United Kingdom until November, delivering many speeches and meeting many prominent Socialists, social organizers, writers, and thinkers. She also joined the British Fabian Society.*

* Formed in January 1884, by teachers, journalists, and clerks, many of whom were active Christian Socialists, it was an eclectic, democratic, gradualist, optimistic movement, aiming to extend democracy, improve the machinery of democratic government, extend government powers to improve the welfare of the community, especially the working-class portion, and promote positive government action to promote equality. Instead of forming a political party, they adopted the concept of "permeation," joining and influencing organizations where useful socialist work could be done. They were, essentially, publicizers of a socialist ideal.

Shortly after her return to New York, she met Prestonia Mann (1861–1945), who wrote for and edited *The American Fabian*. Charlotte promised to write for it and to help organize an American Fabian Movement.* The new editor, William J. Ghent (1866–1942), warmly welcomed her to the movement; the January 1897 issue printed two of her earlier poems and a front-page encomium.[75]

She departed for a lecture tour, at the end of April 1897, and spent a week on a ranch in Eureka, Kansas, at the end of June. She wrote in her diary: "State weak, but fall to work in sheer despite for article about economic basis of woman question. Get hold of a new branch in my theory on above subject—the biggest piece & saw it. Now I can write the book."[76]

Writings

"Human Nature"†

[. . .] I wish to assert that Human Nature is *the result of Social Conditions* far more than the conditions are the result of the nature!

What is it, pray, that has made all the forms of life differ from each other and differ from their own earlier forms? Why *conditions* to be sure!

The world was all fire once, and once it was all water—hot water at that! When the first life forms appeared they found themselves surrounded by conditions, and as the conditions changed the lifeforms changed—they *had* to, or die!

When the first men appeared they found themselves surrounded by conditions; by cold and heat, by pleasure and pain, by hunger and thirst, by love and hate, by danger and success. And

---

* American Fabianism was woven from the writings of George, Lloyd, and Ely; the Social Gospel (or Christian Socialist) movement; and British Fabianism. Its main organizer was W. D. P. Bliss (1856–1926), formerly a member of the Knights of Labor and the Nationalist movement. Following a trip to England, he established the Fabian Society of Boston and *The American Fabian*. Though his plan for an American Fabian League was never officially launched, the newspaper continued to publish until 1900.

† Lecture presented to the Pasadena Nationalist Club, June 15, 1890, pp. 16–45, handwritten manuscript in Gilman papers, folder 163.

according to their conditions and to their power of adaptibility they grew and changed and developed and progressed.

But there is a difference between man and his lower brothers.

They *find* their conditions, and live accordingly. He *makes* his —at least a large part of them, and therein is the only hope of the prophet and preacher.

If the poverty and sickness and vice we live in today were solely the result of *natural* conditions, we might sit down helplessly and wait for evolution to take care of us. But they are not! We make them ourselves.

There is a factor in Human Nature that we do not find in any lower form.

Originally, ages and ages since, man was so helpless as they, but somewhere—sometime—somewhen [sic]—there came into his body a brain, into his brain a soul, into his soul a power we call the will. The names are all confusing and inadequate. The things itself may be simply stored up energy, accumulated reflex action, reserved nerve force; it may differ from the lower animals only in degree—but it is there!

Natural conditions work *upon* the other animals—they work *through* man.

Because of our power of communication in the present by which each can take advantage of the experience of all; because of our power of communication with the past by which we can take advantage of the experience of all those who went before; because of our power to *make things,* to create, to produce, to embody ideas; we stand alone, above, in a place apart. *We create conditions and they react upon us.*

We can find no physical or mental trait in the lower animals which their natural environment does not account for.

We find in man the great preponderance of his nature accounted for, not by his natural environment—but by his *Human Environment*—He is what he is because of what he has done!

The animals *take from* the outer world—man adds to it. What does one animal do to another that alters or changes him except by slow unconscious transmission?

But one man can put forth work into the world that lifts and helps and changes his fellow beings more than centuries of natural developement—and work that curses and degrades!

I am scientist enough to know that man with all his brain is an ordered product of evolution; I am naturalist enough to know that law rules everywhere, that the subtlest action of the soul is resolvable by long and careful study, back to the simplest elements of life; I am poet enough to know that the natural world is divine and the divine world is natural; but look at it how you will, account for it how you will, man, today, stands above the animmals, and is in large and ever larger measure the arbiter of his own destiny!

We are *conscious,* we can think as well as feel, we can realize, remember, and foresee. We do not have to act from immediate pressure of circumstance; we act, if we choose, from *remembered* circumstance or *foreseen* circumstance. We can act under fear of results which have never before happened, but which we foresee will happen from collateral knowledge.

When you follow life back to the lowest forms you find but one instinct—to seek pleasure and flee pain.

To follow the line of least resistance; to do what is easiest—that is the simple force which has with slow and constant miracle turned protoplasm into personality. As each form specialized it developed the instinct proper to the organism.

Instinct, mind you, is the result of habit—not habit of instinct. It is the transmitted effect of repeated actions and can be changed like every other form of life. Look at the instinct of the wild dog and the instinct of the tame dog. Who gave the dog what we now call his *"nature"*—faithful, obedient, self-sacrificing? Why *we* did. The wild dog is not faithful, obedient, self-sacrificing. We have developed those instincts by making the creature perform the action whose repetition formed the instinct.

It is the law of all living things, the law of every slightest current of thought or feeling, the law of every action, the law of reproduction—the undying impulse of every thing that is—to *grow*—to *go on*—to *do itself again.*

It is this force that man has used upon the animals—what

we call "training." It is the same force he makes use of with his children, and calls it "education." It is the same steady undying force which urges us all to troop like sheep, to live like slaves, to die like any helpless cattle—the impulse to *do what we have done before, to do what others do, to do what we are told*—to accept and submit and swallow whole what we have given to us!

But that is not *Human* nature. *Human* nature is the nature of man *as distinguished* from the other animals! And this blind folly of submission and helpless acceptance, this dull clamor that we are what we are and cannot help it, this pitiful existence of disease and crime, is not from our *human* nature, but from that old foundation of common nature which we share with the beasts, yes, and the vegetables.

Now let us make a few illustrative distinctions, let us define a little.

The nature of a cat is the inherited result of such actions as the cat performs and no other animal performs.

But those actions are the result of the cat's environment—and her power of adaptation; she cannot help being a cat any more than she can help being an animal.

The nature of a man is the inherited result of such action as the man performs and no other animal performs.

But those actions are the result of his environment and power of adaptation *plus* his will, and he can help being a man, though he cannot help being an animal. I have seen persons in gutters who were not men at all for the time being. I have seen persons out of gutters whose every act was due to the helpless submission to their environment of the lower animals.

Much as I grieve to say it, much as I shame to say it, the great mass of humanity is very little human still.

We *have* the power but do not use it. We *are* men but do not live so. We live willless and brainless, doing what we are told, and what our fathers did before us.

But some men are smarter and stronger. They use their brains and count on our *not* using ours.

Thereby does a small proportion of the world grow fat on the foolishness of the rest; the same human power and human character, the same beastlike weakness and folly, that [allows] one man to send a hundred thousand to fight and die for they know not what, enable one man to count his gold by carloads while a hundred thousand live and die in hopeless want.

And when we seek to alter this peculiar and unpleasant condition of things they tell us we must alter human nature.

Why not? Let us by all means alter it. Let them find to their amazement that, though all the fools are not dead yet, there are not nearly so many as there used to be.

It is *the people* who make the world! It is *the people* who *are* the world! And if they will *let* one man take all their bread and butter —why you cannot blame him so awfully. I dare say we would do much the same if we had happened to be smart that way!

Now here is the face of the earth.

And here are people on it with an organism that is capable of great enjoyment, of great achievement, of constant development. We are at the top of this world's ladder now, and we have great hopes of getting still higher in another. And yet we are lower than the beasts. Lower in proportion to what we might be. Sicker and wickeder and weaker, as well as higher and finer and nobler.

Here we all are today, suffering from this and suffering from that and suffering from the other, and calling it "the common lot of humanity"! Lot indeed! Are we trees? Are we houses? Are we stuck in the ground and fenced in that we call life a "*lot*"? It would seem so.

But it is *not* so. We can move and leave that lot, and what is more we can dig and ditch and plow and plant until that lot is a garden of Eden—if we choose.

And we do choose. We heartily object to our lot as we find it, and we propose to so alter that lot that the former owners would not recognize it.

We are living today under social institutions which are left over from former ages. That creative faculty of ours is a stumbling block unless we use it properly.

If we leave off creating and try to abide by what is already created we are worse off than our little brothers, the beasts, after all. For as fast as they develope the earlier forms die and are forgotten; but we carefully petrify ours, and instead of using them as scarecrows and signposts we try to live in them still.

Fancy our friend the horse preserving pictures and statues and descriptions of the time when he was Eohippus and Orohippus, Miohippus and Pliohippus, or even Hipparian Gracile*—and trying to live and look as they did! Our brains can hinder as well as help, and we see to it that they shall! Because we know what we were a thousand years back, we consider it ample reason for never [moving] one year forward.

The progress of the animals is easy and general, what affects one affects all, and when the climate gets colder they grow long hair without any fuss.

But with us? It is absolutely funny!

Here we stand with all history behind us and all that science can tell so far, knowing in large measure just what we are and just what has made us what we are, and yet we have only one race that will so much as allow a man to speak his mind as to our unnecessary evils.

Life grinds hard upon us. We say of our children—"poor little things—let them be happy while they can"! And we say to our children when they don't want to give up "you can't have what you want in this world"!

It takes all our lives to get our living—we haven't anything left over for pleasure or production. [. . .]

Until we can live in comparative ease, until we can get our physical needs supplied without exhaustion—we can not be fully human, can not grow. [. . .]

What is the chance of racial improvement of *any* individual life, when we have to make laws to keep small children out of factories, when the "criminal classes" reach the cradle almost, when in our Christian country babies of *four years old* are taught to sew on buttons—sit sewing buttons all day long—for their bread!

When the struggle for existence presses upon the lion and the lioness, so that they can not get food for their young and their

* The first four are extinct ancestors of the modern horse (Equus), the fifth a horse-like animal, a side-branch.

young have to hunt for themselves, scarce weaned—you may look for a degraded type—decrease in size, decrease in strength —failure and death—and find it.

When the struggle for existence presses on this proud human race till it can not support its young—when our children have to support themselves before they [unintelligible] themselves—before they are grown, here also you may look for a degraded type, decrease in size and decrease in strength, decrease in virtue, decrease in energy, increase of every form of distortion and disease, morbid developements of the poor, thwarted body and mind—premature horrors of vice and crime, premature surrender to every phase of evil—premature death.

You may look for this and find it! Not until we as a race have conquered our food supply, have mastered the necessity of existence, can we *even keep our place in creation*—to say nothing of advancing.

The reason we have maintained our present position so long, is that there were enough of us tolerably well placed to pour a steady stream of normal human life into the mill that throws out at the top those "fittest to survive," the rich, and grinds out at the bottom a steady ever-widening stream flowing toward the poorhouse, the prison, the hospital, the insane asylum, and the grave.

Now nationalism proposes to make life relatively easy. To govern the food supply and the fuel supply and the clothing supply so that all may have a fair share.

Nationalism would not see the sawmills of Washington run off their refuse wood into great piles as large as houses and burning night and day, while we in Southern California pay twelve and fifteen dollars a cord, and we in northeastern cities freeze, and the railroads "charge all the traffic will bear."

Nationalism would not let our fruit rot on the ground by thousands of bushels while the poor of Eastern cities die for lack of it and the railroads "charge all the traffic will bear."

Nationalism means that everybody would share and nobody would suffer.

When you attempt to train and elevate and develop any

animal, you must first *care for him*. If he is left to "struggle for existence" he will *show only those qualities called for by the struggle!* Relieve that pressure—feed and warm him—and he has a reserve of energy to apply to new developement.

We want no master. We are our own masters. But until we can relieve ourselves of the grinding pressure of life today, we can never hope for better life tomorrow. We can not have it because we are not fit for it. We can not be fit for it because our conditions compel us to be what we are. Conditions that were founded long ago upon necessity, but whose foundation has fallen from under them, and which only endure today because we are not wise enough to pull them down.

We know what human life might be. Heaven may come in its season, but let us see to it that we do God's will *here* before we talk of the hereafter.

We know, I say, what human life might be. Give us health and pessimism is gone. Give us happy industry—work that we love, the creative output of a willing soul and idleness and crime are gone. Give us love, pure happy freely given love, love which does not ask "support" on one side or "submission" on the other and immorality is gone.

With health and work and happy love intemperance would go, and Death itself would draw back to his normal limits, back to his rightful ground, back to the peaceful end of ripe old age where the only tears are glad ones for a glad release.

I suppose you think that is an absurd picture. It is the worst proof of our unnumbered years of wrong that we can not believe in better things.

But *study,* study and think, and you will find the sorrows that shorten our lives and the sins that blacken them are *fruits* not seeds! They are *symptoms* not the disease.

What we call human nature—what we groan over and apologize for and exterminate or shriek at as we choose—this tissue of human action about us—is no more human than it is human for sailors starving on a raft to eat each other's flesh!

It is *not* human! It is not natural even! It is the blind pressure of life against conditions unnatural, inhuman, evil and awful in their effects. You cannot fight against them, you cannot *escape* them, but you can cut them down and dig them up, root and branch!

But first you must distinguish between those roots and branches. And then you must find the connection—the trunk—that is the thing to cut through first.

This world has always been full of wailing. And there have always been those to sorrow over it, and cry out upon our sins. But it is for this age, the age of reason, of science, of discovery, and invention; it is for us to give over sorrowing, to stop teaching about sin, to find *why* we live as we do and die as we do.

Go and preach chastity and temperance and honesty and truth in the New York tenements, or on Fifth Avenue and Madison Square.

In neither will you succeed.

Human virtue and human happiness are matters of cause and effect; they do not grow on thistles nor grapes on thorns; *through* and *by* the laws of nature must all good come, and we must learn those laws and follow them. And it is not so hard.

Out of the earth comes *all* that we have, *all* that we are, the food and drink that keep us alive, the clothes that cover us, the roof that shelters us, *every thing!* I heard a man say once, arguing before a Lyceaum, that the Indians had a natural right to live but no natural right to the soil! Did he expect the Indians to live in the water?

We all have a right to live, and that means a right to the soil.

The hour when one man claims the soil as *his*—the hour when a child born into the world has no right to a foot of ground to lie on alive or dead—when a man must pay another man for his very grave!—in that hour begins slavery and crime and suffering without an end.

Those who own land own life. Those who do not own land must buy their lives of those who do *at their own terms.*

So begins the strife of our business world.

To live you must get money.

How do you get money? Where do you get money? It does not grow on trees. You must get it from other people. How can you get it? By giving them something for it. Suppose you have nothing to give for it? Go work for them, give them your time and labor—be their slave. Suppose they do not want your time and labor—they have enough? Then you are not even a slave—you are a criminal—or a dead man.

To sell!—to sell! To sell! You have to sell more than you buy or you don't make a living! You *must* sell and you must make people buy! So comes adulteration. Only to sell—to outsell the others, to sell on any terms, no matter if those who buy buy death—and so comes advertisement. Our whole business world boils over in advertisement! To sell—to sell! To sell! no matter if those who buy buy sin!

What else can you do? You must live. That is the first law God put into the world. And when we live *on each other*—as we must—when some few hold the face of the earth from us—what can you expect but just what you see!

Nationalism has struck a great taproot in striking at our business system, the root of the struggle between man and man. Cut that, and you shall see a mighty fall of foliage and flower and fruit—the luxuriant top of rampant crime and corruption.

There is another root as deep—possibly deeper—the struggle between man and woman.

But these things are all marching together today.

The time is coming and coming fast when men and men shall be friends together and blush for shame at the cutthroat folly of the past, and men and women shall be friends together and what joy beyond all shame will fill us then.

Then we shall know what Human nature is. Then indeed the lion shall lie down with the lamb and a little child shall lead them.

Then we can praise instead of pray and thank the underlying all-embracing good that his will *is* done on earth as it is done in heaven!

"Our Place Today" *

[. . .] Some of you will say again that it is part of the male function in the human race to provide for the family, including

* Lecture presented to the Los Angeles Woman's Club, January 21, 1891, pp. 11–30, handwritten manuscript in Gilman papers, folder 164.

under this head all the varied activities of our race, and the female function merely to serve the family; that for the female to enter real human life would militate against the functional duties—in other words that the whole created human world, church and palace, book and picture, drama and oration, tool and weapon—can be produced only by the male sex, and that the female sex have no power beyond their functional ones!

Who told you this?

How do you know it?

Where is it written?

Alas! It is written in every line and stone and fabric of this man-made world! It is told you down all the centuries by many voices! It is still universally believed.

But it is a lie!

Now I want to make a scientific statement, and then I will try to illustrate and explain it.

Race function does not interfere with sex function. Sex function *does* interfere with race function.

Take some of the lower races—genus felis for instance—take a lion.

What are the characteristics of lions? We all know in a general way. We know the power and ferocity and carnivorous habits of the beast. Does not the lioness share them? Ask a hunter which is the worst to meet, a lion or a lioness—a bear or a shebear?

The lioness is a female. She brings forth her young in due season and suckles them. But she is a *lion* first—a *female* second! All that the male lion does the female lion does also and is "wife and mother" beside! Suppose the lioness stayed always in her hole, while only the lion prowled and hunted. Suppose she had no claws or teeth but had to howl for her mate to defend her in any danger! Suppose she could not roam and climb as he did and was afraid instead of brave, pitiful instead of fierce. Nature would get along with it somehow, of course. She would develope the lion in his capacity and the lioness in her capacity—and before long we should have each of them dragging their "masculinity" and "femininity."

That the lioness hunts and fights makes her the *better mother*

—not the worse! She transmits to her young true lion qualities. What manner of lion cubs would you expect if the mother was feeble and timid?

Now do you think it is proven of the human race that the more helpless and ignorant a woman is the better wife and mother she is? The reverse is proven.

We hear a great deal of these holy and wonderful duties of ours. Holy and wonderful they are, but they are only feminine functions—not *human* ones! We share our maternal instinct and our mating instinct with the other animals—away down the line all you come to [is] the unisexual things and the egg-laying creatures which never know their young.

Womanhood is a fine thing, but it is not Humanity anymore than childhood is Humanity. The dominant soul—the clear strong accurate brain, the perfect service of a healthy body—these do not belong to *sex*—but to *race!*

When the Soul stands before God it is not judged as a male soul or a female soul but as a *human soul,* and I doubt much if any feminine weakness will excuse us there for failing in our share of the world's work.

Whether you believe in The Day of Judgement, or whether you believe in Karma or whether you just know scientifically that force is never wasted—put it on any ground you please our life here on earth is our working day, and the work we do tells for or against not only ourselves, but all our kind!

Now are you sure that a life of domestic service is a woman's whole duty in life? Are you sure that you are the best wives by having no work and no interest beyond your own four walls— and your neighbors? Are you sure you are the best mothers by each of you consecrating twenty years to the care of your own children *whether you are fitted for that care or not?* [. . .]

Is there any proof whatever that the way we women fulfill our duties as wives and mothers is *the best way?*

Just look at the facts. As far as faithfulness goes, and house-keeping, most women do their duty as wives. But is that *enough?* Is simply being a female and being on hand when you are wanted a wife's whole duty? Or keeping the house clean and the dinner hot and having a smile hung on the front door to greet your husbands with?

Does a man want nothing but a *woman* for his life companion —does he not want a *person* too—a human being—his equal in every sense?

To be *equal* does not mean to be *alike,* you know. A perfectly developed woman is the equal of a perfectly developed man, though different.

And as to mothers—well!

I am a mother myself, so you must forgive me if I hit pretty hard; but really do you think that the rate of infant mortality is any credit to our maternity? Half the children born die under five years. Half those under one year.

Think what that means. *One child out of two!* For every baby that we give our very heart's blood to, and face death to bring to life—for every one that lives—another dies! And of those that remain what is their health? How many children do you see that are always well? We talk of "children's diseases" as if God made measles and sent them flying after the children to bring them back to heaven!

Let us not blame God for our diseases—diseases come from sin—and God does not sin nor make sin! When a child is born scrofulous is that God's fault or *ours?*

Let me tell you a fact that may open your eyes a little. Among savages children do not die as ours do. They may practice infanticide, but save for that the babies live. Catlin* tells of a tribe he knew where *only three children had died in ten years;* and of examining Indian burial places—where the bodies are placed on high scaffolds—and finding only six or seven child skeletons among hundreds!

They might talk of being mothers—brag of it—but I never heard they did!

We proclaim it as our first business in life—and look at us.

My friends, do you know what is the first duty of a mother? (I have said this thing before and mean to again.)

* George Catlin (1796–1872) painted hundreds of pictures and wrote dozens of books on Native American peoples.

For what does the horse-trainer select a brood mare? For anything that she may do to the colt after it is born? No. *For the qualities that she transmits to it!*

The first duty of a mother is to be a mother worth having.

Even as far as our functional duties are concerned, we do not fill our places now; we cannot properly fill them while we are wives and mothers *and nothing else.*

You cannot be a male or female thing unless you are the thing first—the female fox is a fox as well as a female, the female eagle is an eagle as well as a female, and the female of the race of man must be an independent integer of that race as well as the female thereof! She must, that is, if she is ever to wholly fill her place on earth.

We are half the human race.

We are responsible to God and man for our half—for half the ignorance and folly, half the shame and sin. I do not say we *commit* half the sin—statistics prove we do not. Women, I believe, are about one-fifth of "the criminal classes." But we are responsible as human beings for the condition of the race.

There is not a living soul on earth—nor ever has been, but was once a child of ours! Even the Immaculate Conception leaves motherhood its crown!

The whole living world is just a lot [of] grown-up babies—*our* babies—and it is our concern what manner of lives they lead—their glory is our glory—their shame our shame! How do we hold our trust?

Do you know what the Koran says of woman? "Thy wife is thy tillage!" [2:223] We have been the soil from which men grew. We women—children that we raised were simply more soil to raise more men—we were the world-producers—men the world!

If this was the best way to make humanity great I would not say a word, but it is *not.*

Take the Turkish woman, that ultra-female thing whose very face must be hidden; does she, the blind and soulless slave of the harem rear nobler sons, or the English and American women in their comparative freedom?

Did you ever notice the high advance in human intelligence

during this century? The immense speed of knowledge and invention, science and discovery?

The world has never seen its equal.

And did you ever compare this fact with the other—that it is just about within this century that women have learned to read? It stands to reason that you get a wiser child from a wise man and a wise woman than from a wise man and a fool.

You cannot be a perfect wife till you belong to the human race with your husband.

You cannot be a perfect mother till you belong to the human race with your son.

You cannot belong to the human race till you do *human work*.

As independent human beings, members of the state, integers, citizens, so only can we be real wives, real mothers, to a race of men.

What is human work? Construction and communication.

How do human beings work? How are the steamships made, the palace cars, the newspapers? By one man working alone in his own four walls? By working *together*.

How have we learned to care for and cultivate fruit and flower, beast and bird?

By each man raising his grandfather's kind of cabbages in his own back garden—rearing hens and horses as his ancestors did in the privacy of his own barn? NO!—*By working together!*

The glory of our race is its power of *communication*. We share our strength and knowledge and rise as one; we share our failure and weakness and help each other bear it. [. . .]

A hundred women in a hundred homes doing a whole woman's work each at houseservice.

Put those hundred women *together*—divide the work—give each woman what she can do best—add invention and improvement—and ten women do that work a hundred did before in one tenth the time!

Did you ever see a woman yet who was cook, housemaid, nurse, seamstress, and housekeeper, and yet *had time* to do anything else? By working together you would save half of your time—about six hours in a working day! You could grow a little then. [...]

It is time we mothers held up our heads and looked our duties squarely in the face.

It is time we learned the one great secret of all human improvement—*working together.* We must learn it before we can improve. And when we use our common brains as well as our individual hearts we shall consider a dead baby as a brand of shame upon our motherhood! [...]

And now you may ask, when the housework is made reasonable and easy so that we save nine tenths of our lives from the greasy whirlpool of the tub and pan, and when motherhood is made reasonable and easy so that we can cheerfully count on raising more than half our children, and without the sacrifice of their mothers' lives, then what are we to do—what is our place if not confined to the home duties?

What is a woman's place?

By the side of man!

It is not good for man to be alone!

After God had made the human race in his own image, male and female, then "God blessed them, and God said unto them Be fruitful and multiply and replenish the earth and *subdue it*" [Genesis, 1:28]. *They* were to subdue it and to have dominion over it—*they,* not *he.*

You live in the city of Los Angeles. You know, some of you, what manner of city it is.

It is composed half of men and half of women. It is your city as much as theirs.

How much do you know about it? How much do you know of the city government, the city business, the city sin? It does not concern you, some will still answer, our field of work is in the home. Well, you all stay at home and work at home, you and your daughters forever. Your husbands and your sons do not stay at home or work at home, they go out alone to meet what is called "the world"—it is not good for man to be alone!

So long as man works alone you will find on one side of him

—the patient domestic ignorant wife, and on the other—Alameda Street!*

Don't you see that if women were all independent conscious citizens, and were united as "a Class"—woman supporting woman, that there wouldn't be any Alameda St.?

If the city government does not properly attend to the city drainage and your home is invaded by disease—is not that your business? If the city government does not provide suitable ventilation and illumination and desk apparatus and teachers in the public schools, is not that your business?

There is nothing in the created world which is not your business, directly or indirectly. The country is your country, the government is your government, you are half the world in your own persons, and mothers of the other half—can anything happen to the world which does not concern you?

By virtue of our humanity the interests of humanity are ours.

By virtue of our womanhood those interests are doubly ours. Twofold as wives. Million fold as mothers.

And the place in which we stand today is awful in its importance.

We are new to our responsibility, fresh and unbiased in judgement, like a race from another planet. Only within a century have we known anything of common life. And we have come to life in an era more rich in possibility—more fraught with danger —more big with hope—than any the struggling world has ever seen.

We have been held back like a reserve force, while half the army fought alone. It has fought, the other half, most manfully, but fought in darkness, crippled and stunted by the great division.

And now, just as the press has brought humanity into communication, while steam and electricity annihilate time, while education and suffrage are practically universal, we come into the field.

Man has done great things to accomplish all this alone—great things! But what things are they? Has human life grown and improved in this triumphant progress of material power? Is human

* A notorious red-light district in Los Angeles, from about 1870 to 1909.

happiness more deep and lasting in silk and broadcloth than it was in homespun or in skins? Does the railroad and telegraph keep your babies alive or your hearts from breaking?

The gains of humanity are gains in *feeling*. Where Christianity has really taught us to love each other, there we are better off.

Love and Truth, Goodness and Beauty—these are gains.

And you well know what noble part we have held in these things, ignorant houseservants or sensual slaves though we have been.

Man has done the best he could alone, but look at the result today! The savage world I need not mention, but look at the civilized world—at Europe and America and Australia. Don't look at the church or the state, though they are both instructive spectacles; don't look at Commerce or Service or Art or Culture. *Look at the people!* Are they well and happy? What a few persons have clutched for themselves is not the gain of a race. All over Europe and here in free America—look at the people?

There is hypocrisy in the church, corruption in the state, and in every family a "skeleton in the closet"!

Man has fought disease and conquered it, as you cut heads off a hydra*—the old ones are somewhat mastered; the new ones laugh at science.

Man has fought human error with civil laws, and he cannot make them fast enough to keep up—crimes increase faster than we can make laws to cover them.

He has done his solitary best, and look at it! It is not good for man to be alone!

By the side of man where God placed us—doing the work of the world of which we are half—mothers who can raise live children and strong ones—wives who can hold love forever because he stays of choice—women who can stand alone and therefore can help men and help each other—in the forefront of a race which has no sovereign save God—this is Our Place Today!

* In Greek mythology, a nine-headed monster, one of which was immortal. Slaying it was one of the twelve labors of Hercules. But each time he struck off a head, two would grow in its place. Finally, he burned away eight of the heads and buried the immortal one under a large rock.

The Labor Movement, a prize essay read before the trades and labor unions of Alameda County, Sept. 5, 1892.*

Introduction

When the Trades and Labor Unions of Alameda Country were arranging for the celebration of Labor Day, September 5th, 1892, the delegates from Federal Labor Union No. 5761, suggested the ideas of procuring a gold medal to be given to the woman who should write the best essay on "The Labor Movement." The following essay was awarded the medal, the only trophy of its kind ever given to a woman for similar effort. In doing this, Organized Labor recognizes the fact that "the hand that rocks the cradle, rules the world."

Oakland, Cal., May 15th 1893.

COMMITTEE.

[Herbert] Spencer has defined evolution, in words that open limitless fields of thought, as a progress from indefinite, incoherent, homogeneity, to definite, coherent, heterogeneity, by a series of differentiations.

The evolution of society, in common with that of every other organism, follows this process.

The conception of society as an organism, with the individual man merely as a cell in the structure, is essential to the understanding of any human problem.

The peculiarity of man's position in this respect is that he has a separate consciousness, a separate will. This gives him an immeasurable advantage over lower forms of life.

Where you have intelligent voluntary co-ordination of particles the process of evolution is quicker and easier than where the particles are inert; but if instead of intelligent co-ordination, you have intelligent resistance of particles, the process of evolution is much impeded.

Man holds the advantage of supplementing the action of

---

* Oakland, Calif.: Alameda County Federation of Trades, [1893]; *History of Women*, reel 943, document 8563.

evolutionary law by his own individual co-operative force, but he also labors under the disadvantage of opposing evolutionary law by individual resistance.

This is why human evolution is so confusing a spectacle. It is so swift and perfect at times, at others so slow and confused, so involved in local retrogression and temporary hindrance.

No wonder the thinker from the individual standpoint has so often given up the riddle, and sought a key to life's confusions in the answer—death.

But the collectivist, one who views humanity as an organic whole, can understand the problem and go far to solve it.

Man in his savage state was in a condition of indefinite, incoherent homogeneity. The individual savages were indefinite—unspecialized—one was as good as another.

They were incoherent—unorganized—each for himself.

The man was homogeneous; split up a savage nation, geographically, and the pieces could thrive and grow like the fragments of a zo-ophyte—one part of the race was as good as another—a protoplasmic mass. But man, to-day is definite, coherent, above all heterogeneous. The individual is specialized to such an extent as to be unable to exist without the social body. We cohere by a thousand ties, faintly to the uttermost parts of society, more and more closely to those nearest us in affinity and we are heterogeneous to an extent beyond the highest comprehension of our parent savage.

In this process of social development, the organic evolution of society, the labor movement holds an important part.

As a distinct historical phenomenon, it may be defined as the effort of the different crafts to maintain and improve their own positions.

As an individual phenomenon it is simply the effort of each separate man, by organization, to maintain and improve his own life.

But from the collective standpoint, the labor movement becomes far more interesting; it is seen in its true importance as the organic evolution of the body politic.

Let us study this. Human labor is the voluntary conscious

exertion of faculty, the application of the will to organ or member, causing it to perform its functions. By labor has the individual man grown from a naked cannibal to a civilized human being; and by the co-ordinate labor of all men has society, the collective man[,] become possible at all.

But that great creature is not yet a conscious, living thing. It is being slowly evolved; it is not yet fully alive. In this evolution, the labor movement is precisely analogous to the development of organ and function in earlier forms of life.

Primitive man was a functionless, protoplasmic body. He acted individually, but not collectively. Each one supplied his own needs, and the death of one was no loss to the others, rather a gain—as he left more to eat.

Primitive man was a consumer and not a producer. Modern man is so specialized that the individual does not, and, in the very nature of life, cannot supply his own needs.

In the division of labor which is our collective strength, we have lost the power of the savage to provide for himself, precisely as the specialized cell in the body is unable to provide for itself as does the ameboid cell in the water.

Modern man in some cases devotes his whole energy to the performance of functions which cannot possibly apply to himself —as for instance the dentist, the obstetrician, and many others.

We are to-day highly specialized cells in the social organism; our labor being useful rather to society than to ourselves; and our living depending on society rather than on ourselves.

The more perfectly this specialization is carried out, the more powerful is our collective existence.

The individual we may consider as a cell, but the body of individuals belonging to any one trade or profession, is, to the community, an organ.

It follows that the growth and perfection of each trade-union, guild, and craft, is analogous to the growth and perfection of eye, hand, foot, stomach—any organ of the body.

For civilized society to exist, requires the specialization of bodies of men to perform the various functions of such an organism.

Primitive society was simple, like the earlier forms of animal life. There was the parasitic stage when formless bodies of savages lived on the other animals—mere microbes there.

There was the somewhat higher form when society had developed a nutritive apparatus, the farming and trading class, organs of offense and defense—the fighting class, and a species of head —the ruling class. A very poor head it was too, for many ages; a thick-skulled, home-crowned, butting head, getting the poor body into many a war.

But year after year we have been enlarging and perfecting our social organism until we begin to see what human life may become.

It is not size we need—the age of the megatheirum* is past.

It is not teeth and claws we need, nor scaly hides—our military and police forces are relics of an earlier age.

The growth of man is toward a higher organized, industrial society, successful through relation of parts; a delicate and powerful organism, fit instrument for the further workings of the Great Law. To this end is the labor movement, and there is no other movement in all the human world to be mentioned in the same breath. What a man does is of no account to him save as it moulds and developes his character and constitution. What mankind does is of no account to him save for the same reason.

History, with its tale of war and waste and who was king, is like some interesting story of [']How Mammoth and Mastodon fought'—'The Adventures, of the Ichthyosaurus'—'Which was the Wisest Dodo?[']

History is of value as material for Sociology, as stories of the behavior of certain animals are valuable in zo-ology—all part of the wonderful unveiling of science, in which we see how life shot up through gross reptilian and fierce carnivorous forms, up and up to this crowning creature who reigns undisputed over the lower races by virtue not of size, not of ferocity, not of armor and weapons, not even of ingenuity, solely, but by virtue of parts which gives [sic] him the the power and persistent vitality to supplant all others.

* Large ground sloths of the Miocene and Pleistocene epochs.

It is organic evolution in man, the development and correlation of parts, which makes him master of the elephant; and it is the labor movement, the organic evolution of society, which is making modern civilized man a collective entity which shall surmount and survive all lower civilizations.

It is the labor movement which is doing this, not the labor alone. We have had skilled labor for uncounted ages. Those workmen in the lost arts could do things we can not, just as spiders can do things we cannot.

It is the development of organic relation between different classes of labor, which gives us the advantage.

The workmen of India can make better rugs than the workmen of Lowell [Massachusetts]; but the workmen of Lowell are constituent parts of a higher organism.

The dominance of the Anglo-Saxon race is due not so much to superiority in special faculties as to superiority in co-ordination of faculties. As a perfectly organized army of inferior men can overcome a miscellaneous horde of athletes; so is society permanent and dominant according to its correlation of parts rather than according to the development of its special organs.

The labor movement has by no means realized its mighty use thus far. For the most part it has been an unconscious enlargement of self-interest to include the interests of those related by similar occupation.

But it is just that form of affiliation which establishes the real cohesion of society. The labor movement has heretofore often blindly endeavored to maintain and advance the interests of a special craft at the expense of the others.

But it is just that form of organic limitation which establishes the real definiteness of society.

So has the labor movement, even in its cruder forms, helped in that progress from indefinite, incoherent homogeneity, to definite, coherent heterogeneity, which is the path of social evolution.

And now, when the extension and perfection of our social nervous system or electric wire has brought us all into close contact; when we are realizing our social unity more fully every day, is the labor movement which, more than any other, establishing our brotherhood—our oneness, the world over. Kings still rule, soldiers still fight—feeble survivors of more ancient social systems; and the parasites of society wax fatter than ever in their destructive gluttony; but under it all society is organizing and developing in lines of truest health and beauty.

That the Kansas farmers send flour to the Homestead strikers* is a more important fact than that [Andrew] Carnegie [1835–1919] sends a barrel of whisky to [President Benjamin] Harrison [1833–1901; President of the United States, 1889–1893] or that Andover [Theological Seminary] sends missionaries to Hindostan.

What kings and millionaires and preachers do, is as nothing compared to what the people do; and the people, to-day, are doing what is right.

This is the real work of the labor movement—to increase the functional activity of organized society, and the consciousness of our collective life; to perfect the social usefulness of every craft, and establish its co-ordination; it is the growth of humanity, and its record is the morphology of civilization.

In this world-raising movement are encountered certain obstacles; enormous, apparently immovable; which have, so far, greatly impeded our progress.

One of these is the misconception of the status of labor, which we owe, indirectly, to the hereditary influence of the dim past; and directly, to the educational influence of the Hebrew Scriptures.

The hereditary influence we could outgrow; every fact in modern life contradicts it; but the educational influence of a prevailing religion is re-imposed upon us in every generation.

In primitive ages, labor was mainly performed by slaves. The prisoner of war, the vanquished one, the inferior, labored. While the predatory life was the most successful—the warrior was superior to the worker. Armed men hunted and fought for food,

* The Amalgamated Iron and Steel Workers struck the Homestead, Pennsylvania, plant of the Carnegie Steel Corporation, in July 1892, after their wages had been cut twenty percent. The company locked out the workers; the workers surrounded the plant; and Pinkerton detectives were hired to drive away the workers. In the ensuing gunfight, three detectives and ten workers were killed. The state militia was sent in, the plant reopened under armed guard, and the strike was called off in November.

and the women labored alone. The warrior could live without working; the worker must have defense while he worked. Labor required co-ordination from the first.

Thus the feeling that to labor is to admit inferiority, and subjugation had its first basis.

Conditions have changed. We no longer live by bloodshed. Labor is now the prevalent condition of existence, rapidly rising into more dignity and honor.

The time is coming when the military and judiciary will become extinct forms of human energy; when government will become organization, and the work of the world go on as naturally and unconsciously as the heart beats and the blood circulates.

But the time has not come, and its coming is hindered by the lingering impression that it is better to be worked for than to work.

Added to this is the Hebrew idea, held in common with all early races, that labor was a curse. Their notion is based on the same phenomena as those above mentioned, but its weight with us is due to our receiving it as a religious truth.

What we might outgrow as an inheritance it is difficult to combat as revelation. It is time we let the wisdom of modern scientific truths annul the folly of ancient religious falsehood, and erase from our minds the thought that labor is a curse.

Labor is the distinctive function of humanity; not only a blessing as poetically called, but an absolute condition of existence.

As well call swimming a curse to the fish, flying a curse to the bird, breathing a curse to the lungs, as labor a curse to man.

This obstacle removed, we shall find the progress of social evolution far more steady and rapid.

But there is another, a larger, stronger, deeper rooted. An obstacle so great that because of it the labor movement is still held back to conditions of savagery and violence, the one thing that, more than all others retards our growth. This is the idea embodied in the well known text—"IF A MAN WILL NOT WORK, NEITHER SHALL HE EAT." It is the conception of labor as a means and wages as an end; of labor as a cause and pleasure as a result; it is the practical, deadly form of the most radical error in our religion—the idea of life as an endurance, an exception, and heaven as a reward.

In simplest form it is the idea of "living for what there is in it."

This is utterly unscientific. It is disproven by the growth of every individual; and the life of the individual epitomizes that of the race. To eat—to receive comes first. To labor—that highly specialized faculty of modern man—comes last. For nine months the dawning life receives all and gives nothing.

For twenty years, if conditions are right, the immature man is fed and clothed and loved and taught, with no commensurate return.

After that it is the business of the mature man to work, not for what he is to get, but BECAUSE OF WHAT HE HAS HAD.

The surplus energy of the individual prompts him to labor, to produce. If he has not the surplus energy, he cannot produce, he can only consume.

The superiority of the higher forms of animal life over the lower, is due to the fact that by their complex, co-ordinate activity, they can more easily obtain food and distribute it throughout the organism. Only an organism so fed is capable of such activity. So with organized society. Because of its power to obtain and distribute the necessary supplies to all its parts, are the parts enabled to co-exist and form society. Organized society owes to the individual every possible form of nutrition and education, precisely as the body owes nutrition to the cell. It is the right of the individual to be so cared for, because he is a constituent part of society. He, in return, owes to society all the labor which nutrition and education have made possible to him.

We are not born into a world which has the right to say to us "work—or you shall not live!" We are born into a world which has the duty of maintaining us alive in order that we may work. As in the military stage of society we taught the young boy that he owed his life's best service in the battlefield to the country which protected him; so, in the industrial days, we shall teach our children, boys and girls, that they owe their live's [sic] best service in the field of labor to the country which made them what they are. A devotion absolutely filial will result in this relation between the parent, society, and its child, the man. But the supply must come first, the return after. Our wages must be paid in advance.

I know that it will take a definite and powerful effort of that constructive faculty we call imagination to conceive of life under such conditions. We are so used to considering labor as belonging to that order of effort used in "the struggle for existence," and to think that what we get should be proportioned to the amount and value of our labor—"the survival of the fittest."

Impress your mind with the conviction that all this phase of thought applies only to our relation with nature, outside humanity, to our collective action in maintaining racial existence, but our relation to each other has reached a stage of complete interdependence and common interest where such idea of struggle and survival is preposterous. To illustrate: consider a buffalo, diligently eating grass, or running away from an enemy.

What is the buffalo's part in the struggle for existence? According to his success in eating and running is his survival, his fitness.

But meanwhile, inside the buffalo, many concerted acts are carried on.

The heart beats, the stomach digests, the blood circulates, the lungs breathe, the nerves transmit—all these processes and many more, in order that the whole buffalo may eat and run and so survive; and, more remotely, that the myriad cells composing his great bulk may also live. Horn, hoof and hide, bones, juices, tissues,—if they live at all, can only live as parts of that great body. But they do not struggle for existence; that effort has long left the part and become the duty of the whole.

So with that great body which is man.

Those acts which we perform collectively to maintain, defend, and improve our lives, are in the nature of a struggle for existence.

For man to produce food from earth and sea; for man to overcome the wolf, the tiger, the rabbit, the flea, the cotten [sic] scale, the microbe; for man to avoid disease, remove danger, postpone death; these are acts by which we maintain our existence; by which we as the fittest race on earth, survive.

But every act which men perform FOR EACH OTHER—every social function—all that wondrous flood of benefit which, by virtue of our humanness, one man or woman can give the rest— these efforts are not the struggle for existence, nor to be associated with the idea of personal gain.

If men consumed more than they produced; if they had no functional relation to each other; if their common food supply was insufficient, or if they were cannibals, then it would be in the struggle for existence for them to fight with each other.

But it is ages now since man learned to produce more than he consumed; he has reached a stage in functional relation where interdependence is absolute; and his food supply has become a store of surplus wealth. Therefore it is ignorance or folly for us to speak of the interrelative activity of man as a struggle for existence.

Human labor to-day has its legitimate part in the struggle for existence only where it is concerted action for the common good, against the common foe.

Human labor in all our infinite usefulness to each other, should be orderly, unconscious, involuntary—the peaceful interaction of men—the parts in the organic life of man, the whole.

Seeing this—and the labor movement points so clearly up the path of right progression that one can scarcely fail to see, seeing the direction and means of growth, what hinders an advance! Here is labor organizing and inter-organizing, the wide world over; men of all lands, of all races, learning swiftly and surely that their interests are in common, their work is one.

Intelligence and education are now behind the hands of labor —we who work can think.

What, then, keeps us back?

There are some who will answer, Government! Some, Religion! Some, Society! Most all, perhaps, The Rich! Of the first three it may be said at once that government, religion and society, are in our hands, to be modified and developed as we are able.

Of the last I want to say a special word. A needed word, an earnest, heart-felt, carefully considered word; a truth that should be spoken everywhere in these days when the struggle waxes bitter and bloodshed is already upon us. An intense class-hatred is growing up among us, mainly an imported article, but thriving finely here,—a dull rage against the rich.

We speak of them with scorn, with fury, with sharp satire and stinging ridicule.

We act as though they were in our way.

To the political economist the class is represented by the word "Capital."

That is an imposing word, but the fact it covers is, that in our blindness we have allowed a few men to have more than their share of what we make. It is owing to a diseased condition in the social organism that such a thing is possible; and the depraved cells, the morbid tissues, are not to be blamed for their unhappy state.

In the healthy activity of interhuman function, these so-called rich are functionless, inactive, helpless.

In the power and pride of productive capacity, real human value, they are wanting. In the path of progress, the rising line of evolution, they stand very far back and low—relics of a time when man could only kill and eat and grow fat, and could not MAKE.

A human being that does not work, is a human being ungrown, not fully alive, or else decadent—retrograde—beginning to die. And it is these helpless ones, these infantile or senile weights on society, whom we allow to appropriate more than their share of human wealth! Whom we allow! And then blame them for being what they are!

They are the inevitable result of the wrong condition underlying our whole industrial system, and we have no right to hold ill-feeling against that part of the body where the disease shows most.

If we should undergo a surgical operation, as did France a century ago [during the revolution of 1789], and use the knife to remove our tumerous [sic] growth of millionaires, it would only crop out in another place.

We are all affected with the financial sickness of which these rich are the fever, and the poor the chill.

So long as we believe that a man must work before he eats—
that what we get is a reward of, and should be in proportion to
what we do—so long will the smarter man get more than his
brother, and, once that difference admitted—there is no stop-
ping-place between letting the smart man have one dollar more
and letting him have two hundred million dollars more. The
smartest man can do more—that is his glory; but it is no reason
that he should get more.

What we get should be in order that we may do—not
because of what we have done.

The combined effort of all parts of the body is in order that
the body may thrive, and so the parts thrive also.

The combined effort of all men is in order that the race may
thrive, and so the men may thrive also.

The trouble with the body politic is lack of common consciousness. Once we have that—once we fully realize that we are
one and our interest in common, then we shall see the absurdity
of allowing the nutrition of the body to be diverted from the
active organs which make it, and poured in unhealthy accumula-
tions into these excrescences—the Rich. It cannot be good for
the body to have one part of itself better nourished than another.
It cannot be good for man to have one part of himself better
nourished than another. But it is beneath the dignity of this vast,
intelligent body of humanity to waste energy in wincing and
whining under its disease, or in striking viciously at the sore
places.

It is one of the most laughable pages of history to see this
irresistible, all-conquering thing—The Human Race, spending so
much time over an infinitesimal fraction of itself—this handful of
poor rich. Why, the working population of the world could easily
afford to put all its millionaires in an elegant park by themselves,
build for them the houses they cannot make, cook for them the
food they cannot cook, write for them the books they cannot
write—maintain them forever as interesting relics of barbarism
—so that we go on about our business—the raising of the world.
We must put an end to the causes of this millionaire disease, and
then the existing crop would not trouble us. They are nothing but

symptoms. We have played at life as a game too long. A game with little yellow counters, to be won by the players. We have no right to be angry if the best players—strictly according to rule, get it all. But we have the right—we have the duty, yes, and we have the power,—to stop our childish game forever and fall to work as man never worked before. To work, not for transient, personal aggrandizement, but for the permanent improvement of the habitable globe. To work, we of the higher classes, the specialized, productive classes, that the world may become a garden, full of stately and beautiful cities, fair towns and lovely villages; that the feeding of humanity be a brief and pleasant task, the clothing and housing it an artist's glory; and the teaching of our constant flood of fresh young life a task for man's noblest effort.

This is our work, to make the world fit place for man to live in, and man fit being to live in it.

Behind us is the record of life, clearly spread in the light of science; before us is the upward path, broad, beautiful and within our power to follow.

Let us stop no longer to grieve over the past or rebel at the present.

As the workers of humanity we hold the world in our hands, and can make it what we will.

Forward then, in the light of truth and the warmth of mutual love! Forward in man's one work!—To help God make man better.

"What the People's Party Means" *

[. . .] In the first place it means a new age, it marks an era in history.

Hundreds of years from now those who come after us shall review this age and say, "In the last decade of the 19th century arose the people of the United States, quietly, legally, in good order, and accomplished without bloodshed a revolution more deep, lasting, and effectual for good than any revolution in all history."

* Speech delivered June 9, 1893, pp. 12–18, handwritten manuscript in Gilman papers, folder 172.

That is what the People's Party means. It is not a "mere" offshoot of an old regime, a trifling difference of opinion, a split on some inconsequent idea!

It represents the movement of the age. It stands in plain peaceful legal form for as great an issue as ever led humanity onward.

To be in and to help it is to stand with the heroes and leaders of all time, to be one of those who move the world.

Not to be in it is to rank with the great mass of helplessness and retrogression which has always retarded civilization.

Always there have been the men who could see ahead and move ahead, who have pushed and pulled and struggled on, with humanity hanging its deadweight on the ties that bound them together.

You see we are bound together—we are all one great body, and a part cannot break off and get ahead of the rest.

It is as if we were all harnessed together in a fast team, and some were plunging and pulling to get ahead, some digging their heels in keeping it back as far as they were able, and the majority merely keeping step or serenely hanging by their elbows and letting themselves be carried.

If we were all holding ourselves ready to advance together the work of the leaders would not be so hard and our advance would be faster. The People's Party today is the advance movement of the age. It means more to the real profit of civilization than all other issues of the day together.

That is not putting it before religion or science or art or invention or discovery, save as an immediate need comes first. To kill a bear might be of more profit than to find a gold mine—if the bear came first.

The establishment of the principles on which the People's Party rests means a new inspiration, a new growth, in every branch of human effort.

As it is now all these other fields of life are stunted blasted corrupted injured crushed by the power of evil which is fastened on us all and which the People's Party lives to conquer!

I hardly need to name it. We all know it. Wider than Church or State, stronger than Priest or King, more deepseated wide-spreading, subtle, deadly, and deceiving—holding us all—all—laborer, farmer, artisan, mechanic, artist, scientist, professional and preacher, taking the truth out of religion, the beauty out of art, the joy out of labor, the peace out of life—what thing is this which we fight today?

The Money Power.

The blind bigotry of the rich, the oppression of the purse—that is the most dangerous force at work upon society today, and man's first duty is to resist it!

There are times when much must be risked and spent to gain what to the individual seems little, but to all individuals that little becomes so great that no price would be heavy to have paid for it.

There are times when man must give up peace and safety and rest and love and go forth to effort, danger and death—because of what? To gain what? Because if he did not he would lose what peace and safety he had, to gain the peace and safety of his own loved ones and countless millions more.

Are the men of this day less strong, less brave, less noble than the men of other days?

I do not believe it.

I do not believe it because it is only thirty years ago [in the Civil War] that men still living proved—*proved* before all the world in the ineffacable records of history, that they could so do and dare and suffer.

Some of those men still live. Their sons are our citizens today.

And all that keeps them from the mighty struggle and bloodless victories of today is that they do not understand.

But there are many to teach.

In a few pulpits—on many platforms, in unnumbered books and papers the great principles of human life are being laid before us.

We have our religious life.

We have our political life.

We have our industrial life.

In the first two we have made ourselves free, but because we are slaves in the last we are helpless in all.

Religious freedom is a mockery to men whose industrial life makes them dishonest, heartless, shallow and mean as surely as the slum breeds the criminal.

Political freedom is a mockery to men whose industrial freedom makes their hardwon power mere power for others to use, voting this way or that as their masters direct, voting in idiotic triumph for the very measures that hold them down—mere cat's paws for the artful ape behind.

Industrial freedom is the basis of all freedom; there is none without it.

Industrial freedom makes honest reality of political freedom, and living truth of religious freedom.

Industrial freedom is the watchword of the age, and that is what the People's Party means! [...]

"The Ethics of Woman's Work"*

[...] Work is the natural exercise of expanding faculties, of surplus energy, and comes as naturally to man as singing to birds.

Work is a condition of growth, and growth a condition of existence. The life of the race is in its work.

It is not sufficient to enjoy the fruit of others' labors—if we were supplied with all we wanted by extra human agency we should as inevitably sink as if we went without.

It is that we have artists which make us human—not that we have pictures. The picture is the fruit of the artist and to be enjoyed, but it is the painting of it which is his right, his privilege, his duty.

Here is where women are robbed of their place in the path of progress by being denied that development of industry which means as much to them as it does to men and this injury to women is felt as seriously by the race as if it was done to men.

To have all our mothers woman servants lowers the race level as much as it would to have all our fathers manservants.

Women need progressive organized industry as much as they

* Lecture presented on February 1, 1894, pp. 15–20, handwritten manuscript, Gilman papers, folder 171.

need education or food or air—it is a condition of human existence and progression. That they should be deprived of such industry and relegated eternally to the performance of the nutritive and excretory functions of the body politic, and those at the most primitive level, is wrong—grievously wrong to humanity, and to be carefully considered in the ethics of woman's work.

What work then *should* women do? First of all, like the work of all human creatures, it should be healthful, done for reasonable hours, under right conditions, and not such as to injure either the general human nature or the special woman nature.

(And let me say here in parentheses that housework, with its frequent heavy lifting, its long hours, its nerve-exhausting variations and repitions [sic], its constant having of the hands in water, its endless stepping and standing, is about as trying to the alleged weakness of woman as most kinds of labor.

We hear much of the shop girls who cannot sit down, but we are too familiar with it to notice the exhausted housewife who drops into her chair at dinner for the first time since breakfast, and then has to get up a dozen times during the meal!)

Woman's work should be adapted to her physical health, of course, and to her mental health as well.

Second it should be such as in no way to interfere with the duties of maternity. Sweeping, washing, scrubbing and all such violent exertions—washing of windows and carrying of pails and hods—cooking and ironing with their overheating of the blood —these are no occupations for the prospective or the nursing mother.

A woman who is to be a mother should have no exertion demanded of her, but the housewife cannot cease her endless round of necessary labor for any such incidentals of pain as childbearing.

When women each have some business of their own they should arrange a vacation for these primal duties.

The women whose trained industry it is to serve, teach, watch, or entertain children, should have no other business whatever, especially of a dirty and dangerous sort like housework.

Third, and aside from these considerations, every woman

should do that work to which she is best adapted (so that it be *good work*), in order that she may contribute her share to the transmission of acquired traits by which the race advances.

This is really the most important view of the question, ethically.

Our largest duty is to the race of which we are a part.

To be and do the best we can that we may be and do the most for our kind—that is the human duty—that is what God set us here to do.

We are to grow—to develope—to follow the radiant line of progress which he has set before us; lit with Truth and built on Law; and that path is not to be followed by rite and ceremony, by sacrifice and abasement, by any arbitrary behavior assumed as especially pleasing to the distant Deity; but by the virtue and uplifting of our common business—by the work which we do in the world!

In his work is man's advance on earth and approach to Heaven.

In her work is woman's also, not as the body servant of humanity, but by the side of man in every step of the way— companion, comforter, sister, wife—equal always, on earth as in Heaven.

That is the reason why housework is not sufficient for a sex. [. . .]

"First Class in Sociology: Third Lesson" *

Teacher: "Very well. Who is ready this morning?"

The Individualist: "I am, sir. I have been studying this question of Socialism for some time and am quite prepared to speak on it."

Teacher: "Proceed. Let us hear where you are in your studies."

Individualist: "Socialism is a proposed system of government in which all citizens are compelled to work for the community and the community in return provides for all its citizens. This

---

* *The American Fabian*, 3 (May 1897), pp. 7–9. This introduction to socialism began in the January issue and continued into 1898, encompassing seven lessons in all.

method—could it be carried out—would no doubt insure a certain amount of creature comfort to the soulless slaves composing such a community. My objection, sir—and the objection of all true Americans—is that it would destroy all Individuality and reduce life to a dead level of hopeless monotony!"

Teacher: "I am very glad to see you in the class, my friend. You have stated your views very fairly, and I shall endeavor to answer them to your satisfaction. But I would like you first to be a little more explicit as to just *how* such a system would deprive us of the quality you value so highly—with good reason. You are not, I hope, under the vulgar error by supposing that people are to be provided for by means of barracks, uniforms and rations?"

Individualist: "No, sir. I have passed that."

Teacher: "You understand that with the continued Socialization of Society people will be more and more free to gratify their most diverse personal wants—far more so than at present?"

Individualist: "I had hardly thought that, sir. I supposed that —that a certain similarity in provision must be established. You are confronted, you see, sir, by an economic difficulty in supplying to a whole population the naturally desired luxuries which are now possible to so few; and—if you assume the ability to meet that—by the further difficulty of effecting any fair distribution of publicly owned wealth to meet the thousand caprices of individual desire. No, sir! It cannot be done!"

Teacher: "You are still in ignorance even of the theories of present writers on Socialism—to say nothing of the principles of it, with their inevitable results. Let me explain to you temporarily —prior to a further lesson I shall assign you—that according to the views of one school of Socialists each man shall be ensured the opportunity to labor to the full extent of his powers, and guaranteed the proceeds of his own labor. Another school maintains that all men shall not only be assured of the opportunity to labor, but shall be guaranteed all that they need for life's best development, whether their individual labor is considered an equivalent or not. This doctrine is expressed in the formula: 'To each according to his need; from each according to his ability.'

Under neither of these would Individuality be affected, save, indeed, to develop it."

Individualist: "I must beg to differ with you, sir. The first case, indeed, would not affect it, but it seems to me that such a condition is not Socialism, but simply the just fulfillment of our present system. All we ask now is the right to work and the enjoyment of the proceeds of our own labor. I believe in that myself, and I am a Single Taxer. Nothing could be further from a Socialist! But this second theory you lay down is what I had in mind—that is what I understood Socialists wanted—to sort of lump people together—make 'em all work and reward them all equally."

Teacher: "Not equally, by any means. 'To each according to his need' does not mean that all shall have alike."

Individualist: "But who is to decide, sir, as to what each person needs?"

Teacher: "Himself—or herself."

Individualist: "But—you do not mean that every person is to help himself—or herself—out of a free supply of the products of labor?"

Teacher: "That is the theory I am at present explaining to you. Can you show me how such a condition would destroy individuality?"

Individualist: "I can show you that it is a preposterous idea, sir! An inconceivable absurdity! An impossibility!"

Teacher: "That is not exactly the point. You said that you had studied the question of Socialism and objected to it on the ground that it would destroy individuality. I am asking you to explain how it would do so."

Individualist: "Socialism, sir, as I understand it, consists of a system of forcibly managing the business of the community in the interests of the community—instead of allowing individuals to manage each his own business in his own interests. We should all become a sort of working army—as subservient and automatic as a lot of soldiers—no freedom, no variety, no chance for a man to strike out for himself! Why, sir, just look at the present government officials, the clerks at Washington. Nothing could be more hopelessly stultifying than their existence! Socialism would make us all into a lot of wooden dolls! America would never stand it!"

Teacher: "I can quite understand that any person who continues for a period of many years in a kind of work which offers no room for natural growth would become somewhat as you say. But this is equally true of clerks in other positions than under the government. These government positions are not compulsory. Why do you suppose the victims of such a soul-destroying position remain in office? Indeed, eagerly compete for it?"

Individualist: "Why, of course they do, most of 'em. It's only a very strong man that has sense and courage enough to break away from such a snug berth and go make something of himself. You see its [sic] *sure.*"

Teacher: "Yes. Even with the disadvantages you mention the assurance of payment and the honorable position of working for Uncle Sam direct proves an unceasing attraction. Now, imagine for a moment these things: First, a range of government offices that covered every kind of work necessary to man's happiness. Second, a fully reformed civil service, so that merit was always sure of recognition and promotion. Third, perfect freedom to change from labor that proved distasteful to labor of any other kind. Now, under such conditions as these do you see anything in public service that is destructive of individuality?"

Individualist: "How could a man drop his work and go somewhere else unless there happened to be a vacancy?"

Teacher: "Can he now? My friend, under Socialism we shall still, and always, recognize human limitations. Man can only do now what other people want done. If he tries something else he simply fails in business. So under Socialism, the range of work offered must correspond in some measure to popular needs. Moreover, advanced thinkers among Socialists by no means shut out the principle of individual invention and discovery. The official who shall have some contribution of his own brain to add to human wealth and progress will have ample time and means to work it out."

Individualist: "How so?"

Teacher: "By the exceedingly short hours of required labor, which will leave each individual ample time to develop his own tastes, powers and ideas. And by a public fund, kept to encourage and promote all progress—scientific, artistic or mechanical."

Individualist: "But the individual inventor would have to convince a lot of other men to get hold of the money, wouldn't he?"

Teacher: "Does he not have to now? And he would not be checked by the self-interest of other individuals, who would seek to crush his invention because it interfered with their private gains."

Individualist: "I see what you mean, sir. It sounds very fair. But, after all, the individual does not profit individually by his invention, does he? He has no object, no incentive. *That* is what I mean, sir. Take away the spring of individual self-interest and you take away the incentive of action. No man would try to do anything different when he was just as well off without it! We should remain forever just at the same place—no progress, no individuality!"

Teacher: "I am glad to find you so clear and fair a thinker. You admit that under the theory of Socialism as I present it there is nothing in the method of doing the work or the method of providing for the workers which would destroy individuality; but that, since the contribution of the individual to the good of the community did not result in a specific increase of his own material wealth, therefore he would not so contribute. If this were so, you have some ground for your fears. Do I state your position fairly?"

Individualist: "You do, sir."

Teacher: "Then it remains for me to show that progress, the ever new development of the human spirit, coming as it must through the individual brain, does not depend on the hope of personal material reward. In other words, that the principle of competition, rightly valued by all economists, is not confined in its working to the field of material reward. This requires considerable explanation, however, and I will defer it till the next lesson. [. . .]"

Chapter Three

. . . . .

The Book-Writing Years
(1898–1909)

The Progressive Era

A HOST of reform ideas and groups had appeared in the United States during the 1880s and early 1890s, but the strenuous efforts to merge them had failed. The depression of 1893–1897, the suppression of Coxey's Army* and the Pullman strike in 1894, and the strength the two-party political system demonstrated in the election of 1896, broke the back of most reform organizations and convinced reformers of the failure of industrialism and political parties as progressive forces. However, even though the federal government acted as an agent of suppression during the 1890s, reformers' belief in government as an agency to control business and protect the values being destroyed by unconstrained business activity deepened. Broadly speaking, the idea was to eliminate corporate control of the government and place it in the hands of the educated middle class, who, it was believed, would administer a purified, impartial, moral government.

These "progressive" reformers did not favor partisan political activity or mass organizing, for they distrusted labor unions and parties

* When Congress failed to enact the large-scale public-works program he had advocated, a wealthy Ohio businessman, Jacob S. Coxey (1854–1951), led a peaceful march of 500 people on the Capital. He and fifty of his followers were arrested on their arrival, May 1, 1894.

almost as much as they did corporations. They preferred education, exposure, explanation, and moral exhortation. They tried to organize themselves more effectively, establish clear priorities, and build their expertise to an imposing level through collection and assimilation of data.

A wide strain of moral concern ran through the Progressive reform effort. The Social Justice movement—intellectuals, lawyers, ministers, and reformers such as Jane Addams, Lillian Wald (1867–1940), Florence Kelley, Julia Lathrop (1858–1932), in organizations such as settlement houses, the National Consumers League, the National Child Labor Committee, and the American Association for Labor Legislation—tried to lessen the impact of the industrial age on the less fortunate and insisted that the less fortunate follow a strict standard of moral behavior.[1] That is, they wanted to reform society and the individual at the same time.

Although the Progressives borrowed part of their reform agenda from the Populists, the two movements differed in significant ways: The Progressives were not a political party but a loose coalition of varied organizations; the Progressives were urban-oriented and middle class; the Progressives were less daring and imaginative. Progressivism also represented a clear separation of classes and an elitist approach: middle-class experts and professionals would diagnose the ills of and prescribe the cures for the lower classes, thereby training them to behave as "normal Americans."

Overcoming racial prejudice and eliminating racist institutions did not figure in the progressive program. With the exception of those few whites involved in the National Association for the Advancement of Colored People (1909) and the National Urban League (1910), most Progressives were oblivious of the violent segregation affecting African-Americans, Latinos, Asians, and Native Americans between 1890 and 1910. They were, however, sharply aware of the "new types" of immigrants entering the United States from southern and eastern Europe, and they were determined to train or "Americanize" them.

The women's reform tradition, especially its moral and civic improvement elements, contributed to the Progressive movement, widening woman's sphere rather than eliminating it as a concept. Several key intellectual developments, in social psychology and genetics, offered feminists a means of dissolving woman's sphere, but feminist thinking did not incorporate these findings. Some social psychologists, for example, postulated that sex differences were grounded in custom rather than biology, but most feminists continued to believe in an innate female nature.[2]

Discoveries in genetics also offered the basis for a new strategy for women, but here too feminists either were ignorant of them or unconvinced of their applicability. They continued to accept the scientific consensus that animals adapt to their environment by changing their form and then transmitting those changes to their offspring and proved unreceptive to scientists such as August Weismann (1834–1914), who argued, in his *Essays Upon Heredity* (1889), that the determinant of character was a germ plasm, basically immortal and inviolable, sealed off from the effects of experience.[3] Lester Ward and Edward Ross led the attack on Weismann, and Charlotte and Helen Campbell, among others, approved.[4]

Charlotte's ideology, thus, was not markedly altered by the intellectual and theoretical developments of the new century. She also did not modify her feelings about Marxian socialism and, she told Carolina Severance, "I do not believe in the action of the Socialist party—so far." [5] But she did help organize the Intercollegiate Socialist Society (1905),* spoke frequently at socialist gatherings, and campaigned for Morris Hillquit (1869–1933) when he ran for the United States House of Representatives on the Socialist Party ticket. Her writings were regularly reprinted in the socialist press and her books were used in socialist women's study clubs.[6]

Charlotte wrote very little about working-class women in these years, though she occasionally spoke to Women's Trade Union League† audiences and contributed material to its journal, *Life and Labor.*[7] She also spoke at meetings organized by the Equality League of Self-

---

* It adopted an outlook similar to the British Fabian Society—education for a new social order—and did not function as a section of the Socialist Party. It became the League for Industrial Democracy after World War I.

† The National Women's Trade Union League of America, founded in 1903, was a unique coalition of women workers and wealthy women, dedicated to assisting women wage earners to organize trade unions. For ten years, the WTUL organized women workers, trained them as organizers, and supported their strikes, mainly in the garment trades. In 1913, the organization's emphasis shifted to suffrage activity and protective labor legislation. It dissolved in 1955.

Supporting Women, founded in 1907 by Harriot Stanton Blatch (1856–1940), to provide a forum for women workers to speak on suffrage.

Though she was a consistent spokesperson for suffrage, she repeatedly said that she thought it was too narrow a goal for the organized woman's movement. She agreed to write a weekly column for the suffrage newspaper, *Woman's Journal,* in 1904, "to help make it a broader more representative paper—embracing the whole woman movement and bringing it into relation with the world's movement—at last!" [8]

She did, however, retain her fidelity to woman's clubs. When she married George Houghton Gilman in 1900, and they settled in New York, she joined several clubs and attended regularly.

She had renewed her acquaintance with Houghton, her first cousin,* in March 1897, shortly before she commenced her first book. A friendship bloomed immediately, they saw each other frequently when Charlotte was in New York City, and she wrote him long letters—hundreds of them—when she was lecturing. They are open, witty, flowing, blithe, playful, bantering, and spirited. They include poems and a raft of complimentary comments. Rather quickly they became, for Charlotte, a form of psychotherapy, wherein she revealed her anxieties, conflicts, ambivalences, and the full extent of her approach-avoidance response to emotional intimacy. They were, in short, a test of his capacity to hear the worst about her—and remain devoted—and a test of her ability to overcome her intimacy anxieties.

They were married in Detroit, on June 11, 1900, and Katharine came to live with them at the end of July.† But, Charlotte would write in her autobiography: "For all my happiness at home, and various glories abroad, I remained through all these years [New York, 1900–1922] more sick than well; that is, there was more time spent in dull distress of mind and dreary helplessness than in my natural cheerful activity." [9] But she had learned, by then, what to expect from the depressions and how to endure them.

* A moderately successful patent attorney, he was the son of Katherine Perkins, her father's sister, and William C. Gilman.
† Katharine at first split her time between the Gilmans in New York and the Stetsons in Italy, but then settled in New York, became a painter and sculptor, and married another painter, F. Tolles Chamberlin (1873–1961). They moved to Pasadena and raised two children, Dorothy (b. 1918) and Walter (b. 1920). Katharine died in 1979.

The Books

It all began with economics, an unusual subject for a nineteenth-century woman to address in depth. In fact, it was still struggling to become accepted as a science and a profession in the 1890s. At the time the American Economic Association was founded, in 1885, there were probably no more than two dozen full-time professional economists.[10] None of them were women, although political economy was taught at Vassar, Wellesley, and Smith. As of 1898, four women had earned Ph.D.s in political economy or economics (from Cornell, Minnesota, Wisconsin, and Yale), twenty-two belonged to the 600–member AEA, and only four had contributed articles to the first six volumes of the *Journal of Political Economy* (published by the University of Chicago, beginning in December 1892). During the first decade of the twentieth century, three of the brightest graduate students in economics at the University of Chicago—Katherine Bement Davis (1860–1935), Sophonisba Breckinridge (1866–1948), and Edith Abbott (1876–1957)—had no chance of receiving a university appointment to teach their specialty. They would achieve success and renown in the field of social work.[11]

Charlotte had begun to formulate an economic understanding of women's condition in the spring of 1890, when she contemplated a "serious essay giving views on the economic base of the social evil, and its natural extinction under true economic conditions: lowering of abnormal attractions with more general development, and diminution of fecundity under higher development of all classes."[12] Though she had not read deeply in economic theory—"My reading on social economics is of the vaguest and most general. . . . I have read some of the Fabian Essays. . . . Some of Ely's Economics,* articles here and there —but all together very little"—she believed, as she wrote Houghton, "I've got more than any of them."[13]

In fact, she did not include a bibliography in *Women and Economics,* because, "when it came to making a list of the books I had read bearing on the subject, there were only two! One was Geddes's and Thompson's

---

* Richard T. Ely, *Outlines of Economics* (New York: Macmillan, 1893). She had reviewed it in *The Impress,* November 1893, p. 6.

[sic] *Evolution of Sex,* the other only an article, Lester F. Ward's, in that 1888 *Forum.*"[14]*

And though it was "an enormous new step" in social theory that convinced her she should commence writing the book on women and economics, she noted that she had not read much on that subject and had only "a very vague memory" of what she had read, mentioning only John Stuart McKenzie's *An Introduction to Social Philosophy* (1890). Nevertheless, she wrote Houghton: "I think that with all my lack of proper training, I simply must write it, and I shall look [for] invaluable assistance from you in the way of criticism. It is quite possible that you will see little in it, and consider me another crackbrained enthusiast. . . . But I am solidly committed to my course of thinking [and] shall out with it to the best of my ability."[15]

She began the book on August 31, in Belmont, New Hampshire, writing with astonishing speed, especially considering that she was in a depressed state: 1,700 words the first day, then 2,400, 3,600, 4,000, 9,500. She completed the first draft (35,600 words) on October 8. Small, Maynard Publishers agreed, on November 10, to publish it.[16] She revised the manuscript twice, again in record time, and sent it to the publishers on January 17, 1898. She would say of her writing method in these years:

> Such writing as I have done in those years of free delivery was easy work. An average article, about three thousand words, took three hours to do, a day's work. Sometimes I would have to copy it, or change a little, but usually it was written and sent—like a letter. This is not, in the artistic sense, "literature." I have never made any pretense of being literary. As far as I had any method in mind, it was to express the idea with clearness and vivacity, so that it might be apprehended with ease and pleasure.[17]

Women and Economics, essentially, is a demystification of motherhood, home, and family. It is a critical commentary on the effects of social conditioning, based on evolutionary and biological thinking. It is, how-

* Patrick Geddes and J. Arthur Thomson, *Evolution of Sex* (London: Scott, 1889); Lester Ward, "Our Better Halves," *Forum,* 6 (November 1888), pp. 266–275. The former argued that men and women differed as a consequence of the economy of cell metabolism: men expended energy, hence they were activists; women stored energy, hence they possessed the passive talents. Though the authors posited that these differences were permanent, they stated that the sexes were complementary and mutually dependent and that cooperation was required for human progress.

ever, ahistorical; Charlotte did not trace the evolution of economic systems over time nor did she provide historical data on them. She is also better when she is describing effects than ascribing causes. The key phrase in the book is the "abnormal sexuo-economic relation," but she fails to provide a clear and precise explanation of how normal sex distinction changed into morbid sex distinction in the human species.

The book was widely and favorably noticed in newspapers in all parts of the United States and several in England. It was also reviewed in prestigious academic journals. Jane Addams, Florence Kelley, Inez Haynes Irwin (1873–1970), and Edith Houghton Hooker, among others, ranked it among the significant books of their time.[18] And George E. Howard, when he came to write his massive tome, *A History of Matrimonial Institutions,* called it "one of the most powerful books produced in recent sociological discussion."[19]*

Charlotte proclaimed herself pleased by the number and quality of the reviews.[20] *Women and Economics* went through nine editions in the United States and Great Britain during her lifetime, was translated into seven languages, and made her, according to Degler, "the leading intellectual in the women's movement in the United States during the first two decades of the twentieth century."[21]

Meanwhile, she continued to roam the lecture circuits, mainly in the Midwest. She was offered but rejected a teaching position at Kansas State Agricultural College—because she did not think she had adequate training or a sufficient body of knowledge, because she did not think she could bear the strain of institutional demands, and because she was "simply bursting out into literature."[22] In fact, she was writing dozens of lectures and articles.

In May 1899 she returned to London to attend and speak at the Congress of the International Council of Women. Houghton met her there, and she stayed until the end of August. Despite a deep "misery"

---

* Thorstein Veblen (1857–1929) did not cite any sources for his study of the relationship between evolution and economics in *The Theory of the Leisure Class; an economic study in the evolution of institutions* (New York: Macmillan, 1899). Charlotte, however, had favorably mentioned his "The Economic Theory of Woman's Dress" *Popular Science Monthly,* 46 (December 1894), p. 198) and she would regularly cite *The Theory of the Leisure Class.* But, she wrote thirteen years after she first read it, "He fails to note . . . [that] the very ideas of mastery and ownership, are closely identical with masculine nature, while productive industry is in origin a feminine function." *The Impress,* December 22, 1894, p. 11; "Humanness, Chapter VII: Human Specialization," *The Forerunner,* 4 (July 1913), p. 192.

in July, she wrote an upbeat article about the Congress, declaring, "of congresses of women, the more the better—of internationalism the more the better. There is good hope for our dear world when its mother wakes up."[23]

That year she stitched her lectures on children together into a book, *Concerning Children,* that Small, Maynard published in 1900. In it, Charlotte delivered her most extensive critique of traditional forms of raising children, by discipline and obedience, and called for the creation of a process and environment that encouraged them to think. She wove together her evolutionary and religious ideas into a moral means and end, and made her strongest statements on behalf of transmitted traits. She devoted sixteen pages to a critique of Weismann, arguing that race improvement must be made between the years fifteen and twenty-five —"the most important decade of a lifetime," since those were the years when a person could acquire "a keen new consciousness of personal responsibility" and then transmit that characteristic to his or her children.[24] She did not, however, carefully distinguish between the effects of heredity and those of the environment.

Although it was much less widely reviewed than *Women and Economics,* Charlotte wrote that it "was warmly received and widely noticed."[25] There was a second printing (1901), a British edition, and German and Dutch translations.

Charlotte suffered from extended low periods in January, February, and October 1901, and January 1902. For the first time, her work may have been a factor. She had begun a book on work in February 1900, and was experiencing difficulty expounding its central idea, "that of the organic nature of society, with God and Progress sure [guides] of Human Conduct."[26]

In August 1902 she put aside the manuscript on work and began to plan a book on the home. She had first conceived the idea in the fall of 1898, telling Houghton "how beautifully I can do it, hurling every idol from its shrine."[27] Since she was in the process of writing a series of lectures on the home, this manuscript proceeded smoothly and quickly, and she finished the last chapter in December. McClure, Phillips agreed to publish both the home and work manuscripts.

The Home appeared in 1903. Charlotte thought it was "the most heretical—and the most amusing—of anything I've done."[28] It was a further, more focused, demystification of the central symbol of Victorian culture. She demanded the transformation of the home from a workshop into a retreat, thereby releasing women and their productive forces for the betterment of society. It was reviewed or noticed in over fifty newspapers and magazines nationwide. Only a tiny handful were negative, but even the naysayers admitted that the book would arouse discussion and provoke comment and debate. The editors of *Current Literature* noted that she had "perhaps a wider audience of women interested in women's problems than any other writer in the country."[29] There was a British edition, Swedish and German translations, and a reprint in 1910.

Human Work was published in 1904. Charlotte thought that it was "the greatest book I have ever done, and the poorest—that is, the least adequately done." In fact, nine years later she wrote that "the theme was so large, and the author's powers so inadequate, that the presentation proved quite unsatisfactory."[30] She would continue to expand and revise the ideas in it for the rest of her writing life.

It is her least satisfactory book: it does not have the flow of her best and is more hortatory than convincing. Essentially, it is meant to be a corrective to people's misconceptions—"traditions—superstitions, falsehoods"—about the nature of work, which are the direct cause of the "economic distresses so conspicuous among us." It is her most relentlessly evolutionary based effort and the clearest statement to that point that she had become convinced that ideas dominate social behavior and that human will power is *the* lever of social change. If people only understood the essence of work and the nature of social relations, she claimed, they would alter the economic processes and thereby avoid "suffering and promote our growth and happiness."[31]

It was less widely noticed than *The Home* but more widely than *Concerning Children*. Although most of the reviews were positive, they were not enthusiastic. She was disappointed with the sales of both *Human Work* and *The Home*.[32]

She continued to lecture, speak, debate, and preach in a wide variety of forums, support civic reform and suffrage, and participate episodically in the socialist movement. In June 1908, however, she began to fret about the reception of her ideas. Though she had just returned from a suffrage event at Vassar, where, according to Harriot Stanton

Blatch, "no one was more popular . . . . Her *Women and Economics* was, one might say the Bible of the student body,"[33] she believed she needed a new forum to make herself heard. She wrote: "If I could publish and edit myself and preach, I should then be doing all I could for the rest of my life and have a perfectly clear conscience."[34] She and Houghton formed the Charlton Publishing Company, and, in October 1909, Charlotte inaugurated *The Forerunner*.

Writings

*Women and Economics: A Study of the Economic Relation Between Men and Women as a Factor in Social Evolution)**

Preface

This book is written to offer a simple and natural explanation of one of the most common and perplexing problems of human life, —a problem which presents itself to almost every individual for practical solution, and which demands the most serious attention of the moralist, the physician, and the sociologist—

To show how some of the worst evils under which we suffer, evils long supposed to be inherent and ineradicable in our natures, are but the result of certain arbitrary conditions of our adoption, and how, by removing those conditions, we may remove the evils resultant—

To point out how far we have already gone in the path of improvement, and how irresistibly the social forces of to-day are compelling us further, even without our knowledge and against our violent opposition,—an advance which may be greatly quickened by our recognition and assistance—

To reach in especial the thinking women of to-day, and urge upon them a new sense, not only of their social responsibility as individuals, but of their measureless racial importance as makers of men.

* Boston: Small, Maynard, 1898, pp. vii, 38–39, 101–121, and 177–199.

It is hoped also that the theory advanced will prove sufficiently suggestive to give rise to such further study and discussion as shall prove its error or establish its truth.

Chapter II

[. . .] Man, in supporting woman, has become her economic environment. Under natural selection, every creature is modified to its environment, developing perforce the qualities needed to obtain its livelihood under that environment. Man, as the feeder of woman, becomes the strongest modifying force in her economic condition. Under sexual selection the human creature is of course modified to its mate, as with all creatures. When the mate becomes also the master, when economic necessity is added to sex-attraction, we have the two great evolutionary forces acting together to the same end; namely, to develope sex-distinction in the human female. For, in her position of economic dependence in the sex-relation, sex-distinction is with her not only a means of attracting a mate, as with all creatures, but a means of getting her livelihood, as is the case with no other creature under heaven. Because of the economic dependence of the human female on her mate, she is modified to sex to an excessive degree. This excessive modification she transmits to her children; and so is steadily implanted in the human constitution the morbid tendency to excess in this relation, which has acted so universally upon us in all ages, in spite of our best efforts to restrain it. It is not the normal sex-tendency, common to all creatures, but an abnormal sex-tendency, produced and maintained by the abnormal economic relation which makes one sex get its living from the other by the exercise of sex-functions. This is the immediate effect upon individuals of the peculiar sexuo-economic relation which obtains among us.

Chapter VI

[. . .] The evolution of organic life goes on in geometrical progression: cells combine, and form organs; organs combine, and form organisms; organisms combine, and form organizations. Society is an organization. Society is the fourth power of the cell. It is composed of individual animals of genus homo, living in organic relation. The course of social evolution is the gradual establishment of organic relations between individuals, and this organic relation rests on purely economic grounds. In the simplest combination of primordial cells the force that drew and held them together was that of economic necessity. It profited them to live in combination. Those that did so survived, and those that did not perished. So with the appearance of the most elaborate organisms: it profited them to become a complex bundle of members and organs in indivisible relation. A creature so constructed survived, where the same amount of living matter unorganized would have perished. And so it is, literally and exactly, in a complex society, with all its elaborate specialization of individuals in arts and crafts, trades and professions. A society so constructed survives, where the same number of living beings, unorganized would perish. The specialization of labor and exchange of product in a social body is identical in its nature with the specialization and exchange of function in an individual body. This process, on orderly lines of evolution, involves the gradual subordination of individual effort for individual good to the collective effort for the collective good, —not from any so-called "altruism," but from the economic necessities of the case. It is as natural, as "selfish," for society so to live, the individual citizens working together for the social good, as for one's own body to live by the hands and feet, teeth and eyes, heart and lungs, working together for the individual good. Social evolution tends to an increasing specialization in structure and function, and to an increasing interdependence of the component parts, with a correlative decrease through disuse of the once valuable process of individual struggle for success; and this is based absolutely on the advantage to the individual as well as to the social body.

But, as we study this process of development, noting with admiration the progressive changes in human relation, the new functions, the extended structure, the increase of sensation in the socialized individuals with its enormous possibilities of joy and healthful sensitiveness to pain, we are struck by the visible presence of some counter-force, acting against the normal development and producing most disadvantageous effects. As in our orderly progress in social sex-development we are checked by the tenacious hold of rudimentary impulses artificially maintained by false conditions, so in our orderly progress in social economic development we see the same peculiar survival of rudimentary impulses, which should have been long since easily outgrown. It is no longer of advantage to the individual to struggle for his own gain at the expense of others: his gain now requires the co-ordinate efforts of these others; yet he continues so to struggle.

In this lack of adjustment between the individual and the social interest lies our economic trouble. An illustration of this may be seen in the manufacture of prepared foods. This is a process impossible to the individual singly, and of great advantage to the individual in collective relation,—a perfectly natural economic process, advantageous in proportion to the amount and quality of the food manufactured. This we constantly find accompanied by a morbid process of dilution and adulteration, by which society is injured, in order that the individual concerned in the manufacture may be benefited. This is as though one of the organs of the body—the liver, for instance—should deliberately weaken or poison its quota of secretion, in order that by giving less it might retain more, and become large and fat individually. An organ can do so, does do so; but such action is morbid action, and constitutes disease. The body is injured, weakened, destroyed, and so ultimately the organ perishes also. It is a false conception of gain, and the falsehood lies in not recognizing the true relation between individual and social interests. This failure to recognize or, at least, to act up to a recognition of social interests, owing to the disproportionate pressure of individual interests, is the underlying cause of our economic distress. As society is composed of individuals, we must look to them for the action causing these morbid social processes; and, as individuals act under the pressure of conditions, we must look to the conditions affecting the individuals for the causes of their action.

In general, under social law, men develope right action; but some hidden spring seems to force them continually into wrong action. We have our hand upon this hidden spring in the sexuo-economic relation. If we had remained on an individual economic basis, the evil influence would have had far less ill effect; but, as we grow into the social economic relation, it increases with our civilization. The sex-relation is primarily and finally individual. It is a physical relation between individual bodies; and, while it may also extend to a physical relation between individual souls, it does not become a social relation, though it does change its personal development to suit social needs.

In all its processes, to all its results, the sex-relation is personal, working through individuals upon individuals, and developing individual traits and characteristics, to the great advantage of society. The qualities developed by social relation are built into the race through the sex-relation, but the sex-relation itself is wholly personal. Our economic relation, on the contrary, though originally individual, becomes through social evolution increasingly collective. By combining the human sex-relation with the human economic relation, we have combined a permanently individual process with a progressively collective one. This involves a strain on both, which increases in direct proportion to our socialization, and, so far, has resulted in the ultimate destruction of the social organism acted upon by such irreconcilable forces.

As has been shown, this combination has affected the sex-relation of individuals by bringing into it a tendency to collectivism with economic advantage, best exhibited in our distinctive racial phenomenon of prostitution. On the other hand, it has affected the economic relation of society by bringing into it a tendency to individualism with sex-advantage, best exhibited in the frequent practice of sacrificing public good to personal gain, that the individual may thereby "support his family." We are so used to considering it the first duty of a man to support his family that it takes a very glaring instance of bribery and corruption in their interests to shake our conviction; but, as a sociological law, every phase of the prostitution of public service to private gain, from the degradation of the artist to the exploitation of the helpless unskilled laborer, marks a diseased social action. Our social status rests upon our common consent, common action, common submission to the common will. No individual interests can stand for a moment against the interests of the common weal, either when war demands the last sacrifice of individual property and life or when peace requires the absolute submission of individual property and life to common law,—the fixed expression of the people's will. The maintenance of "law and order" involves the very spirit of socialism,—the sinking of personal interest in common interest. All this rests upon the evolution of the social spirit, the keen sense of social duty, the conscientious fulfillment of social service; and it is here that the excessive individualism maintained by our sexuo-economic relation enters as a strong and increasingly disadvantageous social factor. We have dimly recognized the irreconcilability of the sex-relation with economic relations on both sides,—in our sharp condemnation of making the sex-functions openly commercial, and in the drift toward celibacy in collective institutions. Bodies of men or women, actuated by the highest religious impulses, desiring to live nobly and to serve society, have always recognized something antagonistic in the sex-relation. They have thought it inherent in the relation itself, not seeing that it was the economic side which made it reactionary. Yet this action was practically admitted by the continued existence of communal societies where the sex-relation did exist, in an unacknowledged form, and without the element of economic exchange. It is admitted also by the noble and self-sacrificing devotion of married missionaries of the Protestant Church, who are supported by contributions. If the missionary were obliged to earn his wife's living and his own, he could do little mission work.

The highest human attributes are perfectly compatible with the sex-relation, but not with the sexuo-economic relation. We see this opposition again in the tendency to collectivity in bodies of single men,—their comradeship, equality, and mutual helpfulness as compared with the attitude of the same men toward one another, when married. This is why the quality of "organizability" is stronger in men than in women; their common economic interests force them into relation, while the isolated and even antagonistic economic interests of women keep them from it. The condition of individual economic dependence in which women live resembles that of the savage in the forest. They obtain their economic goods by securing a male through their individual exertions, all competing freely to this end. No combination is possible. The numerous girls at a summer resort, in their attitude toward the scant supply of young men, bear an unconscious resemblance to the emulous savages in a too closely hunted forest. And here may be given an economic reason for the oft-noted bitterness with which the virtuous women regard the vicious. The virtuous woman stands in close ranks with her sisters, refusing to part with herself —her only economic goods—until she is assured of legal marriage, with its lifelong guarantee of support. Under equal proportions of birth in the two sexes, every woman would be tolerably sure of obtaining her demands. But here enters the vicious woman, and offers the same goods—though of inferior quality, to be sure —for a far less price. Every one of such illegitimate competitors lowers the chances of unmarried women and the income of the married. No wonder those who hold themselves highly should be moved to bitterness at being undersold in this way. It is the hatred of the trade-unionist for "scab labor."

On the woman's side we are steadily maintaining the force of primitive individual competition in the world as against the tendency of social progress to develope co-operation in its place, and this tendency of course is inherited by their sons. On the man's side the same effect is produced through another feature of the relation. The tendency to individualism with sex-advantage is developed in man by an opposite process to that operating on the woman. She gets her living by getting a husband. He gets his wife by getting a living. It is to her individual economic advantage to secure a mate. It is to his individual sex-advantage to secure economic gain. The sex-functions to her have become economic functions. Economic functions to him have become sex-functions. This has confounded our natural economic competition, inevitably growing into economic co-operation, with the element of sex-competition,—an entirely different force.

Competition among males, with selection by the female of the superior male, is the process of sexual selection, and works to racial improvement. So far as the human male competes freely with his peers in higher and higher activities, and the female chooses the winner, so far we are directly benefited. But there is a racial distinction between sex-competition and marriage by purchase. In the first the male succeeds by virtue of what he can do; in the second, by virtue of what he can get. The increased power to do, transmitted to the young, is of racial advantage. But mere possessions, with no question as to the method of their acquisition, are not necessarily of advantage to the individual as a father. To make the sexual gain of the male rest on his purchasing power puts the immense force of sex-competition into the field of social economics, not only as an incentive to labor and achieve-ment, which is good, but as an incentive to individual gain, however obtained, which is bad; thus accounting for our multi-plied and intensified desire to get, — the inordinate greed of our industrial world. The tournament of the Middle Ages was a brutal sport perhaps, with its human injury, pain, and death, under the cry of: "Fight on, brave knights! Fair eyes are looking on you!" but it represents a healthier process than our modern method of securing the wherewithal to maintain the sex-relation. As so beautifully phrased by Jean Ingelow [1820–1897]: —

> I worked afar that I might rear
> A happy home on English soil;
> I labored for the gold and gear,
> I loved my toil.

> Forever in my spirit spake
> The natural whisper, "Well 'twill be
> When loving wife and children break
> Their bread with thee!"*

Or, put more broadly by Kipling [1865–1936]: —

> But since our women must walk gay,
> And money buys their gear,
> The sealing vessels filch this way
> At hazard, year by year.†

The contest in every good man's heart to-day between the "ought to" and the "must," between his best work and the

---

* Jean Ingelow, "The Letter L," in *Poems by Jean Ingelow* (London: Oxford University Press, 1921), p. 77.
† Rudyard Kipling, "Rhyme of the Three Sealers" (1893), in *Rudyard Kipling's Verse: The Inclusive Edition*, (Garden City, N.Y.: Doubleday, Page, 1922), p. 130.

"potboiler," is his personal share of this incessant struggle between social interest and self-interest. For himself and by himself he would be glad to do his best work, to be true to his ideals, to be brave in meeting loss for that truth's sake. But as the compromising capitalist says in "Put Yourself in His Place,"* when his sturdy young friend—a bachelor—wonders at his giving in to unjust demands, "Marriage makes a mouse of a man." To the young business man who falls into evil courses in the sex-relation the open greed of his fair dependant is a menace to his honesty, to his business prospects. On the same man married the needs of his wife often operate in the same way. The sense of the dependence of the helpless creature whose food must come through him does not stimulate courage, but compels submission.

The foregoing distinction should be clearly held in mind. Legitimate sex-competition brings out all that is best in man. To please her, to win her, he strives to do his best. But the economic dependence of the female upon the male, with its ensuing purchasability, does not so affect a man: it puts upon him the necessity for getting things, not for doing them. In the lowest grades of labor, where there is no getting without doing and where the laborer always does more than he gets, this works less palpable evil than in the higher grades, the professions and arts, where the most valuable work is always ahead of the market, and where to work for the market involves a lowering of standards. The young artist or poet or scientific student works for his work's sake, for art, for science, and so for the best good of society. But the artist or student married must get gain, must work for those who will pay; and those who will pay are not those who lift and bear forward the standard of progress. Community of interest is quite possible with those who are working most disinterestedly for the social good; but bring in the sex-relation, and all such solidarity disintegrates,—resolves itself into the tiny groups of individuals united on a basis of sex-union, and briskly acting in their own immediate interests at anybody's or everybody's expense.

The social perception of the evil resultant from the intrusion

* Charles Reade, *Put Yourself In His Place* (London: Smith Elder, 1870).

of sex-influence upon racial action has found voice in the heartless proverb, "There is no evil without a woman at the bottom of it." When a man's work goes wrong, his hopes fail, his ambitions sink, cynical friends inquire, "Who is she?" It is not for nothing that a man's best friends sigh when he marries, especially if he is a man of genius. This judgment of the world has obtained side by side with its equal faith in the ennobling influence of woman. The world is quite right. It does not have to be consistent. Both judgments are correct. Woman affecting society through the sex-relation or through her individual economic relation is an ennobling influence. Woman affecting society through our perverse combination of the two becomes a strange influence, indeed.

One of the amusing minor results of these conditions is that, while we have observed the effect of marriage upon social economic relation and the effect of social economic relation upon marriage,—seeing that the devoted servant of the family was a poor servant of society and that the devoted servant of society was a poor servant of the family, seeing the successful collectivity of celibate institutions,—we have jumped to the conclusion that collective prosperity was conditioned upon celibacy, and that we did not want it. That is why the popular mind is so ready to associate socialistic theories with injury to marriage. Having seen that marriage makes us less collective, we infer conversely that collectivity will make us less married,—that it will "break up the home," "strike at the roots of the family."

When we make plain to ourselves that a pure, lasting, monogamous sex-union can exist without bribe or purchase, without the manacles of economic dependence, and that men and women so united in sex-relation will still be free to combine with others in economic relation, we shall not regard devotion to humanity as an unnatural sacrifice, nor collective prosperity as a thing to fear.

Besides this maintenance of primeval individualism in the growing collectivity of social economic process and the introduction of the element of sex-combat into the narrowing field of industrial competition, there is another side to the evil influence of the sexuo-economic relation upon social development. This is in the attitude of woman as a non-productive consumer.

In the industrial evolution of the human race, that marvelous and subtle drawing out and interlocking of special functions which constitute the organic life of society, we find that production and consumption go hand in hand; and production comes first. One cannot consume what has not been produced. Economic production is the natural expression of human energy,—not sex-energy at all, but race-energy,—the unconscious functioning of the social organism. Socially organized human beings tend to produce, as a gland to secrete: it is the essential nature of the relation. The creative impulse, the desire to make, to express the inner thought in outer form, "just for the work's sake, no use at all i' the work!" this is the distinguishing character of humanity. "I want to mark!" cries the child, demanding the pencil. He does not want to eat. He wants to mark. He is not seeking to get something into himself, but to put something out of himself. He generally wants to do whatever he sees done,—to make pie-crust or to make shavings, as it happens. The pie he may eat, the shavings not; but he likes to make both. This is the natural process of production, and is followed by the natural process of consumption, where practicable. But consumption is not the main end, the governing force. Under this organic social law, working naturally, we have the evolution of those arts and crafts in the exercise of which consists our human living, and on the product of which we live. So does society evolve within itself—secrete as it were—the social structure with all its complex machinery; and we function therein as naturally as so many glands, other things being equal.

But other things are not equal. Half the human race is denied free productive expression, is forced to confine its productive human energies to the same channels as its reproductive sex energies. Its creative skill is confined to the level of immediate personal bodily service, to the making of clothes and preparing of food for individuals. No social service is possible. While its power of production is checked, its power of consumption is inordinately increased by the showering upon it of the "unearned increment" of masculine gifts. For the women there is, first, no free production allowed; and, second, no relation maintained between what she does produce and what she consumes. She is forbidden to make, but encouraged to take. Her industry is not the natural output of creative energy, not the work she does because she has the inner power and strength to do it; nor is her industry even the measure of her gain. She has, of course, the natural desire to consume; and to that is set no bar save the capacity or the will of her husband.

Thus we have painfully and laboriously evolved and carefully maintain among us an enormous class of non-productive consumers,—a class which is half the world, and mother of the other half. We have built into the constitution of the human race the habit and desire of taking, as divorced from its natural precursor and concomitant of making. We have made for ourselves this endless array of "horse-leech's daughters, crying, Give! give!" To consume food, to consume clothes, to consume houses and furniture and decorations and ornaments and amusement, to take and take and take forever,—from one man if they are virtuous, from many if they are vicious, but always to take and never to think of giving anything in return except their womanhood,—this is the enforced condition of the mothers of the race. What wonder that their sons go into business "for what there is in it"! What wonder that the world is full of the desire to get as much as possible and to give as little as possible! What wonder, either, that the glory and sweetness of love are but a name among us, with here and there a strange and beautiful exception, of which our admiration proves the rarity!

Between the brutal ferocity of excessive male energy struggling in the market-place as in a battlefield and the unnatural greed generated by the perverted condition of female energy, it is not remarkable that the industrial evolution of humanity has shown peculiar symptoms. One of the minor effects of this last condition—this limiting of female industry to close personal necessities, and this tendency of her over-developed sex-nature to overestimate the so-called "duties" of her position—has been to produce an elaborate devotion to individuals and their personal needs,—not to the understanding and developing of their higher natures, but to the intensification of their bodily tastes and pleasure. The wife and mother, pouring the rising tide of racial power into the same old channels that were allowed her primitive ancestors, constantly ministers to the physical needs of her family with a ceaseless and concentrated intensity. They like it, of course. But it maintains in the individuals of the race an exaggerated sense of the importance of food and clothes and ornaments to themselves, without at all including a knowledge of their right use and value to us all. It developes personal selfishness.

Again, the consuming female, debarred from any free production, unable to estimate the labor involved in the making of what she so lightly destroys, and her consumption limited mainly to those things which minister to physical pleasure, creates a market for sensuous decoration and personal ornament, for all that is luxurious and enervating, and for a false and capricious variety in such supplies, which operates as a most deadly check to true industry and true art! As the priestess of the temple of consumption, as the limitless demander of things to use up, her economic influence is reactionary and injurious. Much, very much, of the current of useless production in which our economic energies run waste—man's strength poured out like water on the sand—depends on the creation and careful maintenance of this false market, this sink into which human labor vanishes with no return. Woman, in her false economic position, reacts injuriously upon industry, upon art, upon science, discovery, and progress. The sexuo-economic relation in its effect on the constitution of the individual keeps alive in us the instincts of savage individualism which we should otherwise have well outgrown. It sexualizes our industrial relation and commercializes our sex-relation. And, in the external effect upon the market, the over-sexed woman, in her unintelligent and ceaseless demands, hinders and perverts the economic development of the world.

Chapter IX

[. . .] Motherhood, like every other natural process, is to be measured by its results. It is good or evil as it serves its purpose. Human motherhood must be judged as it serves its purpose to the human race. Primarily, its purpose is to reproduce the race by reproducing the individual; secondarily, to improve the race by improving the individual. The mere office of reproduction is as well performed by the laying of eggs to be posthumously hatched as by many years of exquisite devotion; but in the improvement of the species we come to other requirements. The functions of motherhood have been evolved as naturally as the functions of nutrition, and each stage of development has brought new duties to the mother. The mother bird must brood her young, the mother cow must suckle them, the mother cat must hunt for them; and, in every varied service which the mother gives, its value is to be measured by its effect upon the young. To perform that which is most good for the young of the species is the measure of right motherhood, and that which is most good for the young is what will help them to a better maturity than that of their parents. To leave in the world a creature better than its parent, this is the purpose of right motherhood.

In the human race this purpose is served by two processes: first, by the simple individual function of reproduction, of which all care and nursing are but an extension; and, second, by the complex social function of education. This was primarily a maternal process, and therefore individual; but it has long since become a racial rather than an individual function, and bears no relation to sex or other personal limitation. The young of the human race require for their best development not only the love and care of the mother, but the care and instruction of many besides their mother. So largely is this true that it may be said in extreme terms that it would be better for a child to-day to be left absolutely without mother or family of any sort, in the city of Boston, for instance, than to be supplied with a large and affectionate family and be planted with them in darkest Africa.

Human functions are race-functions, social functions; and education is one of them. The duty of the human mother, and the measure of its right or wrong fulfilment, are to be judged along these two main lines, reproduction and education. As we have no species above us with which to compare our motherhood, we must measure by those below us. We must show improvement upon them in this function which we all hold in common.

Does the human mother succeed better than others of her

order, mammalia,* in the reproduction of the species? Does she bring forth and rear her young more perfectly than lower mothers? They, being less conscious, act simply under instinct, mating in their season, bringing forth young in their season, nursing, guarding, defending as best they may; and they leave in the world behind them creatures as good, or better, than their mothers. Of wild animals we have few reliable statistics, and of tame ones it is difficult to detach their natural processes from our interference therewith. But in both the simple maintenance of species shows that motherhood at least reproduces fairly well; and in those we breed for our advantage the wonderful possibilities of race-development through this process are made apparent. How do we, with the human brain and the human conscience, rich in the power and wisdom of our dominant race,—how do we, as mothers, compare with our forerunners?

Human motherhood is more pathological than any other, more morbid, defective, irregular, diseased. Human childhood is similarly pathological. We, as animals, are very inferior animals in this particular. When we take credit to ourselves for the sublime devotion with which we face "the perils of maternity," and boast of "going down to the gates of death" for our children, we should rather take shame to ourselves for bringing these perils upon both mother and child. The gates of death? They are the gates of life to the unborn; and there is no death there save what we, the mothers, by our unnatural lives, have brought upon our own children. Gates of death, indeed, to the thousands of babies late-born, prematurely born, misborn, and stillborn for lack of right motherhood. In the primal physical functions of maternity the human female cannot show that her supposed specialization to these uses has improved her fulfilment of them, rather the opposite. The more freely the human mother mingles in the natural industries of a human creature, as in the case of the savage woman, the peasant woman, the working-woman everywhere who is not overworked, the more rightly she fulfils these functions.

The more absolutely woman is segregated to sex-functions only, cut off from all economic use and made wholly dependent

* Her order is primate, her class mammalia.

on the sex-relation as means of livelihood, the more pathological does her motherhood become. The over-development of sex caused by her economic dependence on the male reacts unfavorably upon her essential duties. She is too female for perfect motherhood! Her excessive specialization in the secondary sexual characteristics is a detrimental element in heredity. Small, weak, soft, ill-proportioned women do not tend to produce, large, strong, sturdy, well-made men or women. When Frederic the Great wanted grenadiers of great size,* he married big men to big women,—not to little ones. The female segregated to the uses of sex alone naturally deteriorates in racial development, and naturally transmits that deterioration to her offspring. The human mother, in the processes of reproduction, shows no gain in efficiency over the lower animals, but rather a loss, and so far presents no evidence to prove that her specialization to sex is of any advantage to her young. The mother of a dead baby or the baby of a dead mother; the sick baby, the crooked baby, the idiot baby; the exhausted, nervous, prematurely aged mother,—these are not uncommon among us; and they do not show much progress in our motherhood.

Since we cannot justify the human method of maternity in the physical processes of reproduction, can we prove its advantages in the other branch, education? Though the mother be sickly and the child the same, will not her loving care more than make up for it? Will not the tender devotion of the mother, and her unflagging attendance upon the child, render human motherhood sufficiently successful in comparison with that of other species to justify our peculiar method? We must now show that our motherhood, in its usually accepted sense, the "care" of the child (more accurately described as education), is of a superior nature.

Here, again, we lack the benefit of comparison. No other animal species is required to care for its young so long, to teach it so much. So far as they have it to do, they do it well. The hen with her brood is an accepted model of motherhood in this

---

* Actually, it was Frederick II's (1712–1786) father, King Frederick William I of Prussia (1688–1740). His greatest joy and obsession was his Potsdam Grenadiers, a regiment of over 2,000 soldiers, all near seven feet tall. When war, purchase, smuggling, and kidnapping could not meet his demands, he ordered every tall man in his kingdom to marry a tall woman.

respect. She not only lays eggs and hatches them, but educates and protects her young so far as it is necessary. But beyond such simple uses as this we have no standard of comparison for educative motherhood. We can only study it among ourselves, comparing the child left motherless with the child mothered, the child with a mother and nothing else with the child whose mother is helped by servants and teachers, the child with what we recognize as a superior mother to the child with an inferior mother. This last distinction, a comparison between mothers, is of great value. We have tacitly formulated a certain vague standard of human motherhood, and loosely apply it, especially in the epithets "natural" and "unnatural" mother.

But these terms again show how prone we still are to consider the whole field of maternal action as one of instinct rather than of reason, as a function rather than a service. We do have a standard, however, loose and vague as it is; and even by that standard it is painful to see how many human mothers fail. Ask yourselves honestly how many of the mothers whose action toward their children confronts you in street and shop and car and boat, in hotel and boarding-house and neighboring yard,—how many call forth favorable comment compared with those you judge unfavorably? Consider not the rosy ideal of motherhood you have in your mind, but the coarse, hard facts of motherhood as you see them, and hear them, in daily life.

Motherhood in its fulfilment of educational duty can be measured only by its effects. If we take for a standard the noble men and women whose fine physique and character we so fondly attribute to "a devoted mother," what are we to say of the motherhood which has filled the world with the ignoble men and women, of depraved physique and character? If the good mother makes the good man, how about the bad ones? When we see great men and women, we give credit to their mothers. When we see inferior men and women,—and that is a common circumstance, —no one presumes to question the motherhood which has produced them. When it comes to congenital criminality, we are beginning to murmur something about "heredity"; and, to meet gross national ignorance, we do demand a better system of education. But no one presumes to suggest that the mothering of mankind could be improved upon; and yet there is where the responsibility really lies. If our human method of reproduction is defective, let the mother answer. She is the main factor in reproduction. If our human method of education is defective, let the mother answer. She is the main factor in education.

To this it is bitterly objected that such a claim omits the father and his responsibility. When the mother of the world is in her right place and doing her full duty, she will have no ground of complaint against the father. In the first place, she will make better men. In the second, she will hold herself socially responsible for the choice of a right father for her children. In the third place, as an economic free agent, she will do half duty in providing for the child. Men who are not equal to good fatherhood under such conditions will have no chance to become fathers, and will die with general pity instead of living with general condemnation. In his position, doing all the world's work, all the father's, and half the mother's, man has made better shift to achieve the impossible than woman has in hers. She has been supposed to have no work or care on earth save as mother. She has really had the work of the mother and that of the world's house service besides. But she has surely had as much time and strength to give to motherhood as man to fatherhood; and not until she can show that the children of the world are as well mothered as they are well fed can she cast on him the blame for our general deficiency.

There is no personal blame to be laid on either party. The sexuo-economic relation has its inevitable ill-effects on both motherhood and fatherhood. But it is to the mother that the appeal must be made to change this injurious relation. Having the deeper sense of duty to the young, the larger love, she must come to feel how her false position hurts her motherhood, and for her children's sake break away from it. Of man and his fatherhood she can make what she will.

The duty of the mother is first to produce children as good as or better than herself; to hand down the constitution and character of those behind her the better for her stewardship; to build up and improve the human race through her enormous power as mother; to make better people. This being done, it is then the duty of the mother, the human mother, so to educate her children as to complete what bearing and nursing have only begun. She carries the child nine months in her body, two years in her arms, and as long as she lives in her heart and mind. The education of the young is a tremendous factor in human reproduction. A right motherhood should be able to fulfil this great function perfectly. It should understand with an ever-growing power the best methods of developing, strengthening, and directing the child's faculties of body and mind, so that each generation, reaching maturity, would start clear of the last, and show a finer, fuller growth, both physically and mentally, than the preceding. That humanity does slowly improve is not here denied; but, granting our gradual improvement, is it all that we could make? And is the gain due to a commensurate improvement in motherhood?

To both we must say no. When we see how some families improve, while others deteriorate, and how uncertain and irregular is such improvement as appears, we know that we could make better progress if all children had the same rich endowment and wise care that some receive. And, when we see how much of our improvement is due to gains made in hygienic knowledge, in public provision for education and sanitary regulation, none of which has been accomplished by mothers, we are forced to see that whatever advance the race has made is not exclusively attributable to motherhood. The human mother does less for her young, both absolutely and proportionately, than any kind of mother on earth. She does not obtain food for them, nor covering, nor shelter, nor protection, nor defence. She does not educate them beyond the personal habits required in the family circle and in her limited range of social life. The necessary knowledge of the world, so indispensable to every human being, she cannot give, because she does not possess it. All this provision and education are given by other hands and brains than hers. Neither does the amount of physical care and labor bestowed on the child by its mother warrant her claims to superiority in motherhood: this is but a part of our idealism of the subject.

The poor man's wife has far too much of other work to do to

spend all her time in waiting on her children. The rich man's wife could do it, but does not, partly because she hires some on to do it for her, and partly because she, too, has other duties to occupy her time. Only in isolated cases do we find a mother deputing all other services to others, and concentrating her energies on feeding, clothing, washing, dressing, and, as far as may be, educating her own child. When such cases are found, it remains to be shown that the child so reared is proportionately benefited by this unremittent devotion of its mother. On the contrary, the best service and education a child can receive involve the accumulated knowledge and exchanged activities of thousands upon thousands besides his mother,—the fathers of the race.

There does not appear, in the care and education of the child as given by the mother, any special superiority in human maternity. Measuring woman first in direct comparison of her reproductive processes with those of other animals, she does not fulfil this function so easily or so well as they. Measuring her educative processes by inter-personal comparison, the few admittedly able mothers with the many painfully unable ones, she seems more lacking, if possible, than in the other branch. The gain in human education thus far has not been acquired or distributed through the mother, but through men and single women; and there is nothing in the achievements of human motherhood to prove that it is for the advantage of the race to have women give all their time to it. Giving all their time to it does not improve it either in quantity or quality. The woman who works is usually a better reproducer than the woman who does not. And the woman who does not work is not proportionately a better educator.

An extra-terrestrial sociologist, studying human life and hearing for the first time of our so-called "maternal sacrifice" as a means of benefiting the species, might be touched and impressed by the idea. "How beautiful!" he would say. "How exquisitely pathetic and tender! One-half of humanity surrendering all other human interests and activities to concentrate its time, strength, and devotion upon the functions of maternity! To bear and rear the majestic race to which they can never fully belong! To live vicariously forever, through their sons, the daughters being only another vicarious link! What a supreme and magnificent martyrdom!" And he would direct his researches toward discovering what system was used to develope and perfect this sublime consecration of half the race to the perpetuation of the other half. He would view with intense and pathetic interest the endless procession of girls, born human as their brothers were, but marked down at once as "female—abortive type—only use to produce males." He would expect to see this "sex sacrificed to reproductive necessities," yet gifted with human consciousness and intelligence, rise grandly to the occasion, and strive to fit itself in every way for its high office. He would expect to find society commiserating the sacrifice, and honoring above all the glorious creature whose life was to be sunk utterly in the lives of others, and using every force properly to rear and fully to fit these functionaries for their noble office. Alas for the extra-terrestrial sociologist and his natural expectations! After exhaustive study, finding nothing of these things, he would return to Mars or Saturn or wherever he came from, marveling within himself at the vastness of the human paradox.

If the position of woman is to be justified by the doctrine of maternal sacrifice, surely society, or the individual, or both, would make some preparation for it. No such preparation is made. Society recognizes no such function. Premiums have been sometimes paid for large numbers of children, but they were paid to the fathers of them. The elaborate social machinery which constitutes our universal marriage market has no department to assist or advance motherhood. On the contrary, it is directly inimical to it, so that in our society life motherhood means direct loss, and is avoided by the social devotee. And the individual? Surely here right provision will be made. Young women, glorying in their prospective duties, their sacred and inalienable office, their great sex-martyrdom to race-advantage, will be found solemnly preparing for this work. What do we find? We find our young women reared in an attitude which is absolutely unconscious of and often injurious to their coming motherhood,—an irresponsible, indifferent, ignorant class of beings, so far as motherhood is concerned. They are fitted to attract the other sex for economic uses or, at most, for mutual gratification, but not for motherhood. They are reared in unbroken ignorance of their supposed principal duties, knowing nothing of these duties till they enter upon them.

This is as though all men were to be soldiers with the fate of nations in their hands; and no man told or taught a word of war or military service until he entered the battle-field!

The education of young women has no department of maternity. It is considered indelicate to give this consecrated functionary any previous knowledge of her sacred duties. This most important and wonderful of human functions is left from age to age in the hands of absolutely untaught women. It is tacitly supposed to be fulfilled by the mysterious working of what we call "the divine instinct of maternity." Maternal instinct is a very respectable and useful instinct common to most animals. It is "divine" and "holy" only as all the laws of nature are divine and holy; and it is such only when it works to the right fulfilment of its use. If the race-preservative processes are to be held more sacred than the self-preservative processes, we must admit all the functions and faculties of reproduction to the same degree of reverence,—the passion of the male for the female as well as the passion of the mother for her young. And if, still further, we are to honor the race-preservative processes most in their highest and latest development, which is the only comparison to be made on a natural basis, we should place the great, disinterested, social function of education far above the second—selfishness of individual maternal functions. Maternal instinct, merely as an instinct, is unworthy of our superstitious reverence. It should be measured only as a means to an end, and valued in proportion to its efficacy.

Among animals, which have but a low degree of intelligence, instinct is at its height, and works well. Among savages, still incapable of much intellectual development, instinct holds large place. The mother beast can and does take all the care of her young by instinct; the mother savage, nearly all, supplemented by the tribal traditions, the educative influences of association, and some direct instruction. As humanity advances, growing more complex and varied, and as human intelligence advances to keep pace with new functions and new needs, instinct decreases in value. The human creature prospers and progresses not by virtue of his animal instinct, but by the wisdom and force of a cultivated intelligence and will, with which to guide his action and to control and modify the very instincts which used to govern him.

The human female, denied the enlarged activities which have developed intelligence in man, denied the education of the will which only comes by freedom and power, has maintained the rudimentary forces of instinct to the present day. With her extreme modification to sex, this faculty of instinct runs mainly along sex-lines, and finds fullest vent in the processes of maternity, where it has held unbroken sway. So the children of humanity are born into the arms of an endless succession of untrained mothers, who bring to the care and teaching of their children neither education for that wonderful work nor experience therein: they bring merely the intense accumulated force of a brute instinct,— the blind devoted passion of the mother for the child. Maternal love is an enormous force, but force needs direction. Simply to love the child does not serve him unless specific acts of service express this love. What these acts of service are and how they are performed make or mar his life forever.

Observe the futility of unaided maternal love and instinct in the simple act of feeding the child. Belonging to order [class] mammalia, the human mother has an instinctive desire to suckle her young. (Some ultra-civilized have lost even that.) But this instinct has not taught her such habits of life as insure her ability to fulfil this natural function. Failing in the natural method, of what further use is instinct in the nourishment of the child? Can maternal instinct discriminate between Marrow's Food and Bridge's Food, Hayrick's Food and Pestle's Food, Pennywhistle's Sterilized Milk, and all the other infants' foods which are prepared and put upon the market by—men! These are not prepared by instinct, maternal or paternal, but by chemical analysis and physiological study; and their effect is observed and the diet varied by physicians, who do not do their work by instinct, either.

If the bottle-baby survive [sic] the loss of mother's milk, when he comes to the table, does maternal instinct suffice then to administer a proper diet for young children? Let the doctor and the undertaker answer. The wide and varied field of masculine activity in the interests of little children, from the peculiar human phenomenon of masculine assistance in parturition (there is one animal, the obstetric frog, where it also appears) to the manufacture of articles for feeding, clothing, protecting, amusing, and educating the baby, goes to show the utter inadequacy of maternal instinct in the human female. Another thing it shows also,—the criminal failure of that human female to supply by intelligent effort what instinct can no longer accomplish. For a reasoning, conscious being deliberately to undertake the responsibility of maintaining human life without making due preparation for the task is more than carelessness.

Before a man enters a trade, art, or profession, he studies it. He qualifies himself for the duties he is to undertake. He would be held a presuming impostor if he engaged in work he was not fitted to do, and his failure would mark him instantly with ridicule and reproach. In the more important professions, especially in those dealing with what we call "matters of life and death," the shipmaster or pilot, doctor or druggist, is required not only to study his business, but to pass an examination under those who have already become past masters, and obtain a certificate or a diploma or some credential to show that he is fit to be intrusted with the direct responsibility for human life.

Women enter a position which gives into their hands direct responsibility for the life or death of the whole human race with neither study nor experience, with no shadow of preparation or guarantee of capability. So far as they give it a thought, they fondly imagine that this mysterious "maternal instinct" will see them through. Instruction, if needed, they will pick up when the time comes: experience they will acquire as the children appear. "I guess I know how to bring up children!" cried the resentful old lady who was being advised: "I've buried seven!" The record of untrained instinct as a maternal faculty in the human race is to be read on the rows and rows of little gravestones which crowd our cemeteries. The experience gained by practising on the child is frequently buried with it.

No, the maternal sacrifice theory will not bear examination.

As a sex specialized to reproduction, giving up all personal activity, all honest independence, all useful and progressive economic service for her glorious consecration to the uses of maternity, the human female has little to show in the way of results which can justify her position. Neither the enormous percentage of children lost by death nor the low average health of those who survive, neither physical nor mental progress, give any proof of race advantage from the maternal sacrifice.

Concerning Children*

Chapter II. The Effect of Minding on the Mind

[. . .] The rearing of children is the most important work, and it is here contended that, in this great educational process, obedience, as a main factor, has a bad effect on the growing mind. A child is a human creature. He should be reared with a view to his development and behaviour as an adult, not solely with a view to his behaviour as a child. He is temporarily a child, far more permanently a man; and it is the man we are training. The work of "parenthood" is not only to guard and nourish the young, but to develope the qualities needed in the mature.

Obedience is defended, first, as being necessary to the protection of the child, and, second, as developing desirable qualities in the adult. But the child can be far better protected by removing all danger, which our present civilisation is quite competent to do; and "the habit of obedience" developes very undesirable qualities. On what characteristics does our human pre-eminence rest? On our breadth and accuracy of judgment and force of will. Because we can see widely and judge wisely, because we have power to do what we see to be right, therefore we are the dominant species in the animal kingdom; therefore we are consciously the children of God.

These qualities are lodged in individuals, and must be exercised by individuals for the best human progress. If our method of advance were that one person alone should be wise and strong, and all other persons prosperous through a strict subservience to

* Boston: Small, Maynard, 1900, pp. 37–45.

his commands, then, indeed, we could do no better for our children than to train them to obey. Judgment would be of no use to them if they had to take another's: will-power would be valueless if they were never to exercise it.

But this is by no means the condition of human life. More and more is it being recognised that progress lies in a well-developed average intelligence rather than in a wise despot and his stupid serfs. For every individual to have a good judgment and a strong will is far better for the community than for a few to have these qualities and the rest to follow them.

The "habit of obedience," forced in upon the impressible nature of a child, does not develope judgment and will, but does develope that fatal facility in following other people's judgment and other people's wills which tends to make us a helpless mob, mere sheep, instead of wise, free, strong individuals. The habit of submission to authority, the long deeply impressed conviction that to "be good" is to "give up," that there is virtue in the act of surrender,—this is one of the sources from which we continually replenish human weakness, and fill the world with an inert mass of mind-less, will-less folk, pushed and pulled about by those whom the obey.

Moreover, there is the opposite effect,—the injurious reaction from obedience,—almost as common and hurtful as its full achievement; namely, that fierce rebellious desire to do exactly the opposite of what one is told, which is no nearer to calm judgment than the other.

In obeying another will or in resisting another will, nothing is gained in wisdom. A human creature is a self-governing intelligence, and the rich years of childhood should be passed in the guarded and gradual exercise of those powers.

Now this will, no doubt, call up to the minds of many a picture of a selfish, domineering youngster, stormily ploughing through a number of experimental adventures, with a group of sacrificial parents and teachers prostate before him. Again an unwarranted assumption. Consideration of others is one of the first laws of life, one of the first things a child should be taught; but consideration of others is not identical with obedience. Again, it will be imagined that the child is to be left to laboriously work out for himself the accumulated experiments of humanity, and deprived of the profits of all previous experience. By no means. On the contrary, it is the business of those who have the care of the very young to see to it that they do benefit by that previous experience far more fully than is now possible.

Our system of obedience cuts the child off from precisely this advantage, and leaves him longing to do the forbidden things, genereally doing them, too, when he gets away from his tutelage. The behaviour of the released child, in its riotous reaction against authority as such, as shown glaringly in the action of the average college student, tells how much judgment and self-control have been developing behind the obedience.

The brain grows by exercise. The best time to develope it is in youth. To obey does not develope the brain, but checks its growth. It gives to the will a peculiar suicidal power of aborting its own impulse, not controlling it, but giving it up. This leaves a habit of giving up which weakens our power of continued effort.

All this is not saying that obedience is never useful in childhood. There are occasions when it is; and on such occasions, with a child otherwise intelligently trained, it will be forthcoming. We make a wide mistake in assuming that, unless a child is made to obey at every step, it will never obey. A grown person will obey under sharp instant pressure.

If there is a sudden danger, and you shriek at your friend, "Get up—quick!" or hiss a terrified, "Sh! Sh! Be Still!" your friend promptly obeys. Of course, if you had been endeavouring to "boss" that friend with a thousand pointless caprices, he might distrust you in the hour of peril; but if he knew you to be a reasonable person, he would respond promptly to a sudden command.

Much more will a child so respond where he has full reason to respect the judgment of the commander. Children have the same automatic habit of obedience by the same animal inheritance that gives the mother the habit of command; but we so abuse that faculty that it becomes lost in righteous rebellion or crushed submission. The animal mother never misuses her precious authority. She does not cry, "Wolf! Wolf!" We talk glibly about "the best good of the child," but there are few children who are not clearly aware that they are "minding" for the convenience of "the grown-ups" the greater part of the time. Therefore, they suspect self-interest in even the necessary commands, and might very readily refuse to obey in the hour of danger.

It is a commonplace observation that the best children —i.e., the most submissive and obedient—do not make the best men. If they are utterly subdued, "too good to live," they swell the Sunday-school list of infant saints, die young, and go to heaven: whereas the rebellious and unruly boy often makes the best citizen.

The too obedient child has learned only to do what he is told. If not told, he has no initiative; and, if told wrong, he does wrong. Life to him is not a series of problems to be solved, but a mere book of orders; and, instead of understanding the true imperious "force" of natural law, which a wise man follows because he sees the wisdom of the course, he takes every "must" in life to be like a personal command,—a thing probably unreasonable, and to be evaded, if possible.

The escaped child, long suppressed under obedience, is in no mood for a cheerful acceptance of real laws, but imagines that there is more "fun" in "having his own way." The foolish parent claims to be obeyed as a god; and the grown-up child seeks to evade God, to treat the laws of Nature as if she, too, were a foolish parent.

Suppose you are teaching a child arithmetic. You tell him to put down such and such figures in such a position. He inquires, "Why?" You explain the reason. If you do not explain the reason, he does not understand the problem. You might continue to give orders as to what figures to set down in what place; and the child, obeying, could be trotted through the arithmetic in a month's time. But the arithmetic would not have gone through him. He would be not better versed in the science of numbers than a typesetter is in the learned books he "sets up." We recognise this in the teaching of arithmetic, and go to great lengths in inventing test problems and arranging easy stages by which the child may gradually master his task. But we do not recognise it in teaching the child life. The small acts of infancy are the child's first problems in living. He naturally wishes to understand them. He says, "Why?" To which we reply inanely, "Because I tell you to!" That is no reason. It is a force, no doubt, a pressure, to which the child may be compelled to yield. But he is no wiser than he was before. He has learned nothing except the lesson we imagine so valuable,—to obey. At the very best, he may remember always, in like case, that "mamma would wish me to do so," and do it. But, when cases differ, he has no guide. With the best intentions in life, he can but cast about in his mind to try to imagine what some one else might tell him to do if present: the circumstances themselves mean nothing to him. Docility, subservience, a quick surrender of purpose, a wavering, untrained, easily shaken judgment,—these are the qualities developed by much obedience.

Are they the qualities we wish to develope in American citizens?

" 'Superfluous Women' " *

We have not yet fully recognized the social value of the unattached women of our century.

The presence of a large body of single women in a community is an essentially modern condition. Earlier races easily absorbed all their women, adding them to the possessions of some men; as one may read in the Hebrew Scriptures how widows were to be promptly remarried by their brothers-in-law. No, detached women were wanted. When living involved fighting, every household must have a male head, and a headless household naturally fell to some stronger one.

Under a polygamous and patriarchal regime there were no superfluous women; and back of that period they were such valuable property, through being the working members of society, that one might as well speak of superfluous sheep, or cows, or slaves, as of superfluous women in those days.

Modern society, with its monogamic basis and general indus-

* Woman's Journal, April 7, 1900, p. 105.

trial development, on the one hand, forbids the absorption of extra women by plural marriage, and, on the other, makes possible their economic existence by individual industry. Thus we see that although the balance of the sexes is far more equal than in the days when great numbers of males were continually destroyed through warfare and other risks, yet we have to-day a larger class of isolated women than ever before.

This social phenomenon is of immense importance.

It has been measured so far mainly as an evil; the evil to the woman herself in losing her share in the great processes of reproduction, with all the care and happiness involved; the evil to society in the multiplication of opportunity for illicit union in varied forms; and the economic evil to men in having either to "support" or to "compete with" these single women.

The various observers and commentators, each impressed strongly with a given point of view, have failed to reconcile the contradictions involved in these last two charges, and failed also to see the immense benefit of this large and unique class to society.

The economic contradiction is easily disposed of, its error lying in our common assumption that "pay" is the object of working. We think only of the "pay" the man gets, and that, if the woman, too, gets some of the pay, she robs him. Look instead at the plain fact that work is done to make something, or to carry it about. Production or distribution—these are the two great divisions of human labor. Now consider a farmer raising corn, and having six daughters, four sisters, and three maiden aunts depending on him for support. If he alone has to raise corn, they will all be hungry. If these amiable ladies all put a hand to the plow and a shoulder to the wheel, the corn supply is multiplied by thirteen —a visible increase of wealth, whether they eat or sell. A woman consumes goods to a large extent, and, unless she produces them, she is a burden on society somewhere. If, however, our farmer complains that there isn't enough land for them all to work on, and if they work he loses his job—then the economic point to quarrel with is the peculiar shrinkage in the face of the earth— not a surplus of productive labor.

The other two objections to a surplus of unmarried women

are both largely just. It is a pity that any human creature should miss that large field of human usefulness and joy, marriage and the raising of children. But for a thousand reasons some of us must; and the loss must simply be faced and borne like any other deprivations, and, like others, it has its compensations.

The effect on prostitution and kindred evils is a serious one, but largely economic in its nature. The single women most open to this sort of temptation are those unable satisfactorily to support themselves. Given good economic conditions, and the average woman does not succumb to that form of temptation. But when economic advantage is all that way, when the world is added to the flesh and the devil, it is true that a large surplusage of women means an increase in prostitution.

But now let us look upon the bright side of the picture, upon the immense social advantages accruing through this class. For the first time in history, we see women acting freely and as individuals upon the society of their times. Instead of being absorbed, contented, wholly occupied and limited by their own families, we have now the heart and mind and ever serviceable hand of woman turned loose to serve the world in general. The power of love, undrained by its natural recipients, is freed for wider use; the capacity for absolute devotion and unfailing service to one person, is now applicable to a social need; and we have about us in visible record the effect of all this potential motherhood upon society. The educational, religious, charitable, philanthropic, reformatory, and generally humanitarian work of this age, is largely done by single women.

Men, working for themselves, and usually for a cormorant crowd of dependents, cannot in honor "give their services" to these more general needs; but women, long accustomed to give their services, can and do. Thus the superfluous women who are not using all their time and strength in self-support, form the main social force in conscious improvement.

The women who are self-supporting are women even more useful to society at large. Much as we need the woman in times of suffering and disease, personally and socially, we need her more in steady every day contact. Neither sex does its best alone; each needs the influence of the other. To have all the main industries of the world in male hands alone, and women growing more and more content to "be supported," was a vast social evil. The married woman, if her man was poor, was too smotheringly engrossed in her range of industries to see the way out; and the married woman, if her man was rich, was usually too sodden in discontent to be any more useful. It remained for the single woman, reluctant, afraid, utterly unconscious of her noble mission, to creep slowly into the ranks of honorable social service.

Through her presence in common industry, through the visible and growing proof of her ability, comes the slow but steady change in the position of women. The industries change and become more human in their conditions, and the women change and become more human too. They have suffered—much—this vanguard who "were swept away, and their bodies did not even serve to build the bridge," but "they made a path to the water's edge," and over it shall pass "the whole human race."

The Home: Its Work and Influence*

Introductory

[. . .] The sum of the criticism in the following study is this: the home has not developed in proportion to our other institutions, and by its rudimentary condition it arrests development in other lines. Further, that the two main errors in the right adjustment of the home to our present life are these: the maintenance of primitive industries in a modern industrial community, and the confinement of women to those industries and their limited area of expression. No word is said against the real home, the true family life; but it is claimed that much we consider essential to that home and family life is not only unnecessary, but positively injurious.

Chapter V. The Home as a Workshop

I. The Housewife

All industry began at home.

All industry was begun by women.

---

* New York: McClure, Phillips, 1903, pp. 10, 82–103, 166–179, and 183.

Back of history, at the bottom of civilization, during that long period of slowly changing savagery which antedates our really human life, whatever work was done on earth was done by woman in the home. From that time to this we have travelled far, spread wide, grown broad and high; and our line of progress is the line of industrial evolution.

Where the patient and laborious squaw once carried on her back the slaughtered game for her own family, now wind and steam and lightning distribute our provisions around the world. Where she once erected a rude shelter of boughs or hides for her own family, now mason and carpenter, steel and iron worker, joiner, lather, plasterer, glazier, plumber, locksmith, painter, and decorator combine to house the world. Where she chewed and scraped the hides, wove bark and grasses, made garments, made baskets, made pottery, made all that was made for her own family, save the weapons of slaughter, now the thousand manufactures of a million mills supply our complex needs and pleasures. Where she tamed and herded a few beasts for her own family, now from ranchman to packer move the innumerable flocks and herds of the great plains; where she ploughed with a stick and reaped with a knife, for her own family, now gathered miles of corn cross continent and ocean to feed all nations. Where she prepared the food and reared the child for her own family—what! Has the world stopped? Is history a dream? Is social progress mere imagination?—*there she is yet!* Back of history, at the bottom of civilisation, untouched by a thousand whirling centuries, the primitive woman, in the primitive home, still toils at her primitive tasks.

All industries began at home, there is no doubt of that. All other industries have left home long ago. Why have these stayed? All other industries have grown. Why have not these?

What condition, social and economic, what shadowy survival of oldest superstitions, what iron weight of custom, law, religion, can be adduced in explanation of such a paradox as this? Talk of Siberian mammoths handed down in ice, like some crystallised fruit of earliest ages! What are they compared with this antedeluvian relic! By what art, what charm, what miracle, has the twentieth century preserved *alive* the prehistoric squaw!

This is a phenomenon well worth our study, a subject teeming

with interest, one that concerns every human being most closely
—most vitally. Sociology is beginning to teach us something of
the processes by which man has moved up and on to his present
grade, and may move farther. Among those processes none is
clearer, simpler, easier to understand, than industrial evolution. Its
laws are identical with those of physical evolution, a progression
from the less to the greater, from the simple to the complex, a
constant adaptation of means to ends, a tendency to minimise
effort and maximise efficiency. The solitary savage applies his
personal energy to his personal needs. The social group applies its
collective energy to its collective needs. The savage works by
himself, for himself; the civilised man works in elaborate interdependence with many, for many. By the division of labour and
its increasing specialisation we vastly multiply the output; by the
development of business methods we reduce expense and increase
results; the whole line of growth is the same as that which makes
a man more efficient in action than his weight in shellfish. He is
more highly organised and specialised. So is modern industry.

The solitary savage knew neither specialisation nor organisation—he "did his own work." This process gives the maximum
of effort and the minimum of results. Specialised and organised
industry gives the minimum of effort and the maximum of results.
That is civilised industry.

The so idealised and belauded "home industries" are still
savage. The modern home is built and furnished by civilised
methods. Arts, crafts, and manufactures, sciences, professions,
many highly sublimated processes of modern life combine to make
perfect the place where we live; but the industries practised in
that place remain at the first round of the ladder.

Instead of having our pick of the latest and best workers, we
are here confined to the two earliest—the Housewife and the
Housemaid. The housewife is the very first, and she still predomi-
nates by so large a majority as to make us wonder at the noisy
prominence of "the servant question." (It is not so wonderful,
after all, for that class of the population which keeps servants is
the class which makes the most noise.) Even in rich America, even
in richest New York, in *nine-tenths* of the families the housewife

"does her own work." This is so large a proportion that we will consider the housewife first—and fully.

Why was woman the first worker? Because she is a mother. All living animals are under the law of, first, self-preservation, and, second, race-preservation. But the second really comes first; the most imperative forces in nature compel the individual to sacrifice to the race. This law finds its best expression in what we call "the maternal sacrifice." Motherhood means giving. There is no limit to this urgency. The mother gives all she has to the young, including life. In many low organisms the sacrifice is instantaneous and complete—the mother dies in giving birth to the young— just lays her eggs and dies. Such forms of life have to remain low, however. The defunct mothers can be of no further use to the young, so they have to be little instinctive automata, hopelessly arrested in the path of progress.

Nature perceived that this wholly sacrificed mother was not the best kind. Little by little the usefulness of the mother was prolonged, the brooding mother, the feeding mother, lastly the nursing mother, highest of all. Order [class] mammalia stands at the top, type of efficient motherhood.

When human development began, new paths were open to mother-love—new tasks to maternal energy. The human mother not only nursed and guarded the child, but exercised her dawning ingenuity in adding to its comfort by making things.

The constructive tendency is essentially feminine; the destructive masculine. Male energy tends to scatter and destroy, female to gather and construct. So human labour comes by nature from the woman, was hers entirely for countless ages, while the man could only hunt and fight, or prance and prophesy as "medicine man"; and this is still so in those races which remain savage. Even in so advanced a savage race as the Zulus, the women do the work; and our own country has plenty of similar examples near at hand.

As human civilisation is entirely dependent on progressive industry, while hunting and fighting are faculties we share with the whole carnivora, it is easy to see that during all those ages of savagery the woman was the leader. She represented the higher grade of life; and carried it far enough to bring to birth many of the great arts as well as the humbler ones, especially the invaluable art of language.*

But maternal energy has its limits. What those limits are may be best studied in an ant's nest or a beehive. These marvelous insects, perfected types of industry and of maternity, have succeeded in *organising motherhood*. Most creatures reproduce individually, these collectively—all personal life absolutely lost in the group life. Moved by an instinct coincident with its existence, the new-hatched ant, still weak and wet from the pupa, staggers to the nearest yet unborn to care for it, and cares for it devotedly to the end of life.

One bee group-mother, crawling from cell to cell, lays eggs unnumbered for the common care; the other group-mothers, their own egg-laying capacity in abeyance, labour unceasingly in the interests of those common eggs; and the delicate perfection of provision and service thus attained results in—what? In a marvelous motherhood and a futile fatherhood; the predominant female, the almost negligible male—a temporary fertilising agent merely; in infinite reproduction, and that is all; in more bees, and more ants, more and more for ever, like the sands of the sea. They would cover the earth like a blanket but for merciful appetites of other creatures. But this is only multiplication—not improvement. Nature has one more law to govern life besides self-preservation and reproduction—progress. To be to re-be, and to be better is the law. It is not enough to keep one's self alive, it is not enough to keep one's kind alive, we must improve. This law of growth, which is the grand underlying one that moves the universe, acts on living species mainly through the male. He is the progressive where the female is conservative by nature. He is a variant where she is the race type. This tendency to vary is one of the most beneficent in nature. Through it comes change, and, through change, improvement. The unbridled flow of maternal energy is capable of producing an exquisite apparatus for child-

* See Otis Mason, "Woman's Share in Primitive Culture." (New York: Appleton, 1894. Footnote in original.)

rearing, and no more. The masculine energy is needed also, for the highest evolution.

Well it is for the human race that the male savage finally took hold of the female's industry. Whether he perceived her superiority and sought to emulate it is doubtful; more probably it was the pressure of economic conditions which slowly forced him to it. The glaring proofs of time taught him that the pasture was more profitable than the hunting ground, and the cornfield than the pasture. The accumulating riches produced by the woman's industry drew him on. Slowly, reluctantly, the lordly fighter condescended to follow the humble worker, who led him by thousands of years. In the hands of the male, industry developed, The woman is a patient, submissive, inexhaustible labourer. The pouring forces of maternity prompt her to work for ever—for her young. Not so the man. Working is with him an acquired habit, and acquired very late in his racial life. The low-grade man still in his heart despises it, he still prefers to be waited on by women, he still feels more at home in hunting and fighting. And man alone being represented in the main fields of modern industry, this male instinct for hunting and fighting plays havoc with the true economic processes. He makes a warfare of business, he makes prey of his competitors, he still seeks to enslave—to make other work for him, instead of freely and joyously working all he can. The best industrial progress needs both elements—ours is but a compromise as yet, something between the beehive and the battlefield.

But, with all the faults of unbridled male energy, it has lifted industry from the limits of the home to that of the world. Through it has come our splendid growth; much marred by evils of force and fraud, crude, wasteful, cruel, but progressive; and infinitely beyond the level of these neglected rudimentary trades left at home; left to the too tender mercies of the housewife.

The iron limits of her efficiency are these: First, that of average capacity. Just consider what any human business would be in which there was no faintest possibility of choice, of exceptional ability, of division of labor. What would shoes be like if every man made his own, if the shoemaker had never come to his development? What would houses be like if every man had his own? Or hats, or books, or waggons [sic]? To confine any industry to the level of a universal average is to strangle it in its cradle. And there, for ever, lie the industries of the housewife. What every man does alone for himself, no man can ever do well—or woman either. That is the first limit of the "housewife."

The next is the maternal character of this poor primeval labourer. Because of her wealth of power and patience it does not occur to her to make things easier for herself. The fatal inertia of home industries lies in their maternal basis. The work is only done for the family—the family is satisfied—what remains? There is no other ambition, no other incentive, no other reward. Where the horizon of duty and aspiration closes down with one's immediate blood relations, there is no room for growth.

All that has pushed and pulled reluctant man up the long path of social evolution has not touched the home-bound woman. Whatever height he reached, her place was still the same. The economic relation of the sexes here works* with tremendous force. Depending on the male for her economic profit, her own household labours kept to the sex-basis, and never allowed to enter the open market, there was nothing to modify her original sex-tendency to work with stationary contentment. If we can imagine for a moment a world like ours, with all our elaborate business processes in the hands of women, and the men still in the position of the male savage—painted braves, ready for the warpath, and good for little else—we get a comparison with this real condition, where the business processes are in the hands of men, and the women still in the position of the female savage—docile toilers for the family, and good for little else. That is the second limit of the housewife—that she is merely working for her own family—in the sex-relation—not the economic relation; as servant to the family instead of servant to the world.

Next comes her isolation. Even the bottom-level of a universal average—even the blind patience of a working mother—could be helped up a little under the beneficent influence of association.

* See "Women and Economics," C. P. Stetson. [Footnote in original.]

In the days when the ingenious squaw led the world, she had it. The women toiled together at their primitive tasks and talked together as they toiled. The women who founded the beginnings of agriculture were founders also of the village; and their feminine constructive tendencies held it together while the destructive tendencies of the belligerent male continually tore it apart. All through that babyhood of civilisation, the hunting and fighting instinct made men prey upon the accumulated wealth resultant from the labouring instinct of women—but industry conquered, being the best. As industry developed, as riches increased, as property rights were confined more and more closely at home. Later civilisations have let them out to play—but not to work. The parasitic female of the upper classes is allowed the empty freedom of association with her useless kind; but the housewife is still confined to the house.

We are now giving great attention to this matter of home industry. We are founding chairs of Household Science, we are writing books on Domestic Economics; we are striving mightily to elevate the standard of home industry—and we omit to notice that it is just because it is home industry that all this trouble is necessary.

So far as home industry has been affected by world industry, it has improved. The implements of cooking and cleaning, for instance—where should we be if our modern squaw had to make her own utensils, as did her ancient prototype? The man, in world industry, makes not only the house, with all its elaborate labour-saving and health-protecting devices; not only the furniture of the house, the ornaments, hangings, and decorations, but the implements of the home industries as well. Go to the household furnishing store of our day—remember the one pot of the savage family to boil the meat and wash the baby—and see the difference between "home-made" and "world-made" things.

So far as home industry has progressed, it is through contact with the moving world outside; so far as it remains undeveloped, it is through the inexorable limitations of the home in itself.

There is one more limitation to be considered—the number of occupations practised. Though man has taken out and developed all the great trades, and, indeed, all trades beyond a certain grade, he has left the roots of quite a number at home. The housewife practises the conflicting elements of many kinds of work. First, she is cook. Whatever else is done or undone, we must eat; and since eating is ordained to be done at home, that is her predominant trade. The preparation and service of food is a most useful function; and as a world-industry, in the hands of professionals, students, and experts, it has reached a comparatively high stage of development.

In the nine-tenths of our homes where the housewife is cook, it comes under all these limitations: First, average capacity; second, sex-tendency; third, isolation; fourth, conflicting duties.

The cook, having also the cleaning to do, the sewing, mending, nursing, and care of children, the amount of time given to cooking is perforce limited. But even the plainest of home cooking must take up a good proportion of the day. The cooking, service, and "cleaning up" of ordinary meals, in a farmhouse, with the contributary processes of picking, sorting, peeling, washing, etc., and the extra time given to special baking, pickling, and preserving, take fully six hours a day. To the man, who is out of the house during work-hours, and who seldom estimates woman's work at its real value, this may seem extreme, but the working housewife knows it is a fair allowance, even a modest one.

There are degrees of speed, skill, intelligence, and purchasing power, of course; but this is a modest average; two hours for breakfast, three for dinner, one for supper. The preparation of food as a household industry takes up half the working time of half the population of the world. This utterly undeveloped industry, inadequate and exhausting, takes nearly a quarter of a twelve-hour day of the world's working force.

Cooking and sewing are inimical; the sewing of a housewife is quite generally pushed over into the evening as well as afternoon, thus lengthening her day considerably. Nursing, as applied to the sick, must come in when it happens, other things giving way at that time. Cleaning is continuous. Cooking, of course, makes cleaning; the two main elements of dirt in the household being grease and ashes; another, and omnipresent one, dust. Then, there are the children to clean, and the clothes to clean—this latter so considerable an item as to take two days of extra labour—during which, of course, other departments must be less attended.

We have the regular daily labour of serving meals and "clearing up," we have the regular daily labour of keeping the home in order; then we have the washing day, ironing day, baking day, and sweeping day. Some make a special mending day also. This division, best observed by the most competent, is a heroic monument to the undying efforts of the human worker to specialise. But we have left out one, and the most important one, of our home industries—the care of children.

Where is Children's Day?

The children are there every day, of course. Yes, but which hour of the day? With six for food, with—spreading out the washing and ironing over the week—two for laundry, with — spreading the sweeping day and adding the daily dusting and setting to rights—two for cleaning; and another two for sewing —after these twelve hours of necessary labour are accounted for, what time remains for the children?

The initial purpose of the home is the care of children. The initial purpose of motherhood is the care of children. How are the duties of the mother compatible with the duties of the housewife? How can child-culture, as a branch of human progress, rise to any degree of proficiency in this swarming heap of rudimentary trades?

Nothing is asked—here—as to how the housewife, doing all these things together her life long, can herself find time for culture and development; or how can she catch any glimmer of civic duty or public service beyond this towering pile of domestic duty and household service. The particular point herein advanced is that the conditions of home industry *as such* forever limit the growth of the industry so practised; forever limit the growth of the persons so practising them; and also tend to limit the growth of the society which is content to leave any of its essential functions in this distorted state.

Our efforts to "lift the standard of household industry" ignore the laws of industry. We seek by talking and writing, by poetising and sermonising, and playing on every tender sentiment and devout aspiration, to convince the housewife that there is something particularly exalted and beautiful, as well as useful, in her occupation. This shows our deep-rooted error of sex-distinction in industry. We consider the work of the woman in the house as essentially feminine, and fail to see that, as work, it is exactly like any other kind of human activity, having the same limitations and the same possibilities.

Suppose we change the sex and consider for a while the status of a house-husband. He could be a tall, strong, fine-looking person —man-servants often are. He could love his wife and his children —industrial status does not affect these primal instincts. He could toil from morning to night, manfully, to meet their needs.

Suppose we are visiting in such a family. We should find a very rude small hut—no one man could build much of a house, but, ah! the tender love, the pride, the intimate emotion he would put into that hut! For his heart's dearest—for his precious little ones—he had dragged together the fallen logs—chipped them smooth with his flint-ax (there could have been no metal work while every man was a house-husband), and piled them together. With patient, loving hands he had daubed the chinks with clay, made beds of leaves, hung hides upon the walls. Even some rude stools he might have contrived—though furniture really belongs to a later period. But over all comes the incessant demand for food. His cherished family must eat, often and often, and under that imperative necessity all others wait.

So he goes forth to the hunt, brave, subtle, fiercely ingenious; and, actuated by his ceaseless love for his family, he performs wonders. He brings home the food—day after day—even sometimes enough for several days, though meat does not keep very long. The family would have food of a sort, shelter of a sort, and love. But try to point out to the house-husband what other things he could obtain for them, create for them, provide for them if he learned to combine with other men, to exchange labour, to organise industry. See his virtuous horror!

What! Give up his duty to his family! Let another man hunt for them!—another man build their home—another man make their garments! He will not hear of it. "It is my duty as a husband," he will tell you, "to serve my wife. It is my duty as a father to serve my children. No other person could love them as I do, and without that love the work would not be done as well." Strong in this conviction, the house-husband would remain intrenched in his home, serving his family with might and main, having no time, no strength, no brain capacity for undertaking larger methods; and there he and his family would all be, immovable in the Stone [Paleolithic] Age.

Never was any such idiot on earth as this hypothetical home-husband. It was not in him to stay in such primitive restrictions. But he has been quite willing to leave his wife in that interestingly remote period.

The permanent error of the housewife lies in that assumption that her love for her family makes her service satisfactory. Family affection has nothing to do with the specialist's skill; nor with the specialist's love of his work for the pleasure of doing it. That is the kind of love that makes good work; and that is the kind of work the world needs and the families within it. Men, specialised, give to their families all that we know of modern comforts, of scientific appliances, of works of art, of the complex necessities and conveniences of modern life. Women, unspecialised, refuse to benefit their families in like proportion; but offer to them only the grade of service which was proper enough in the Stone Age, but is a historic disgrace to-day.

A house does not need a wife any more than it does a husband. Are we never to have a man-wife? A really suitable and profitable companion for a man instead of the bond-slave of a house? There is nothing in the work of a house which requires marital or maternal affection. It does require highly developed skill and business sense—but these it fails to get.

Would any amount of love on the part of that inconceivable house-husband justify him in depriving his family of all the fruits of progress? What a colossal charge of malfeasance in office could be brought against such a husband—such a father; who, under the name of love, should so fail in his great first duty—Progress.

How does the woman escape this charge? Why is not she responsible for progress, too? By [w]hat strange assumption does she justify this refusal to keep step with the world? She will tell you, perhaps, that she cannot do more than she does—she has neither time nor strength nor ambition for any more work. So might the house-husband have defended himself—as honestly and as reasonably. It is true. While every man had to spend all his time providing for his own family, no man ever had, or ever could have, time, strength, or ambition to do more.

It is not *more* work that is asked of women, but less. It is *A different method* of work. Human progress rests upon the interchange of labour; upon work done humanly for each other, not, like the efforts of the savage or the brute, done only for one's own. The housewife, blinded by her ancient duty, fails in her modern duty.

It is true that, while she does this work in this way, she can do no more. Therefore she must stop doing it, and learn to do differently. The house will not be "neglected" by her so doing; but is even now most shamefully neglected by her antique methods of labour. The family will not be less loved because it has a skilled worker to love it. Love has to pass muster in results, as well as intentions. Here are five mothers, equally loving. One is a Hottentot [Khoikhoi]. One is an Eskimo. One is a Hindoo. One is a German peasant woman. One is an American and a successful physician.

Which could do most for her children? All might compete on even terms if "love is enough" as poets have claimed; but *which could best provide for her children?*

Neither overflowing heart nor overburdened hand sufficiently counts in the uplifting of the race; that rests on *what is done*. The position of the housewife is a final limitation and a continuous, increasing injury both to the specific industries of the place, and to her first great duty of motherhood. The human race, fathered only by house-husbands, would never have moved at all. The human race, mothered only by housewives, has moved only half as fast and as far as it rightly should have done, and the work the patient housewife spends her life on is pitifully behind in the march of events. The home as a workshop is utterly insufficient to rightly serve the needs of the growing world.

Chapter IX. Domestic Ethics

[. . .] Both the teaching of our religion and the tendency of social progress call for a larger love, and the home, in its position of arrested development, primitive industry, and crippled womanhood, tends rather to check that growth than to help it. The man's love for his family finds expression in his labour for other people—he serves society, and society provides for him and his dear ones; so good will spreads and knits; comradeship and fellow-feeling appear, friendship brings its pure height of affection; this is the natural line of development in the great social virtue, love.

But the woman, still expressing her love for her family in direct personal service, misses all that. The primitive father, to feed the child, went forth himself and killed some rabbit—and the primitive mother cooked it: love, in grade A. The modern father, to feed his child, takes his thousandth part in some complex industry, and receives his thousand-fold share of the complex products of others' industry, and so provides for the child far more richly than the savage could: love, in grade Z. But the modern mother—if we can call her so by courtesy—to feed her child still does nothing but cook for it, still loves in grade A; and the effect of that persistence of grade A is to retard the development of grade Z. Mother-love is the fountain of all our human affection; but mother-love, *as limited by the home,* does not have the range and efficacy proper to our time. The home, as at present maintained, checks the growth of love.

As to Truth. This is a distinctly modern virtue. it comes in slowly, following power and freedom. The weak lie, a small beast hides; the lion does not hide. The slave lies—and the courtier; the king does not lie—he does not need to.

The most truthful nations are the most powerful. The most truthful class is the most powerful. The more truthful sex is the more powerful. Weakness, helplessness, ignorance, dependence, these breed falsehood and evasion; and, in child, servant, and woman, the denizens of the home, we have to combat these tendencies. The standard of sincerity of the father may be taught the son; but the home is not the originator of that standard. In this, as in other virtues, gain made in quite other fields of growth is necessarily transmitted to the home; but fair analysis must discriminate between the effect of religion, of education. of new social demands, and the effect of the home as such.

Courage comes along two main lines—by exposure to danger, and by increase of strength. The home, in its very nature, is intended to shield from danger; it is in origin a hiding place, a shelter for the defenceless. Staying in it is in no way conducive to the growth of courage. Constant shelter, protection, and defence may breed gratitude—must breed cowardice. We expect timidity of "women and children"—the housemates. Yet courage is by no means a sex attribute. Every species of animal that shows courage shows it equally in male and female—or even more in mother than in father. "It is better to meet a she-bear robbed of her whelps than a fool in his folly." This dominant terror—the fool —is contrasted with the female bear—not the male. Belligerence, mere combativeness, is a masculine attribute; but courage is not.

The cowardice of women is a distinctly home product. It is born of weakness and ignorance; a weakness and an ignorance by no means essential feminine attributes, but strictly domestic attributes. Keep a man from birth wrapped in much cloth, shut away from sky and sun, wind and rain, continually exhausting his nervous energy by incessant activity in monotonous little things, and never developing his muscular strength and skill by suitable exercise of a large and varied nature, and he would be weak. Savage women are not weak. Peasant women are not weak. Fishwives are not weak. The home-bound woman is weak, as would be a home-bound man. Also, she is ignorant. Not, at least not nowadays, ignorant necessarily of books, but ignorant of general life.

It is this ignorance and this weakness which makes women cowards; cowards frank and unashamed; cowards accustomed to be petted and praised, to be called "true woman" because they scream at that arch-terror of the home—a mouse. This home-bred cowardice, so admired in women, is of necessity transmitted to their sons as well as daughters. It is laughed out of them and knocked out of them, but it is born into them, relentlessly, with every generation. As black mothers must alter the complexion of a race, so must coward mothers alter its character. Apart from fighting—where the natural combative sex-tendency often counts as courage—our men are not as brave as they would be if their mothers were braver. We need courage to-day as much as we ever needed it in our lives. Courage to think and speak the truth; courage to face convention and prejudice, ridicule and opposition. We need courage in men and women equally, to face the problems of the times; and we do not get that courage from the home.

The sense of Justice is one of the highest human attributes; one of the latest in appearance, one of the rarest and most precious. We love and honour justice; we seek in some main lines of life to enforce it, after a fashion; but many of our arrangements are still so palpably unjust that one would think the virtue was but dreamed of, as yet unborn. Justice follows equality and freedom. To apprehend it at all the mind must first perceive the equal, and then resent the unequal. We must get a sense of level, of balance, and then we notice a deflection. As a matter of social evolution our system of legal justice springs from the primitive market place, the disputes of equals, the calling in of a third party to adjudicate. The disputants know instinctively that an outsider can see the difficulty better than an insider. Slowly the arbiter was given more power, more scope; out of much experience came the crystallisation of law. "Justice!" was the cry of the lowest before the highest; and the greatest kings were honoured most for this great virtue.

The field for justice has widened as the state widened; it has reached out to all classes; its high exercise distinguishes the foremost nations of our times. Yet even in the teeth of the law-courts injustice is still common; in everyday life it is most patent.

We have made great progress in the sense of justice and fair play; yet we are still greatly lacking in it. What is the contribution of domestic ethics to this mighty virtue? In the home is neither freedom nor equality. There is ownership throughout; the dominant father, the more or less subservient mother, the utterly dependent child; and sometimes that still lower grade—the servant. Love is possible, love deep and reciprocal; loyalty is possible;

gratitude is possible; kindness, to ruinous favouritism, is possible; unkindness, to all conspiracy, hate, and rebellion is possible.

Justice was born outside the home and a long way from it; and it has never even been adopted there.

Justice is wholly social in its nature—extra-domestic—even anti-domestic. Just men may seek to do justly in their homes, but it is hard work. Intense, personal feeling, close ties of blood, are inimical to the exercise of justice. Do we expect the judge upon the bench to do justice, dispassionate unswerving, on his own child—his own wife—in the dock? If he does, we will hail him as more than mortal. Do we expect a common man—not a judge with all the training and experience of his place, but a plain man —to do justice to his own wife and his own child in the constant intimacy of the home? Do we expect the mother to do justice to the child when the child is the offender and the mother the offended? Where plaintiff, judge, and executioner are lodged in one person; where there is no third party—no spectators even— only absolute irresponsible power, why should we—how could we—expect justice! We don't. We do not even think of it. No child cries for "Justice!" to the deaf walls of the home—he never heard of it.

He gets love—endless love and indulgence. He gets anger and punishment with no court of appeal. He gets care—neglect —discourtesy—affection—indifference—cruelty—and some- times wise and lovely training—but none of these are justice. The home, as such, in no way promotes justice; but, in its dispropor- tionate and unbalanced position to-day, palpably perverts and prevents it.

Allied to justice, following upon large equality and recognition of others, comes that true estimate of one's self and one's own powers which is an unnamed virtue. "Humility" is not it—to undervalue and depreciate one's self may be the opposite of pride, but it is not a virtue. A just estimate is not humility. But call it humility for convenience's sake; and see how ill it flourishes at home. In the circumscribed horizon small things look large. There is no general measuring point, no healthy standard of comparison.

The passionate love of the wife, the mother, and equally of

the husband, the father, makes all geese swans. The parents idealise their children; and the children, even more restricted by the home atmosphere—*for they know no other*—idealise the parents. This is sometimes to their advantage—often the other way. Constant study of near objects, with no distant horizon to test and change the focus, makes us short-sighted; and, as we all know, the smallest object is large if you hold it near enough. Constant association with one's nearest and dearest necessarily tends to a disproportionate estimate of their values.

There is no perspective—cannot be—in these close quarters. The infant prodigy of talent, praised and petted, brings his production into the cold light of the market, under the myriad facets of the public eye, to the measurement of professional standards—and no most swift return to the home atmosphere can counterbalance the effect of that judgment day. A just estimate of one's self and one's work can only be attained by the widest and most impersonal comparison. The home estimate is essentially personal, essentially narrow. It sometimes errs in underrating a world-talent; but nine times out of ten it errs the other way—overrating a home-talent. Humility, in the sense of an honest and accurate estimate of one's self, is not a home-made product. A morbid modesty or an unfounded pride often is. The intense self-consciousness, the prominent and sensitive personality developed by home life, we are all familiar with in women.

The woman who has always been in close personal relation with someone,—daughter, sister, wife, mother,—and so loved, valued, held close, feels herself neglected and chilly when she comes into business relations. She feels personal neglect in the broad indifference of office or shop; and instantly seeks to establish personal relations with all about her. As a business woman she outgrows it in time. It is not a sex-quality, it is a home-quality; found in a boy brought up entirely at home as well as in a girl. It tends to a disproportionate estimate of self; it is a primitive quality, common to children and savages; it is not conducive to justice and true social adjustment.

Closely allied to this branch of character is the power of self-control. As an initial human virtue none lies deeper than this; and here the home has credit for much help in developing some of the earlier stages of this great faculty. Primitive man brought to his dawning human relation a long-descended, highly-developed Ego. He had been an individual animal "always and always," he had now to begin to be a social animal, a collective animal, to develop the social instincts and the social conduct in which lay further progress.

The training of the child shows us in little what history shows us in the large. What the well-bred child has to learn to make him a pleasing member of the family is self-control. To restrain and adjust one's self to one's society—that is the line of courtesy —the line of Christianity—the line of social evolution. The home life does indeed teach the beginning of self-control; but no more. As compared with the world, it represents unbridled license. "In company" one must wear so and so, talk so and so, do so and so, look so and so. To "feel at home" means relaxation of all this.

This is as it should be. The home is the place for personal relief and rest from the higher plane of social contact. But social contact is needed to develop social qualities, constant staying at home does not do it.

The man, accustomed to meet all sorts of people in many ways, has a far larger and easier adjustment. The woman, used only to the close contact of a few people in a few relations, as child, parent, servant, tradesman; or to the set code of "company manners," has no such healthy human plane of contact.

"I never was so treated in my life!" she complains—and she never was—at home. This limits the range of life, cuts off the widest channels of growth, overdevelops the few deep ones; and does not develop self-control. The dressing-gown-and-slippers home attitude is temporarily changed for that of "shopping," or "visiting," but the childish sensitiveness, the disproportionate personality, remain dominant.

A too continuous home atmosphere checks in the woman the valuable social faculties. It checks it in the man more insidiously, through his position of easy mastery over these dependents, wife, children, servants; and through the constant catering of the whole *menage* to his special tastes. If each man had a private tailor shop in his back yard he would be far more whimsical and exacting in his personal taste in clothes. Every natural tendency to self-indulgence is steadily increased by the life service of an entire wife. This having one whole woman devoted to one's direct personal service is about as far from the cultivation of self-control as any process that could be devised.

The man loves the woman and serves her—but he serves her *through his service of the world*—and she serves him direct. He can fuss and dictate as to details, he can develop all manner of notions as to bacon, or toast, or griddle cakes; the whole cuisine is his, he supports it, it is meant to please him, and under its encompassing temptation he increases in girth and weight; but not in self-control. He may be a wise, temperate, judicious man, but the home, with its disproportionate attention to personal desires, does not make him so.

No clearer instance could be given of the effect of domestic ethics. In this one field may be shown the beneficent effects of the early home upon early man, the continued beneficent effects of what is essential in the home upon modern man; and the most evil effects of the domestic rudiments upon modern man. The differing ages and sexes held together by love, yet respecting one another's privacy, demand of one another precisely this power of self-control. Children together, with no adults, become boisterous and unruly; adults together, with no children, become out of sympathy with childhood; the sexes, separated, tend to injurious excesses; but the true home life checks excess, develops what is lacking, harmonises all.

What does the morbid, disproportioned, overgrown home life do? It tends to develop a domineering selfishness in man and a degrading abnegation in woman—or sometimes reverses this effect. The smooth, unconscious, all-absorbing greed which the unnaturally developed home of to-day produces in some women, is as evil a thing as life shows. Here is a human creature who has all her life been loved and cared for, sheltered, protected, defended; everything provided for her and nothing demanded of her except the exercise of her natural feminine functions, and some proficiency in the playground regulations of "society."

The degree of sublimated selfishness thus produced by home life is quite beyond the selfishness we so deplore in men. A man may be—often is—deplorably selfish in his home life; but he does not expect all the world to treat him with the same indulgence. He has to give as well as take in the broad, healthy, growing life of the world.

The woman has her home-life to make her selfish, and has no world life to offset it. [. . .]

The home is the cradle of all the virtues, but we are in a stage of social development where we need virtues beyond the cradle size. The virtues begun at home need to come out and grow in the world as men need to do—and as wom[e]n need to do, but do not know it. The ethics of the home are good in degree. The ethics of human life are far larger and more complex.

Our moral growth is to-day limited most seriously by the persistent maintenance in half the world of a primitive standard of domestic ethics.

Human Work*

Chapter XVI. Our Position To-Day

[. . .] That the unproductive consumer should believe the absurdities on which his absurd position rests is comprehensible; but that the producer, not properly supplied with social nourishment, and overtaxed in the production of the very supplies he does not get enough of, should accept the basic fallacies which hold him in his even more absurd position,—this is not so comprehensible.

Perhaps what does account for it is this: that with all his labour and suffering the worker after all *is* Society; he is in the main performing great service; he has a right to be more contented than the ex-man who does not work. He is in the more normal position, though he does not know it; and the sociological laws are always stronger in their action than our notions. As a matter of fact the working class, which does not mean merely the "labouring class" of our present terminology, but which includes

* New York: McClure, Phillips, 1904, pp. 358–364, 368–375, and 383–386.

all workers with hand and brain, is the world. They are the acting factors in those processes which constitute social life.

Through all these centuries of unbelief and misbelief they have done the things which kept the world alive. They have clothed the world, fed the world, housed the world, taught the world, beautified and improved the world; yes, and have lifted it from savagery to its present level. To-day in our democracy they need only enlightenment to see a further duty to the world in a better organisation of its economic processes. Thrilled as they are by the swiftly growing current of social consciousness, conscious as they are that things are wrong, anxious as they are to set things right, they are still hindered by these economic errors of us all.

Under the Ego concept they speak of "every man's right to the product of his own labour," a sociological absurdity. In the first place no member of Society has an "own" labour, our labour is all collective and co-ordinate. In the second place it is not the product of his fraction of our labour that a man wants, but the product of the labour of many other persons, of all times and places. In the third place it is not even "the equivalent" of his fraction of our labour that a man wants, it is a previous supply of the social product bearing no relation to his subsequent output except that of nourishment and stimulus.

In short, there is no true class-distinction in acceptance of those deep-seated errors which together modify the conduct of mankind so injuriously. The false classification we are treating is *the product of those errors.* With right economic belief and action there would be no division of Producer and Consumer, no Leisure Class, no Working Class, no serried ranks of Capital and Labour. All would produce, all would consume; all would work and all would have leisure; all would share in the social capital and the social labour,—both elements of social advantage.

The economic relation of the sexes is of enormous importance in our present day problems, as I have endeavored to point out in my previous book, "Women and Economics." The economic dependence of the female on the male, her food being obtained, not in industrial relation with society, but in the sex relation with the individual male, affects the race not only through the ensuing overdevelopment of sex, but through an artificial maintenance of primitive ideas and feelings in economics. The woman's artless attitude of taking all that is given her and frequently asking for more, without ever entertaining the idea of return in kind, of paying for her keep, maintains in the race, as we have previously shown, the tendency to inordinate consumption, the quenchless appetite of a parasite. This parasitic appetite is the invariable result of economic dependence. We need not wonder at the evolution of a parasitic class when we maintain, or seek to maintain, a parasitic sex.

As we have seen in an earlier chapter, another effect of this condition is, by its resultant exaggeration of the sex nature of the male, to maintain in him the belligerent and destructive tendencies which belong to a remote period of race improvement through sex competition, a period of animal individualism, and which work much evil in a period of constructive and co-ordinate industry. Where wealth and progress depend on the cordial intelligent interdependence of the group, it is most deteriorating to have maintained this primitive attitude of sex combat. Again, the male, being obliged to provide goods for several persons besides himself, and yet being limited in goods to the amount he can himself produce, the natural desires of the individual are augmented by the accumulated desires of the whole family, yet gratified only through him; and each man faces the world, with the output of one, yet requiring the income to support six—or whatever number he represents! According to the Want theory* this is a beautiful provision of nature for augmenting the man's output. In the light of fact it does nothing of the kind. It simply augments his desire to get—in no way adding to his power to give. That moving mirror of life, our literature, is one long picture of the effects of this incarnate appetite at home, dragging ever at the man's purse strings, and pushing hard against social honour, social duty, all the high traits of citizenship.

The child, most important of all, reared in this atmosphere of continual demand, seeing his father looking on the world as a

* The principle that people work to gratify their desires (wants).

place to hunt for prey for his mate and young, seeing his mother do nothing whatever but minister to the family needs, inevitably grows up to look at life in the same way. To his growing soul, the world appears to be a number of houses with families in them. The business of life appears to be to keep house for these families. The mother does this in a life of personal service. The father does it in mulcting "the world" as far as he is able.

If, on the contrary, a young human being grew up to see his father regarding his work for humanity as the chief duty in life, his mother with the same attitude, both regarding the consumption of goods as but a means to further and better work, and those goods always explained to him to come, not from the individual exertion of his father "wrestling with the world," but from the combined exertions of that world—that great, rich, kind ever-fruitful, and generous world of willing workers which feeds all its children so well,—but I stray into consideration of future conditions instead of present.

At present we have for the common lot of humanity that painful exhibition known as "the round man in the square hole." Of all human troubles, none is so universal as this—a man's work does not fit him. His income is insufficient, his output is insufficient, and he does not healthfully enjoy the process of living. A general condition of misadaptation, with necessary results of malnutrition and malproduction,—that is the prominent and visible symptom of our deep-lying psychological errors.

Consider the life of a typical average man.

He is misborn, misfed, mistaught, misclothed, misgoverned, to a varying degree. Instead of having a clear view of the social life and his place in it, he has a false and distorted view of his personal life, and only sees the social action as it infringes on him. He is surrounded from infancy with poor workmanship, the grudging product of those unhappy misplaced men in square holes. The education which should be his introduction to the great and beautiful facts and laws of life, is too often a "bread-winning" process, practised by celibate women, as being more respectable than other work, and introducing him merely to a mass of unrelated facts and old ideas. The higher the field of social service, the less does "whip-dodging" or "bread-winning" help, and none is higher than teaching.

Thus mishandled, the boy grows up without the aid of that subtle discernment and delicately applied special training which would have brought out his best faculties. He is a blurred indeterminate, self-contradicting group of faculties, he has no unerring organic preference to lead him to his work. He is the nearest approach we can make to that "all-around man" we hear so much of; but the intricate duties of social service do not furnish us with one-sized cylindrical holes for our machine-made pegs. Into some hole he must go, we will not feed him else; so in he pops, and "settles down for life."

That is our common phrase for a permanent establishment in the active service of Society, otherwise known as "self-support," "earning one's living," "maintaining a family." Our average man is not expected to love his work, to enjoy it, to grow continually through it. He does all this sometimes, but too rarely. Our methods of education have been especially esteemed, not because they taught the child to like what he did, but taught him to do what he did not like. We take it for granted that he will not like his life work, and so seek to fit him for continued application to distasteful service.

In such work as this, there is a continuous waste of nerve force. Compelled attention, and action that is not led by interest and fed by the natural discharge of energy along preferred lines, are suicidally wasteful. In Nature's effort to reduce this steady leakage of life force, she transfers the action to the domain of habit as rapidly as possible; and the sufferer experiences that much relief. Dislike, the exhausting effort of enforced attention, and the plunging and kicking of more normal impulses toward other activities, give way at length to a dull contentment, a patient submission to monotonous routine, and some pale pleasure in its monotony.

There are three large distinct evils to Society in such an artificial misplacement of its members. First, the work done is not as good nor as plentiful as if it were done on lines of true organic relation, by the men specialised in power and preference for that work. In the second place, the man is weakened and worn out prematurely by the unnatural effort to do what he does not like, what he is not fitted for, what is not his own special work; thus further reducing the output. And in the third place, the overtaxed and unhappy worker requires all manner of extra inducements and palliations to keep him at his unsuitable task. He has to have rest, more and more vacations and changes, or breaks down sooner. He has to have various fictitious excitements in his work —making it a game, a race, or a fight; to make up for its lack of normal interest.

And he has to have "amusement" and "recreation" also of an unnatural, morbid kind—heavy doses of social stimulus coarsened and concentrated to suit his exhausted nerves. All this beyond the prominent well-known evil of the resort to physical stimulant and solace, such as alcohol and tobacco. These last rapidly deteriorate the physical stock of the race; again injuring Society in the stuff it is made of; but the degraded and excessive amusements injure the very soul of Society; lowering every kind of art which caters to them, and so demoralising the highest lines of advancement.

A thousand minor lines of injury may be traced, such as the increase in defective children, owing to exhausted parents, and its accompanying tax upon Society's resources; but these main lines stand forth clearly: The limitations and degradation of the social output, and the deterioration of tissue in the constituent members of Society.

The deterioration of human stock is twofold; partly due to the strained, unnatural position of the worker; and partly due to the effect of inferior supplies furnished by his degraded product. In the more directly useful human products there is less injury than in the higher forms. In food and clothing and carpenter work it is easier to detect fault and falsehood, and there is less of it; though even in these departments our adulterated food, shoddy clothing, and jerry-built houses do harm enough; but in the more advanced professions, the evil is enormous. The faults and false-hoods in product, in literature, art, religion, government, and education, that spring, first, from their being done by the round man in the square hole, and second, from their being done for the unhealthy demands of the other round men in square holes,— these work incalculable harm.

Here is the girl who is trained to be a teacher because it is reputable, and who accepts her square hole and does her unsatisfying work as patiently and fruitfully as she can. It is excellence we want in work, not a patient and dutiful inferiority. This inferior quality of teaching is further lowered by the unwise demands of the misplaced people who pay the teacher, and so a continuous morbid action is generated. It would be a hard task to show one human grief, one human sin, that does not find part of its cause and maintenance in this so general condition of our life to-day. See the comparative result in our physical organism if we set fingers to serving as toes, eyes as ears, lungs as livers. If any such misplacement were conceivable, it would involve so low a degree of development in the various parts that it was possible to exchange services, and one of them could do good service.

In the social organism such high specialism and efficiency as we have is due to the progressive force of our economic development, calling forth such positive preference in some men that they will do the work they like best. All the world's great servants and helpers have been thus driven from within, by the rising flood of social energy, specialised to one burning focal point of expression. Such men work without reward, and regardless of opposition; work their lives long, often live and die poor and unhonoured, simply because they were true to their fundamental duty as human beings—to serve Society in the function for which they were evolved. In spite of their neglect, abuse, and injury, they are not to be pitied; for, on the one hand, they had the enormous joy of serving humanity; and on the other—even if they were not aware of that high pleasure—they had the intense functional satisfaction of doing the work they were made for.

We are so used to "the dull level of mediocrity," and the labour whose noblest height is conscientious effort, that when we do find a strongly specialised individual so highly fitted to perform one service that he can do no other—we call him a genius. So great is the power of working in these "geniuses"—the happy lavish outpour of social energy through a natural channel—that we have put the cart before the horse as usual, and defined genius as "the capacity for hard work." There are a thousand hard workers for one genius, but a fact like that does not worry our shallow generalisers. Unfortunately, owing to our lack of true education and the crushing weight of the false, only the exceptional genius now and then succeeds in forcing his way to his true place, and he does it by breaking through the poor, blundering, reward-and-penalty system with which we obstruct social development, and by letting out what is in him, producing his natural fruitage of work, quite irrespective of pay or punishment.

Thanks to this quenchless functional vigour of Society we are never without some natural work; and thanks to our vast facility of transmission we all share in the products of genius to a greater or less extent. Yet it is but a painful and niggard harvest compared to the universal crop we might enjoy if we would let it grow. Happiness to the individual is in fulfilment of function, it is as much in farming as in fiddling, if you like it—"every man to his taste." And the benefit to society lies in every man's working "to his taste"; as beautiful and desirable a combination as need be imagined.

This does not mean that all would manifest transcendent genius, but that each, in his place and degree, would have that strong instinctive tendency, that vivid delight in fulfilment of function which should accompany human work in every department.

Chapter XVII: The True Position

[. . .] Now, what, in the light of truths as at present open to us, is the best way to improve the human race, and therefore our highest duty? Recognising the organic relation of Society; that our very life, to say nothing of our improvement, rests on our becoming properly related to each other in the specialised service which constitutes a human life; and to perform that service ever better —the first duty of a human being stands prominently forth. It is this:

To assume right functional relation to Society, to one another. Not charity, not philanthropy, not benevolence, not self-immolation or self-sacrifice or self *anything;* but simply to find and hold our proper place in the Work in which and by which we all live.

To do one's right work involves all the virtues. Our virtues are always matters of interrelation; they concern our attitude toward each other, our treatment of each other. An individual man, alone, can manifest no virtues beyond those of a clean beast. Human life is interrelative, and all its virtues, i.e., distinctive qualities, are interrelative. Once accept this basic duty in fulfilment of specialised services, and all those virtues, we, as individuals, have been so fatuously striving for, appear in us, as natural corollary of that right relation. Conversely our "sins," namely, our various forms of social disease, manifest in the bewildered individual, will of themselves go out as naturally as the virtues come in.

Classify our sins. One enormous mass we call sins against property; all forms of theft, robbery, and the larger and subtler kind of dishonest appropriation. This class is the natural result of our perverted distribution of social products. It is one of the many weak spots of the Want theory that an absence of the essentials of life, instead of promoting industry, often produces more direct and injurious methods of transfer. Quite the larger part of our legal machinery is devoted to the maintenance of the local congestion of wealth on the one hand, and to the prevention of the breaking-down of the social tissues under the pressure of that congestion on the other. Given a surplus of wealth in some places and a deficit in others, and the fabric of human nature breaks down in a given proportion.

Want makes men steal quite as naturally as it makes them work, indeed more so, as being the earlier custom. Our political economics founded on the Want theory should give half their pages to a study of the proportionate relation between Want, Theft, and Wealth, after the learned discussion of Want, Work, and Wealth. One is as legitimate a fact in economics as the other.

That normal distribution of social products which would provide the growing individual with all that he needed to bring out his best powers, and which would teach him clearly where and how to use those powers in return, would drop out of the world completely this class of sins. The supply coming *first,* the child growing up to measure his conduct as a return for what has been given him; taught from infancy to see in the world, behind and around him the endless Giver, and himself as the product of it all and owing his output to those now alive, and more especially those to come—that child, that man, will have no comprehension of theft, major or minor. In a word: All illegitimate acquisition of property rests on the illegitimate retention of property. Remove the cause, and you remove the effect.

What remains? Sins against the person. Part of these are based on property also,—all murder and violence done "with the interested motives," or in revenge for previous injury to property, or denial of property. A large majority of the sins against the person would go, too, when we establish the right distribution.

There remain the sins based on the sex relation. The right economic position for women will remove the greater part of these. When women no longer make their living out of their loving, the prostitute, and that more successful specialist, the mercenary wife, will leave the world. The reduction of sex-attraction from its present fever-height to a normal level, and the perfect freedom for true marriage resultant upon right distribution of property, will take away the cruder and more violent forms of sexual sin, and give us pure monogamy at last.

I do not say that *all* sin would leave the world upon our assuming right economic relations; nor even that this great mass would disappear in a night; but the cause of the disease being removed, the healthy social currents would flow calmly on and we should soon outgrow these evils too long endured. Social disease will eliminate itself by right living as does physical disease.

"Sins" are always phenomena of defective social relation—they are not individual matters at all, an individual can no more do wrong than he can do right. The beasts have no morals because they have no Society. Human conduct is all interrelative; and right or wrong *as it affects the others*. Given any wrong relation in Society, and a certain proportion of sin works out among its members, now here, now there, according to the nature of the diseased relation.

The despot breeds the sycophant, the liar, the assassin; the rich man breeds the thief; the woman who makes her living by marriage, the prostitute. And these sins cannot be checked in the point of expression, the individual, any more than you can cure scarlet fever with salve.

We are good, or We are bad, — with remarkable disconnection of personal circumstance. The thieving produced by the clot of wealth may not break out in the immediately surrounding tissue if that is pretty healthy, but creeps along the line of least resistance, and appears through the brain least able to resist it.

No man liveth to himself, and no man dieth to himself, again.

If, then, this great field of evil, and a thousand as evil concomitants, may be cleared off the world by the adoption of more healthy social processes; if those healthy social processes consist in each person's being in his right place, and doing his right work in Society; if, too, it clearly appears that to the individual consciousness this right place and right work represent Happiness, — Happiness such as we have never been able to conceive in our little ego-stunted brains; then human duty looms up large and clear.

To find your right place, do your right work, here is the basis of all virtue, joy, and growth. [. . .]

With a prospect like this before us, what prevents a sweeping and instant change? Nothing prevents a sweeping and instant change in the minds of some of us; a recognition of the nature of human life and human work which sees it all natural, all healthful, all good in itself; and the bad only an evanescent mistake, easily to be avoided in future; but to spread that recognition in the minds of all of us means time and effort, and cannot become general at once.

Meanwhile, it is open to us, without waiting for all to see alike these patent truths, to go to work on such changes in economic condition as shall soonest check the decay in social tissues so dangerously apparent at both ends of our present "Society," and bring up, as soon as may be, those whose growth has been arrested for ages.

The world is full of aborted people, aborted by the crushing pressure of these old lies in economics; people crippled in mind, people crippled in body, people swollen and distorted from being oversupplied and underworked; people shrunken and distorted from being overworked and undersupplied. These can be helped at once by those of us who see the wisdom of improving the race without waiting for them to understand and accept the principles on which the change in condition rests. We did not wait for all the citizens of America to believe in the principles involved, before giving them the public school and public library. Many do not, when questioned, even now believe in those principles. But they are not reluctant to avail themselves of the provision made; and the advantageous results of the provision are apparent in our citizens, whether they understand why or not.

There are some most comforting facts, meanwhile, in our social relationship, which enable us to attack the concrete problems of our time with courage and patience. Seeing that our gain is social, and not individual, and that it is rapidly transmissible as far as the brain is open to transmission, we have but to develop the brain of our laggard members to bring them into possession of the whole great field of social advance. The wealth of Society, steadily augmented as it is by the very individuals who need so much more social return than they have ever had, is quite equal to any drain which may be necessary to pay up our arrears of debt to the worker. A conscientious and aroused society, seeing how unjustly neglected have been its most valuable constituents, cannot do too much to bring to them, and to their children, all the social nourishment they can absorb; i.e., to provide the best possible educational environment for the children who need it most. [. . .]

There are certain physical conditions in the social body, brick and mortar conditions, which are affecting us all for evil, and which can be readily changed. There are, also, certain economic relations in that body, affecting us all for evil, that can equally be changed. We need to see these in their true importance; as affecting not only the immediate individuals concerned, but as so affecting the whole structure of Society as to inexorably produce the conspicuous evils with which we are so painfully familiar. Once recognised, our duty is clear—a glad, swift, forward movement bringing joy and gain to all.

What are these general conditions?

One is the economic position of woman, which involves false sex relations, including all forms of prostitution; maintains primitive individual instincts and checks social ones, and is largely responsible for the morbid action of social economics. Another is the maintenance of domestic industry; which, as I have shown in another book [*The Home*], prevents the development of the home, the progress of woman, the right education of the child, and the normal progress of man.

Combined, these two conditions find material form in that hotbed of primitive egoism, the cumbrous, expensive, inadequate dwelling house of our time, or rather, of past time, of the most remote and barbarous time, most injuriously preserved in this. It is true that each human being needs a wholly private and personal room to rest in; that solitude, pure individual solitude, is a social necessity. It is also true that the great primal group, the family, needs its group of rooms, its private home. But the point of divergence is in the Work involved.

Work is social, it does not belong to the person nor, in any advanced degree, to the family. That so much human work is at present performed in and for the separate family is an enormous condition of social evil. It maintains, beyond all the efforts of religion and science to combat, the selfishness of the primeval Pig.

Social consciousness and its great currents of love and enthusiasm, of power and pride, cannot find room in brains continually cramped by application to the most ignominiously personal concerns.

It is not only that the family could have a far simpler, purer, and more private life if they would but take advantage of our immense social facilities, but so could the individual men and women; born and reared in families, to be sure, but born and reared as members of Society, active and responsible factors in social progress.

These men and women, if the families they grew up in were in true social relations, instead of each one keeping up a little down-drawing whirlpool of antediluvian individualism, would be a thousand times more valuable citizens. While the minds of our women are exercised only, or mainly, in impression and expression of a purely personal nature, they and their stunted children and heavily handicapped men cannot properly receive and discharge the vivifying currents of social consciousness.

That consciousness forces itself out here and there through specially sensitive individuals, usually at great personal sacrifice. These special individuals, heavily charged with the social spirit, push and struggle, work and fight, suffer and die, trying to stir to equal life the great ego-bound mass of unawakened Society. Much work has been accomplished, great good has been done, the world is incomparably better off for the presence of these better developed members, but our gain is as nothing to what it would be if the progress was shared by all. [. . .]

"Domestic Economy"*

One of the strongest intrenchments of our piously defended system of household industry is its supposed economy. "The careful housewife" is our ideal of a wise and judicious expender of money, some even going so far as to call her a "partner" in the business of housekeeping. A recent defender of this view, Mr. Robert Webster Jones, writing in the March *House Keeper*, says definitively:

> In the ideal marriage husband and wife are equal partners. Two departments engage the energy and attention of the firm, the earning department and the home department. One is as important as the other. Each requires an expert, industrious, watchful manager if the home is to be successful. . . . His wife is doing just as much as he is for the success of the firm, if not more.†

If this is a true position, it does, indeed, go far to justify our methods of living, even if they are archaic. But is it?

* *The Independent*, 56 (June 16, 1904), pp. 1359–1363. See also "The Beauty of a Block," *Ibid.*, 57 (July 14, 1904), pp. 67–72; and "Housing for Children," *Ibid.*, August 25, 1904, pp. 434–438. Later, she wrote two articles on town planning: "Applepieville," *The Independent*, 103 (September 25, 1920), pp. 365 and 393–394; and "Making Towns Fit to Live in," *Century Magazine*, 102 (July 1921), pp. 361–366.

† The *Readers' Guide to Periodical Literature* did not index the articles from this journal, and the one extant copy of this edition, at the Library of Congress, was "not on the shelf," so I have been unable to annotate the title, volume, and pages.

Let us give a fair examination to this particular point, the economy of domestic industry, not touching on any other aspect of the question.

Merely as a matter of business, is it good business?

What is, exactly, the business we are to study?

It is that of catering to the personal physical needs of the human animal, caring for the health of the body, providing shelter, warmth, food and cleanliness. There are additional minor clauses and there are some very important psychic associations; but we will only discuss here the material side.

The home is intended to furnish shelter and protection to the family—sleeping accommodations, food, and those cleansing processes so essential to all civilized life. The business of the home is in the rent or purchase and replenishment of the place and plant; the provision of supplies for consumption; the preparation and service of food, and all kinds of cleaning. What is commonly called "housekeeping" really embraces this group of industries, arbitrarily connected by custom, but in their nature not only diverse, but grossly incompatible.

We are familiar with each as a business by itself; as in the service of cooked food, long practiced in the many forms of eating house; in the furnishing of shelter and rest at night, as in lodging house or dormitory; the cleaning of the person and of clothing, as in bath-house or laundry; the nursing of the sick, as in hospitals; the care and training of children, as in nursery or school. All these forms of specialized human business are known to us, with their skilled officials; but in our common thought—and practice—we hold that they are better done in the lump, at home.

As separate businesses we can plainly see their incompatibility. No man advertises a "Restaurant and Laundry," or "Bakery and Bath-house"—the association of fresh food and soiled linen or unclean bodies would not be pleasant to our minds. Neither should we patronize a "Kindergarten and Carpet Cleaning Establishment" or "Primary School and Dressmaking Parlor," and, above all, should we avoid a dormitory for adults which was at the same time a nursery for infants. In the care of the sick, for their sakes as well as other interests involved, we isolate them as

far as possible; a hospital naturally striving for quiet and cleanliness.

Yet we carry on all these contradictory trades in one small
building, and also live in it!

Not only do we undertake to have all these labors performed
in one house, but by one person.

In full ninety per cent. of our American homes there is but
one acting functionary to perform these varied and totally dissimilar functions — to be cook, laundress, chambermaid, charwoman,
seamstress, nurse and governess.

But one character in history or fiction can approach this
position, the sole survivor of the shipwrecked "Nancy," who so
cheerfully relates:

> O I'm the cook and the captain bold,
>   And the mate of the "Nancy" brig;
> And the bo'sun tight and the midshipmate.
>   And the crew of the captain's gig!*

The average housewife can similarly boast:

> O I'm the cook and the seamstress neat,
>   And the nurse when ills betide;
> And the laundress jade and the chambermaid
>   And the governess beside!

The person who is expected to achieve this miracle is not
some specially selected paragon of varied ability, but merely the
average woman; neither is she prepared for her herculean tasks
(Hercules was never required to perform his twelve labors all at
once!) by a rigorous course of training, but is supposed to be fitted
by nature for their successful achievement, aided perhaps by
instruction from a similarly well prepared predecessor. Under
these circumstances the wonder is that even half of us live to
grow up, that our average of intelligence and ability is so good,
and that our common standard of comfort and cleanliness, of
health, vigor and peace of mind is as high as it is; that any degree
of family happiness remains to us; and it is no wonder whatever,
but an inevitable consequence, that the waste and incompetence

* Unable to identify.

manifested in this pitiful business constitute so huge a loss and injury. Let us examine the waste first. Wealth is increased by productive labor. Whatever checks, reduces or weakens that labor is a loss to us. Wealth is diminished by unnecessary expenditure in time, labor or money. Our domestic administration wastes nearly half the productive labor of the world, and costs three times what it need cost in time, labor and money.

This method of running six great businesses in one unsuitable shop, by one unsuitable person, is expensive. The labor of the world is performed by men and women. In harems, it is true, women are exclusively maintained for purposes other than economic, and in our scanty proportion of "upper classes" the same ideal is upheld: but in the great majority of the population the woman, vigorous and valuable, works, as she has done from the beginning of human life. The proportion of women in America who keep even one servant is shown by our last census to be about one to sixteen.

The fact that most women are not paid for their labor does not deprive them of economic value, tho [sic] it does of economic independence. Slaves were not paid, yet were worth good money in the market.

Half the labor of the world is woman's labor.

The waste under discussion is this: We take half the people of the world and set them to wait upon the other half, thus limiting the output of their labor exactly as it would that of a lumber camp if half the men were assigned to wait upon the other half instead of chopping wood; or of an army if half the soldiers were "keeping tent" instead of fighting; or of a ship's crew if half the sailors were cooks.

In any body of civilized men specialized labor meets the needs of the group, a certain number being employed in each industry; and as machinery and organization improve, it takes fewer numbers to do the same work, thus setting free more human power to meet higher needs and increasing wealth.

In savagery each man, wholly unspecialized, spends all his time and labor on his immediate physical needs, and not only can do nothing else, but does this most miserably. For each man to require one other man to thus take care of him is but one degree better than savagery, and the degree is not raised by the other man's being a woman. The amount of productive labor wasted is that between the number of people really required to carry on their trade in proper business methods and the present number —half the adult population.

Among the rich in our cities, or wherever servants are kept, we increase the waste of labor, and also that of purchasing and depreciation of plant.

In the primitive family group, where the wife is the servant, many interests combine to make her exert herself to the best advantage, to do as much and spend as little as possible. The enlarged group, where two or more women are doing this same kind of work, adds to every element of expense and loses the earlier tendency to cautious economy.

We should also recognize in this connection that a superior family with servants involves an inferior family to furnish them. Where all families are well to do, no servants are obtainable.

The real unit of domestic industry is the family itself. Where servants are added we have a sort of feudal group, and in admiring the smooth workings of a large, well managed, wealthy household we should hold clearly in mind those subsidiary cottages or tenement rooms in which reside the tributary families without whose assistance the large one could not exist.

Let us consider the economic aspects of this business of housekeeping in a residential block in New York, a group of well-to-do families, where the income is five or six thousand dollars a year.

Such a block has about one hundred families, to which we will give the census average of two adults and three children. Here is a schedule of their expenses, a conservative and low average, well within the limits of fact: Labor is given as that of three house servants, cook, second maid and nursemaid, at $5, $4 and $5 a week, and an outside man to clean sidewalks and attend to the furnace, etc., at $50 a year. Food is allowed at $4 per capita per week—not that it need to cost that, but that, with a group of eight and the waste incidental to servants, it generally does.

Interest and depreciation on plant the housewife will recognize better as breakage and wearing out. We have made a very modest allowance for it. Laundry expense we will allow at $3.50 a week —a woman for two days and two meals—this will be included in the labor item. The schedule stands thus:

	Per annum.	
	Per family.	Per block.
Rent.............................	$1,500	$150,000
Food.............................	1,664	166,400
Labor	960	96,000
Fuel and light	50	5,000
Interest and depreciation	50	5,000
	$4,224	$422,400

Let us now see how these ends could be better served. We will assume the following treatment of the block and its businesses:

One hundred houses average six floors, counting the cellar; say, twelve rooms. The cellar and basement floor are now generally used as the workshop part of the domestic plant, the top floor for children and servants, leaving the family the dining-room and parlor floor and two floors of bedrooms. Now let the cellar and basement be eliminated from the domestic scheme entirely, and the top floor (save one room), with the roof, be devoted to the children; that leaves to the family proper all the space it had before.

The underlying space, equal to that of thirty-three entire houses (note that a full third of our living space in a crowded city is now devoted to the domestic trades!), we will use as follows: Space of two entire houses for kitchen; not a small, dark, dirty place with the cellar below, the laundry in or adjacent, and all manner of unpleasant concomitants, but a white, light, high-ceiled, well ventilated, beautiful and scientifically appointed laboratory, with its allied offices. The space of another house for a laundry, equally attractive and well fitted; of another for the heating plant of the block, and of one more for offices and rooms of such resident workers as were necessary. This leaves the space of twenty-eight houses, or, spread out as it is in two lower floors, a little more than both the long sides of the block, to be fitted up as gymnasia, swimming pools, ball room, club rooms of all sorts, for the use of the residents.

The roof space—entirely freed from smoke and dirt by the removal of kitchen and cellar from under our houses, the one heating plant and food laboratory carefully consuming all smoke and waste—becomes an ideal playground for children. The upper floor is also fitted for child culture; large, sunlit nurseries and other accommodations with rooms for resident attendants. Space of one room on this floor might be reserved to each house, with its little hall and entrance to this children's department, so that the family would have precisely the space it has now, minus only the workshop and servants' rooms. At what cost and by what service may the needs of the family be met better and more cheaply?

Let us assume the entire block to be owned by one man, previously yielding him $150,000 a year in rents.

He now lets to the families seven rooms each—the same space formerly occupied—for $120,000. This includes heat. He lets the upper floor (minus the one room and small hall and stair) and roof to the manager of the children's department for $20,000. He lets the cellar and basement to the food laboratory, laundry and manager of the recreation rooms for $20,000.

Thus the landlord gets $10,000 a year more than he did before, which may be applied to cover the expense of his large heating plant, etc. (tho, to be sure, that ought not to cost more than a hundred small ones!) At any rate he will not lose by the change.

For the family rent is now somewhat reduced. The bill for fuel and light we will roughly cut in half, for lack of exact figures, the heat being supplied as in an apartment house, but the family using light as before. The interest and depreciation on plant go down tremendously, all the waste and breakage of 300 incompetent servants and 100 separate plants being replaced by the efficient small corps in one kitchen, one laundry, one "cellar." It may be estimated at $500 a year each in the three—$1,500 in all—

something less than the $5,000 now paid by the block! But the main items are food and labor.

The laundry work was done by 100 women working two days a week for each family at $1.50 a day and dinner; $3.50 a week, per year $182, for the block $18,200. This allows ten dozen pieces to each family. This work could be done by twenty skilled workers in a proper shop at $10 a week each, for $104 per family; $2 a week—20 cents a dozen.

The cleaning essential to a neat and sanitary home of seven rooms could be done in an hour a day by two skilled workers at 25 cents an hour—$3 a week—$156 a year per family.

The outside man, whose labor we estimated at $50 a year per family, has resolved himself into the reduced bill for heating, and a contract to clean sidewalks for the block, which might be $500 a year—something less than the present $5,000 paid to 100 men by 100 families.

The food bill itself we can at once reduce by half. Where eight people, with the waste of three servants and the laundress, and the hopelessly extravagant individual buyer—100 small purchasers of no special training—make this item average $4 a week per capita, one expert purchaser buying for 500, with a special dairy, a special truck farm or equivalent arrangement with butcher, grocer and market gardener, would easily reduce it to $2 and give better food.

Now for the kitchen labor. Here we will be extravagant. No crude, ignorant, fluctuating horde of 100 low class women will be intrusted with the health of 500 people. Our food laboratory will be served at this rate: [table appears on opposite page]

This establishment, it will be observed, is not a restaurant. It does not have to pay rent for eating space in the business part of the city, nor to allow for an immense margin of waste with varying customers. It has a steady number of patrons, who can order their preferred dishes in advance if they choose, or pay somewhat less for a well arranged *menu* which shall make of the weary housewife a cheerful guest, or both. You carefully order your dinner—by telephone, of the manager—all at once, instead of ordering it of a number of tradesmen after discussion with the cook. That

Food for 600 (allowing for one servant)				$62,400	
The families paid for this number			$124,800		
Rent				2,000	
The families paid for kitchen space, girls' room, etc., equal to two floors			50,000		
Fuel, etc.				500	
The families paid			2,500		
Interest and depreciation				500	
The families paid			5,000		
Labor:					
1 manager, per week	$30	$1,560			
1 bookkeeper, per week	5	780			
1 head cook, per week	25	1,300			
2 cooks at $20 per week	40	2,080			
12 cooks at $15 per week	180	9,360			
10 assist's at $10, per week	100	5,200			
Delivery service at $10 per day		3,650			
		$23,930		23,390	[23,930]
The families paid 100 cooks at $5 per week, board at $4 per week			46,800		
Total of food company				$88,330	[89,330]
Total by domestic method			$231,100	[229,100]	
			88,330	[89,330]	
			$142,770	[139,770]	
Food served at dumbwaiters and dishes removed: 3 meals a day at $3 per capita per week				$93,600	
				88,330	[89,330]
Annual profit for food company				$5,270	[4,270]

dinner, perfectly prepared and hot, comes into your pantry by the dumbwaiter, as it does now. What difference does it make to your family happiness that it was not steaming through the halls beforehand? It is better food, far better cooked. If your devout regard for the privacy of the family leads you to insist on a stranger in the room to wait on you, that may be had by paying for it.

Perhaps the "simple living" for which so many sigh will lead us to be content with fewer dishes and our own mutual service.

The soiled china returns, as it came, by dumbwaiter.

And what is to become of the servants? They can learn to be higher grade workers. It is no advantage to society to maintain an immense number of extremely inefficient persons.

One other item remains, the nursemaid. As one feature in the labor expense we paid her $5 a week and board, $4—9 X 52 = $468 a year; for the block, $46,800. Let us call this item child culture and see what we might get for the money.

Of our 300 children, some 200 will be of nursery age. For their care and training we will now engage, not an ignorant and irresponsible young girl, but as fine a woman as love can lead and long study and training fit to care properly for little children.

Such a woman, as tho starting a private school, hires the children's department of the block for $20,000 a year. This is fitted up with all nursery and kindergarten appointments, with sand and sun and water rooms, gymnasia for little ones, and the great playgrounds and gardens on the roof, at an expense of $50,000, on which is paid a yearly rent of $5,000.

For attendance we will have ten skillful, experienced women at $25 a week each, ten at $15, and service at $10—$50 a week, $2,600 a year. The head of such an undertaking should have an income of $4,000, making the total $55,000. Among 100 families $550 each. This is $82 a year more than is now paid for the nursemaid, but it includes kindergarten and also roof privileges for older children. The difference in value received is appreciable, and if further saving is wanted it could be found in doctor's bills. The health and happiness of these little ones would be cheap at a far greater price.

The $300 our families have saved on rent goes to cover "club dues" in the recreation rooms below. Instead of having under all our houses dark and disagreeable holes, where no one goes who does not have to, we have now places of rest and amusement. The aggregate of $30,000 yearly would provide a good deal of healthful amusement for two hundred people—a quiet domestic casino in each block.

Now, how does the account compare?

By the domestic method:

Rent $1,500
Food 1,664
Labor 960
Fuel and light. 50
Interest and depreciation 50
$4,224

This sum is paid for crowded houses full of ill-adjusted industries, for uncertain, low class labor, and constant care and worry.

By organized industry:

Rent $1,200
Food, served 785
Fuel and light 25
Laundry and cleaning 265
Child culture 550
Club dues 300
$3,120   [3,125]

The saving in cold cash is not great, only $1,104 [1,099]; but the gain in value received is vast. If a servant is still kept—at $5 a week and $3 for food—that reduces the savings to $688 per family—$68,800 for the block. But even that, with such improvement in accomodation, is worth considering.

Of course, all these figures are approximate and arbitrary, based merely on estimates of what families like this now pay, and what can be done in somewhat similar combinations. It should be noted that the family is in no way interfered with; the children remain at home—and have more of a home than they ever did before. The economic advantages are impressive enough, but the added ease and happiness in living, especially for children, is the main point to be considered after all.

"Why Cooperative Housekeeping Fails" *

We all know the difficulties of ordinary housekeeping, its increasing complexity and expense, the unpreparedness of the housewife and inefficiency of the servant; and many of us think we know the reasons why this world-old business is so often a failure.

Under pressure of its many disadvantages we see women break down and flee to sanitariums for rest and recuperation; men, too, are often exhausted in the struggle to maintain the rising standard of living. Frequently the effort is relinquished, the home given up, and the family take to living cheaply in a boarding-house, or expensively in a hotel, because it is so much easier.

Boarding-house and hotel life is unsatisfactory to most of us, and the pendulum swings back again to the abandoned home, only to find its difficulties and expenses have increased in the interval.

Our list of patent medicines is scarcely longer than that of home-making or home-mending suggestion and advice. The literature of amelioration piles up around us; and the scientific investigator burrows in statistics and penetrates our kitchens in disguise to find out what really is the matter.

Under these conditions it is quite natural, indeed it is inevitable, that suggestions should be made by active minds as to better ways of living.

Thoughtful persons, impressed by two main items—the unnecessary expense and unnecessary labor of the old system—have seen a great light, and cried: "Let us buy our supplies together! Let us have our work done together! Let us cooperate!" And, where enough could be found like-minded, and conditions made it possible, they have cooperated.

The results so far have been almost always failures, painful,

* *Harper's Bazaar*, 41 (July 1907), pp. 625–629.

pointed, public failures. Why? What is the matter with cooperation?

Is it one of those things of which the purblind say, "It is all
right in principle, but it doesn't work in practice"?—which is
nonsense.

If a thing is right in principle it will work. If it does not work
there is something wrong with the principle.

In this matter of cooperative housekeeping several elements
are involved, and so far the cooperators, while quite correct in
their figures as to expense and labor, have failed to understand
other equally vital interests concerned.

Therefore each of their attempts but adds weight to the
argument of the reactionary, of the blind, submissive transmitters
of old customs, who raise again their standard of triumphant
immobility—until they cease triumphing temporarily to go to the
sanitarium.

Thus the matter stands. The cooperators—those who have
not tried it, that is—prove conclusively the waste of money and
waste of labor in our "domestic economy," and point out its
ceaseless cares and halting execution.

The isolators, still an overwhelming majority, admit these
facts, but maintain that, with all its faults, they love the private
home and will have it—and that as for the golden vision of the
cooperator—it is always a failure.

Both parties are right! The isolators because they uphold an
institution grounded on essential human needs, and refuse to give
it up even for admitted material advantages; the cooperators
because they clearly see disadvantages which are becoming a
deadly menace to society, and some of the reasons for them.

The trouble with the isolators is that they will not admit the
possibility of growth and improvement in their beloved institution,
will not hear to reason, will not study conditions, make reasonable
experiments, or do anything but maintain the sanctity of the
home, on one hand, and wail about the difficulty of housekeeping,
on the other.

The trouble with the cooperators is not so serious. They have dared to look ahead, they have been strong enough to defy old habits, they have worked out a plan of improvement and been willing to try it.

Their failures will stand high in history as leading to the great successes which will presently remodel our home lives and so remake the world.

Let them take heart, then, like any scientific investigators, not doubt the truth they have, but look for more; not think themselves utterly wrong in principle, but learn that there are more principles than one involved.

Here is the position.

The human race is gradually evolving a system of monogamous marriage; our own recent stock, liberally called the "Anglo-Saxon," has maintained it for some time.

Monogamous marriage and the family life going with it have been proved to be the best means of rearing children yet practised, and also the most conducive to personal happiness in the parties concerned. This form of family requires for its maintenance a home, a place to live in by itself. All this we commonly believe— and we are right.

But what we do not understand—the great body of us—is that the work done in and for the home is no real part of that home, and may be quite as well done, even far better done, by other persons, in other places. And what the cooperator does not understand is that while the work may very properly be organized, the families may not.

This is the whole secret of the failure of cooperative house-keeping. It does not go far enough. It still assumes that this work must be done by the family, and as it is proven difficult and expensive for a family to do it alone, therefore it will be easier and cheaper for families to do it together.

Here is where the principle is wrong, and therefore sure to fail in practice.

Families cannot work together. Each family is a self-centred group; with its own separate interests and purposes, it is and it ought to be. But those interests and purposes are not industrial— not now. Once they were. Once the family was a social unit—

the social unity—all the social unit there was. All labor was then domestic, done in the family, by the family, for the family. But this was long, long ago, in prehistoric ages, only to be seen now in scattered remnants of primitive peoples—nomadic, kingless, without national entity—living only in families.

In the course of social evolution all this is outgrown. We see now great nations highly organized, widely efficient; we see industry spread even beyond national limits—the manufacture and commerce of a world.

But the family—bless its old heart!—has failed to observe the little fact that ninety-nine out of a hundred of its whilom occupations have gone from it, and hangs on to its one dwindling remnant of primeval industry as stoutly as if it had never lost anything.

So convinced are we of the identity of love and marriage, of marriage and the family, of the family and the home, of the home and housework—that if one daringly suggests the elimination of housework, we run back up the bracketed list and cry, "This will ruin the home!—break up the family!—destroy marriage!— banish love!"

In reality the isolators and cooperators should join hands on the first three pairs of these long-linked ideas, and together cut the connection at the last. Come!—even from a sense of word values!—is it not clear that such words as love, marriage, and the family are in a totally different class from housework?

But "home" forms the connecting link, we say; home is, on the one side, family—on the other side, housework.

Oh no, it isn't! When we sing, with tears in our eyes and a catch in our voices, "Home, sweet home, there's no place like home!" we do not mean, "Housework, sweet housework, there's nothing like housework!"

Love is physical and psychical, marriage is social, the family is physiological and psycho-social, the home is psycho-physical, but housework is industrial—a thing of an entirely different order.

Because the family, in a very low stage of human life, did work at home is no reason it should now—in fact, is a very good reason it shouldn't. But the cooperator, far-seeing in one way, is blinder in another way than the very people he is trying to help. He expects persons who have made a failure of keeping house alone to succeed in keeping house together! It is pathetic—and it is amusing.

Whereas the very essence of the trouble lies in the inefficiency of the unspecialized workers, most cooperative colonies consist of persons less capable in this line rather than more; a combination of housekeepers below the average—where the average is so painfully low.

No wonder they fail.

A social structure of any sort is composed of individuals—not of families. The family remains at the base of society, making individuals, in whose myriad interactions and interrelations arises the social organization, but the families themselves remain separate. Put them together, and the essential characteristics of family life hold them apart; there is friction, tension, dissension, disintegration.

Cooperative housekeeping is fundamentally wrong in its assumption of a capacity in families for common responsibility and common action.

The family is no longer a proper business agent, even separately, and it was never a proper element of combination.

How, then, are we to harmonize the undeniable truth of the cooperator's facts with the as undeniable truth of the isolator's feelings?

By leaving the separate family in the separate home, and by taking the housework out of it.

This is blank foolishness to most of us. We cannot conceive of such a thing—so persistent is the force of associative idea. Cheer up! We have outgrown many ancient convictions—we shall outgrow this. Once we could not conceive of a country without a king. The Turk finds it as hard to think of a home without a harem as we do to think of a home without a kitchen.

Yet the harem has been eliminated—and the home remains. So will it remain, loved and honored, though kitchenless.

What we need is not convocations of discouraged families to establish committees of multiplied incompetence to meet incessantly divergent wants; but the appearance of capable persons, skilled persons, trained persons, to do cheaply and well what now we do so ill and so expensively.

Where now our work is done by the lowest grade of labor, we need the highest grade of labor, the best the world affords.

"But we could not afford to pay for it!" Oh yes, we could! We pay more now. We pay—a hundred families of us—a thousand dollars a week for our cooks, our hundred cooks. That is, five dollars in cash and five dollars in board and lodging— which we forget to count.

A thousand dollars a week is good wages; we ought to command excellent service for that. A hundred families means on the average five hundred people, and five hundred people could be well and easily cooked for by fifteen cooks.

Of these, one *chef* might be given sixty dollars a week, two lesser lights forty each, two others thirty, and the remaining ten, twenty; making four hundred dollars a week instead of a thousand.

The wages would thus be reduced by sixty per cent., and the standard of cooking raised as much as wages were lowered.

"But who is to hire these fifteen cooks? Is not this leading us again into the proven pitfalls of cooperation? How is such a corps of competent specialists to be brought to bear on our several dining-rooms?"

It is evident that they cannot be brought to bear on our several kitchens.

The kitchen must go.

But the private dining-room will remain long after the private kitchen has followed the hand-loom and spinning-wheel into wider fields.

There must be, for family service, distributing kitchens, arranged with due regard to the permanent comfort of the family.

But the service should be related to the family only as is the service of the confectioner and baker of whom we now purchase food; or of the grocer and butcher from whom we buy the raw materials.

This is the essence of the change in a nutshell. We are going to buy food, cooked food, instead of raw materials. The cook-shop will no longer be trailing its amateur inefficiency at the heels of every family, a dwindling rudiment of ancient customs; but become a clean, scientific, businesslike place, well officered and well manned, furnishing food of a standard of excellence rising steadily from year to year. Here we meet loud protest.

"How do we know it will be good? Who is to judge this standard of excellence? Are the revelations of basement bakeries and the sights, sounds, and smells of cheap restaurants any promise of better things? Is the price-list of the great hotels a hope of economy? Better our 'home-cooking,' with all our present evils, than the horrors of cheap commercialism."

There is a good deal of sense in this protest. If we had to give up our kitchens merely for a restaurant style of living it would be small gain. But there is a wide difference between the old business of running a restaurant or a hotel for transient patronage and this new business of regularly preparing food for a limited number of constant patrons. Consider the dimensions of the work, these kitchens specially arranged for family service, and so numerous as to employ about eight per cent. of the adult population.

That seems a godly [sic] number, does it not?—eight persons out of every hundred in this one business. But in our present method over fifty per cent. are so employed—a full half the adult population—practically all the women!

In fifteen-sixteenths of our population the man's wife cooks for him; in the other sixteenth the man employs one or more subsidiary women to cook for him, each man requiring one or two or more women in this service—an entire half the world cooking for the other half!

Fancy any kind of male combination—an army, a navy, a railroad gang, a lumber camp—in which half the men were detailed to cook for the rest!

Our cooking half being women, we have not noticed the percentage of human life given to this one business, and the waste so involved.

When our habits of eating are wiser and simpler we may reduce the number still farther, but to meet the present wants eight per cent. would do, and that means a large and important trade.

This trade would not have to pay the high rental of the restaurant or hotel—it is a cook-shop, not an eating-house.

It would not have to meet the waste of uncertain patronage, but merely to cook to order for a known number of people. Each family could order with the same freedom it does now, only instead of ordering its food raw, from butcher, grocer, baker, confectioner, fishman, iceman, milkman, and fruiterer, it would order of one shop—and receive it ready to eat.

Many persons dislike the trouble of this everlasting ordering —it is one of the things that try the housewife most. To such these kitchens would submit *table d'hôte* menus, open to additions; and in these the various kitchens would vie with one another in competitive excellence. They would make a speciality of proper food for children, for invalids, for particular tastes, and under pressure of our increasing demand for pure food and right nutrition they would offer a "balanced ration" based on scientific knowledge.

In cities the delivery would be by dumb-waiter to the pantry or dining-room; in the country by overhead-trolley service to the door—a method in wide use in mining regions, and popularly known as the parcel delivery in our great stores.

In any country place where twenty families lived within a mile radius, a central kitchen with three cooks could supply meals in this way.

On widely isolated farms or ranches it would be impracticable —as are many other of the benefits of civilization.

The two immediate opportunities for undertaking this work are in summer resorts and summer schools, or similar places, where tired women would be glad of relief for a while from their "home duties"; and, in cities, in apartment-houses built and arranged for the purpose. Something could also be done in cities and towns, in a door-to-door delivery, such as the citizens of Montclair, New Jersey, are now proposing to organize.* This calls

* The Montclair Historical Society has no record of such a home-delivery project.

for an extensive plant and delivery system of great excellence. Yet such are the enormous profits to be obtained in this business that even this could be managed if we would but recognize the opportunity. [. . .]

This is the true line of advance; making a legitimate, human business of housework; having it done by experts instead of by amateurs; making it a particular social industry instead of a general feminine function, and leaving the private family in the private home where it belongs.

This is not cooperation, but it is good business.

It is one of the greatest business opportunities the world has ever known.

Now let us see whether women, who have followed this trade from the year one, or men, who have merely developed all the rest of the world's work, will be the first in the field to succeed.

"A Suggestion on the Negro Problem"*

Transfusion of blood is a simple matter compared with the transfusion of a civilization; yet that is precisely what is going on between us and the negro race.

They were forcibly extradited from a distant country, from a status far lower than our own; and we for our own purposes gave them a compulsory introduction into our economic group, and made them working factors in our society.

The results proved increasingly disadvantageous. The first arbitrary relation has been laid aside, but the sociological problem is not solved because one answer is seen to be wrong.

Admitting that in a certain number of cases the negro has developed an ability to enter upon our plane of business life, and further admitting, most cheerfully, that this proves the ultimate capacity of the race to do so; there remains the practical problem of how to accelerate this process.

We have to consider the unavoidable presence of a large body

* *The American Journal of Sociology,* 14 (July 1908), pp. 78–85. Within a two-year period, the *Journal* published two articles and four comments by Charlotte. See 12 (March 1907), pp. 690–691 and 717–714; 13 (March 1908), p. 644; 13 (May 1908), p. 781; "How Home Conditions React Upon the Family," 14 (March 1909), pp. 592–605.

of aliens, of a race widely dissimilar and in many respects inferior, whose present status is to us a social injury. If we had left them alone in their own country this dissimilarity and inferiority would be, so to speak, none of our business.

There are other races, similarly distinguished, whose special standing in racial evolution does not embarrass us; but in this case it does. These were imported, much against their wills, for our supposed advantage; and as their inferiority was the very condition of our advantage, making possible their exploitation, no complaint was then made of it.

The laws of economic evolution proved that this supposed advantage was counterbalanced by such heavy disadvantages that it did more harm than good; and with many blunders and much suffering and loss we put an end to the economic relations in which the negro had been held, and set him free; free—an alien race, in a foreign land; under social, economic, political, and religious conditions to which he was by heredity a stranger. By consummate mishandling of the crucial period of change, the break in the relations between blacks and whites became a gulf, and has since widened. We now have an immense area of country in which are found two races, of different degrees of social advancement, living side by side, only partially serviceable to one another, and in many ways antagonistic.

On the field of economic competition into which the negro was so suddenly thrown he does not, as a whole, in fifty years, show equality with us—which is not remarkable. That so many negroes, in this brief time, have made such great progress, is the element not only of hope, but of security in facing our problem. The problem is this:

Given: in the same country, Race A, progressed in social evolution, say, to Status 10; and Race B, progressed in social evolution, say, to Status 4.

Given: That Race A outnumbers Race B as ten to one.

Given: That Race B was forcibly imported by Race A, and cannot be deported.

Given: That Race B, in its present condition, does not develop fast enough to suit Race A.

Question: How can Race A best and most quickly promote the development of Race B?

This problem need not be confused by the element of injury and offense. It is true that Race B in many ways retards the progress of Race A, and grievously offends against it; but it is also true that Race A was the original offender, and has a list of injuries to Race B, greatly outnumbering the counter list. It is also true that both races have served each other in many ways. These points may be laid aside. They arouse our feelings and do not clear our thoughts.

The problem—the question of conduct—the pressing practical issue—is, What can we do to promote the development of the backward race so that it may become an advantageous element in the community? This is not a question of "equality" in any sense. Society is an organic relation, it is not composed of constituents all alike and equally developed, but most diverse and unequal. It is quite possible to have in a society members far inferior to other members, but yet essential to the life of the whole.

A man would rather lose all his ten shoes than his two eyes; and both feet than his eyes and ears. Our special senses are far "superior" to our meat and bones; yet it is quite essential to the body's life that even its least important parts be healthy.

If the negro population can become entirely self-supporting and well behaved it ceases to be a "problem" and a menace. If it becomes more than self-supporting, contributing its quota to the general good, then it will be a valuable part of the body politic, an advantage to all. The fact that so many negroes have reached this position is the proof that social evolution works more rapidly than the previous process of natural selection. The African race, with the advantage of contact with our more advanced stage of evolution, has made more progress in a few generations than any other race has ever done in the same time, except the Japanese. That splendid instance of this process of self-conscious social evolution shows the irresistible power of direct transference of institutions, and their result. Our own general history, with its swift, resistless Americanization of all kinds of foreigners, shows the same thing. The evolution of society, while based on natural conditions and forces, has long since reached the stage where it is directly promoted by society's own efforts. From the foreigner of every sort the American is made by sharing with him the advantages of our institutions — even by compelling him to partake of that advantage. This brings us again to our direct question: How can we best promote the civilization of the negro?

He is here; we can't get rid of him; it is all our fault; he does not suit us as he is; what can we do to improve him?

At last the suggestion: Let each sovereign state carefully organize in every county and township an enlisted body of all negroes below a certain grade of citizenship. Those above it — the decent, self-supporting, progressive negroes — form no problem and call for nothing but congratulation. But the whole body of negroes who do not progress, who are not self-supporting, who are degenerating into an increasing percentage of social burdens or actual criminals, should be taken hold of by the state.

This proposed organization is not enslavement, but enlistment. The new army should have its uniforms, its decorations, its titles, its careful system of grading, its music and banners and impressive ceremonies. It is no dishonor but an honorable employment from the first, and the rapid means of advancement. Men, women, and children, all should belong to it — all, that is, below the grade of efficiency which needs no care. For the children — this is the vital base of the matter — a system of education, the best we have, should guarantee the fullest development possible to each; from the carefully appointed nursery and kindergarten up to the trade school fitting the boy or girl for life; or, if special capacity be shown, for higher education.

This at once stops the lowering process — it leaves the state only the existing crop of low efficients to handle, and insures the higher efficiency of the next generation. Those old enough to work should be employed as follows: enough should be placed on farms to provide for the entire body. These farms should be model farms, under the best management, furnishing experiment stations, and bases for agricultural instruction, as well as the food for the whole army and all its officials; and where cotton and such products were raised, they would be a further source of income.

As a large percentage of the negro population is best suited to agricultural labor, and this would prove a very important working base for the institution. By modern methods of advanced agriculture the land would be improved; the best results obtained from it, and the laborers continually taught their business. The surrounding country would be benefited by these stations.

Another large number, in mills and shops belonging to the undertaking, would make clothing, uniforms, etc., for them all; and another detachment would assist in the necessary building.

All these are but the internal functions of the new body; its direct service to society would be in meeting the crying need of the whole South for better roads, harbors, river banks, and the general development of the country. Construction trains, carrying bands of the new workmen, officers, and men, with their families, with work for the women and teaching for the children, would carry the laborer along the roads he made, and improve the country at tremendous speed.

With proper food, suitable hours of work, rest, and amusement; without the strain of personal initiative and responsibility to which so many have proved unequal, a great amount of productive labor would be thus brought to the service of the community. As fast as any individuals proved themselves capable of working on their own initiative they would be graduated with honor. This institution should be compulsory at the bottom, perfectly free at the top.

Each company would have its clerk, each individual would have his separate account as soon as his labor passed the amount necessary for the support of the institution; and, when above that amount, a wage fund should accumulate credited to each, furnishing a small capital to start with when graduated. Many who would not perhaps prove capable of entire personal responsibility, could be organized in small post-graduate groups of farms or shops, and so remain until they went on to higher efforts; or perhaps came back into the army.

What this amounts to is simply state organization of the negro, under conditions wholly to his advantage, and therefore to ours. Some persons, hasty in speech, will now be asking "Who is to pay for all this?" To which the answer is, "The same who paid for all the comforts and luxuries of the South in earlier years— the working negro."

Applied labor is wealth.

The unorganized negro does not seem capable in many instances of utilizing his own forces. This organization provides the machinery best to elicit and apply the working force of this great mass of people: and would do so at no loss whatever. If any man, privately, were allowed to govern the labor of, say, a thousand negroes, to his own advantage, he would not be asking "who pays for it?"

The funds necessary to start an undertaking of this sort would, in the first instance, have to be advanced by the several communities interested, but would promptly be returned, and thereafter the organization would be no expense to the community but would pay for itself. Meanwhile the applied labor would result in improvements to the country of endless value, and the improvement in the negroes themselves would add steadily to their value as constituents of the body politic.

A certain percentage of degenerates and criminals would have to be segregated and cared for as they are now, only far more wisely. But the saving to the state in cutting off the supply of these degenerates would go far to establish the economy of the proposition.

Here is at present an undeveloped country and an undeveloped race. Here is potential labor that will not apply itself, and the need for labor unmet. This plan brings the labor to the place where it is wanted, and benefits the laborer in the process. There should be nothing offensive in the whole undertaking. Compulsory education we demand for all in many states; this would enforce it more thoroughly, that is all.

The enlistment would be compulsory, but so is enlistment in the army in highly civilized lands, and that is not held dishonorable. To be drafted to a field of labor that shall benefit his own race and the whole community, need not be considered a wrong to any negro. The whole system should involve fullest understanding of the special characteristics of the negro; should be full of light and color; of rhythm and music; of careful organization and honorable recognition. It should furnish good physical training and as much education as each individual can take.

Every negro graduated would be better fitted to take his place in the community. Every negro unable to graduate would remain under wise supervision, would be really self-supporting, and also help in the great work of raising the people.

Then someone will ask "What will you do when the roads and harbors are all done—when the rough work is exhausted and the country all properly developed?" By the time that happy end is accomplished there will probably be no negro problem.

"But in the meantime," says the questioner, "How are you going to be sure this great undertaking will be managed wisely, honestly, efficiently? Where are you going to get your superior teachers, your managers and superintendents? What is going to prevent the establishment of an immense system of peonage, of state slavery, of enormous profits wrung from these compulsory enlistments? Of 'Army scandals' beside which those of Europe will be as nothing?"

This is a somewhat deterrent suggestion.

If Race A, in Status 10, cannot so behave itself as thus to elevate and improve Race B, in Status 4, it is somewhat of a reflection upon its superiority.

If we, with all our boasted advancement, are incapable of administering a plan of such visible usefulness to both races, of such patent economy and permanent benefit, then we need some scheme of race betterment ourselves. But it does not call for any superhuman virtue.

By the same methods in which a state or county arbitrarily provides for its poor, its defective, or for the education of its children; so it could now bestir itself to provide for this large class of comparatively backward citizens. If the arrangement were made very clear and visibly attractive, and volunteers were called for, with some special honor and recognition for them, it is quite possible that numbers would enlist of their own accord. It might be called the bureau of Labor and Education, or of Labor and Improvement, and arranged on a military basis, with its construction camps, its base of supplies Nos. 1, 2, 3, etc.; it would form a continuous school for all ages, slowly shrinking and withdrawing as the younger generation of colored people showed their ability for voluntary co-operation or entirely individual effort.

Especial care should of course be given to the management, that it be "kept out of politics," and that the finances of the institution be continually open to the public, that full annual reports be printed, and that every means be taken to ensure a fair and just administration.

A training-school for domestic service might be part of each stationary base; and individuals could be sent from this on probation as it were—perfectly free to remain out in satisfactory home service, or to improve their condition as they were able. In case of unsatisfactory service they should be reinlisted—and try some other form of labor.

A plan of organized labor that would make all negroes self-supporting; a plan of education that would make the whole race rise in social evolution; a plan of local development that would add millions to the value of the southern land, and all within the independent power of each state—surely such a plan is worth considering.

"Feminism" *

Feminism is a term applied to what was previously known as "The Woman's Movement," and still earlier, as "Women's Rights."

That Movement, in its largest sense, consists in the development of human qualities and functions among women; in their entering upon social relationships, instead of remaining, as has been almost universally the case, restricted to the sexual and domestic. It is in large part individual and unconscious, but is also increasingly conscious and organized.

* Typescript, "written for Encyclopedia of Social Reform, Wm. P. Bliss," ca. 1908–1909, Gilman papers, folder 175. This article did not appear in The New Encyclopedia of Social Reform . . .," William D. P. Bliss and Rudolph M. Binder, eds., enlarged and revised edition (London and New York: Funk and Wagnalls, 1908) nor in the third edition, 1910. I have not been able to locate a copy of the second (1909) edition.

Our whole historic period is almost exclusively androcentric, (man-centered), showing women in various stages of subjection according to race, class, period, religion, and other modifying influences. Whenever a comparative equality of condition between the sexes has existed, as in high birth, in wealth, in education, there has of course appeared with it a degree of social progress among women; but the general tradition of exclusive masculine supremacy was too strong to allow of any permanent gain.

In the nineteenth century, however, conditions of far wider general education, of rapid economic development, and of the enlightening discoveries of science; together with the new spirit and practise of liberty in the world, following the American and French Revolutions, conduced to a more definite and general uprising among the subject sex.

At first this was shown in individuals, with separate demands, along various lines, as for higher education, freedom to practise trades or professions, or removal of legal injustices and disabilities. Several strong protagonists of the movement arose, most notably John Stuart Mill [1806–1873] with his great book on "The Subjection of Women" [1869]; while others were so convinced of the importance of these changes as to appear on the lecture platform in their defense.

The wider activities of women in charity, reform, especially in the temperance movement, and, in our own country, among the Abolitionists, helped to enlarge their range of emotion, clarify their ideas, and habituate them, to organized action. As a result of all this a Convention was called in 1848 at Seneca Falls, New York, U.S.A., to discuss the "Rights of Women." At this Convention the demand for political equality was first publicly made, and this claim, widely urged by both speakers and writers, was for long the most daring advance of Feminism.

In spite of this simple justice, the obvious necessity, and the conspicuous advantages of political equality, claims sufficiently strong to quite satisfy most of the workers for woman's advancement, there were some who recognized further needs. Economic as well as political independence was demanded, and a swift outpouring of women workers into practically all trades, businesses and professions, marked a change fully as important as that of their enfranchisement.

Some saw that the restriction of the majority of women to domestic industry was an injury, not only to them and to their families, but a severe economic handicap to both sexes, limiting the industrial productivity of women, and loading the men with heavy unnecessary expenses, a waste amounting to forty percent of the world's labor and about half of the cost of living.

Others studied the condition of the relation of the sexes, showing that women were exploited for the pleasure of men, not only in that publically deplored abuse, prostitution, but also in their helpless subservience in marriage. It was shown that this condition was not only an evil to women but to men, also an injury to the child, and so to the state. On this ground arose a special phase of revolt demanding a single standard of morality, and self-government in sex for women, as well as legal, educational, economic, and political equality.

This broad and varied advance has gone on with increasing speed in ever-enlarging numbers in many states and nations, until at present we find places where all the earlier claims are already satisfied and the later are being rapidly approached. Feminism today is in a position of sufficient acceptance to be open to the fullest study.

Yet even so, with all the changes in its front, in its terminology, in its specific demands, we have but begun to grasp the full meaning of the progress involved. We have now a biological base for Feminism, a knowledge of Sociology in the light of which to study it, a wider reading of History, showing the relative position of women in all races, and its consequences; and a new recognition, vaguely felt, of the tremendous import to the world of a conscious, organized, socially responsible Motherhood.

In what may be termed Neo-Feminism, the most important contribution is in the work of the great American Sociologist, Lester F. Ward. In his *Pure Sociology,* Chapter 14, on "The Phylogenetic Forces,"* he shows that throughout nature the female is

* Lester F. Ward, *Pure Sociology: A Treatise on the Origin and Spontaneous Development of Society* (New York: Macmillan, 1903), pp. 290–416.

the race-type, being in reality the earlier organism; the male developing later in the interests of cross fertilization; and that ours is the only species wherein the female is subjected to and exploited by the male.

It is easy to trace to this unnatural position most of the evils which distinguish the relation of the sexes in the human race, to explain the already recognized fact that a civilization advances in proportion to the improvement in the condition of women; and to forecast further improvement when the collective activities of the human race are more fully influenced by the true race-type.

The tremendous value of this view in our popular psychology is that it completely supersedes that prevalent folk-myth, the underlying base of all our false ideas about women, to the effect that she was made as an afterthought, subsidiary to and dependent upon man.

A socially responsible and collectively efficient Motherhood may be given as the farthest and fullest purpose of Feminism.

So broad a movement, involving millions of people of all nations, classes, religions and schools of thought, must of course present many phases, with the excesses and abuses common to every far-reaching social change. Among these abuses the most regrettable are to be found in that small but quite audible group of Feminists who mistake the old evil of sex-license for a new freedom. Certain well-known writers distinctly advocate such license, seeming to consider monogamy as a tyrannical invention of man instead of the perfectly natural and highly evolved form of mating it really is; and we find some conscientious and intelligent women, as well as thoughtless and ignorant ones, thus deliberately perpetuating the worst conditions of their past and playing into the hands of their previous masters. This is called by its supporters "the New Morality," yet it is hardly to be distinguished from the old immorality.

The opposition to Feminism, which was at first practically universal, resting on mental inertia and the unquestioned social traditions, diminished in volume but increased in intensity with the steady success of the movement. And as, in all ages, people willingly believe all evil of a thing they fear and hate, so the

Woman's Movement has been accused of the worst intentions and results.

As each forward step was made and the dreaded change became an established fact, without the alleged evil results, the charges were transferred to the next demand, and today we find the rapidly increasing extension of the franchise to women charged with the same evils long ago attributed to their having a higher education or a chance to earn their livings.

The latest and highest form of Feminism has great promise for the world. It postulates a womanhood free, strong, clean, and conscious of its power and duty. This means a selective motherhood, the careful choosing of fit men for husbands, with full knowledge of the necessary qualifications and conditions. It means a higher standard of chastity, both in marriage and out, for men as well as women. It means a recognition of the responsibility of socially organized mothers for the welfare of all children.

Further, it brings into the world in full representation the essential feminine principle, Motherhood, which means a wider organization of our economic, educational, religious, and political life than we can yet forecast.

Chapter Four

· · · · ·

The Forerunner Years, 1909–1916

Just as Charlotte Perkins Stetson had cut her domestic ties in 1895, and commenced a lone lecturing path, so too in 1909 did Charlotte Perkins Gilman cut her commercial journalistic ties and embark on a lone publishing path. She did so because she believed that though her thinking had developed and grown, its market value had shrunk. "Social philosophy, however ingeniously presented, does not command wide popular interest," she wrote. "I wrote more and sold less.... [M]ore and more of my stuff was declined. Think I must and write I must, the manuscripts accumulated far faster than I could sell them, some of the best, almost all—and finally I announced: 'If the editors and publishers will not bring out my work, I will!' "[1]

For the next seven years and two months, Charlotte wrote, edited, and published a monthly magazine, filling it with her verses, stories, essays, criticism, and sermons. It fluctuated between twenty-six and thirty-four pages for the first fifteen months, and became a 28–page journal in February 1911. Published by the company she and her husband had founded, the Charlton Company, 67 Wall Street, New York City, it cost $.10 an issue, $1 a year. There was no newsstand edition: one either subscribed or purchased it from the several political organizations that distributed it. Probably between 5,000 to 7,000 people read it.[2] As a reviewer in *Putnam's Magazine* noted, these readers received "a good deal of C. P. Gilman" for $1.[3] For some, like the writer Mary Austin, it was too much: "Everything she wrote was in the same key.

... I had to drop her magazine with its terrible sameness, its narrow scope."[4]

In fact, Charlotte's commentaries ranged over a wide range of topics, but the central theme never varied—social and human development were hampered by sexual disfunctions that could only be removed when women were perceived and treated as human beings and human beings were recognized as integral parts of the social organism. There could, however, be a sameness of tone in her writing voice, especially when she used a sermonizing form, as she increasingly did. But when she analyzed social consciousness and human behavior, her voice regained its clear, powerful, critical, and plangent sound.

Six book-length pieces of nonfiction appeared in *The Forerunner,* one of which, *The Man-Made World; or, Our Androcentric Culture,* was published in book form in 1911. It represented her effort to separate the sexual attributes of male and female from the cultural attributes of masculine and feminine. She critically examined the effect of masculine dominance on the family, health and beauty, art, literature, games and sports, ethics and religion, education, society and fashion, law and government, crime and punishment, politics and warfare, and industry and economics. The purpose was to demonstrate the negative impact on society of masculine dominance and prophesy the beneficial effects of a world in which men and women had equal power.

Its writing matched the verve of *The Home,* and it was well reviewed. There was a British edition, a Swedish translation, and a second printing in 1914.

"Our Brains and What Ails Them" (1912) was a study of human stupidity, viciousness, unhappiness, and sickness, of the behavior of people not trained to reason or think, and a prod to the enlightened middle class to eliminate the factors that blocked the brain development of women and "the masses." The 1913 serial, "Humanness," was an effort to give direction to social consciousness, thinking, and action through a critique of individualism, personality, personal selfishness, and egoism. "Social Ethics," the 1914 series, focused on her belief that ethics was *the* science of social conduct and the failures of the ethical systems taught by organized religion. In "The Dress of Women" (1915), she urged women to stop submitting to the "senseless dominion of fashion" and to recognize that cloth was a "social tissue," used to magnify sex, limit social development, impose suffering on animals, waste economic resources, and adversely affect the mind of women.[5] And, in her most optimistic series, "Growth and Combat" (1916), she discussed the trend away from a male-driven, competitive, pain-inflicting society toward a women-carried process of social growth.

She worked hard to keep the magazine afloat, undertaking lecture tours of the United States in 1911 and 1915, and Europe in 1913, while en route to and from the International Suffrage Convention in Budapest, and writing for other periodicals. The magazine earned only half of its production costs, and she eventually had to borrow money from Houghton to keep it going.[6]

Several articles were devoted to a critique of perhaps the only other woman in the world whose credentials as a feminist theorist matched hers: Ellen Karolina Sofia Key (1849–1926). Key was born into a Swedish aristocratic family; both her parents were reformers. An avid reader, mainly educated by tutors, Key knew the works of Darwin, Spencer, and John Stuart Mill. A devout Christian when she was young, she came to consider herself a socialist, though she did not join any socialist organizations. In fact, the only organization for which she ever worked was the Society for Married Women's Property Rights. She thought that organizations were "the burying ground of ideas."[7]

She taught at a progressive school in Stockholm, spoke out publicly for woman's suffrage, supported dress reform and woman's property rights reforms, and wrote essays on female novelists for the first Swedish women's magazine. She achieved prominence in 1896, when her lecture "Misused Womanpower and Natural Areas of Work for Women" was printed as a pamphlet. It contained the core of her philosophy: that women are different from men and should develop their special capacities; that a woman had to make "the essence of her being the departure point for her striving after liberation"; and that women who tried to become men's equals, who competed with them, misused their energies. She accused the women's movement of spreading a dogmatic view of women that actually restricted their liberty and limited their influence by prescribing masculine standards of behavior for them, and insisted that it was as mothers that women would lead the "revolt against everything evil in society."[8]

The book that brought her worldwide attention, *Barnets århundrade*

(*The Century of the Child*), was published in 1900. In 1903, she began lecturing abroad, achieving her most significant influence in Germany, where she helped organize the Mother-Protection Movement in 1905. That year the first article about her appeared in a United States Journal, *Review of Reviews*,[9] and her first major United States article, "The Woman of the Future," was published in the fall of 1907.[10]

The Century of the Child appeared in English translation in 1909, followed by seven others between 1911 and 1916, and five magazine articles in 1913 and 1914. The feminist writer Rheta Childe Dorr (1866–1948) wrote: "everybody who used to read Charlotte Perkins Gilman was now reading Ellen Key. I read 'Love and Marriage' and 'The Century of the Child,' and thought them both queer and old-fashioned, almost reactionary.' " (Dorr traveled to Sweden to interview Key, and found the conversations interesting, inspiring, and obscure.)[11]

Charlotte reviewed *Century of the Child* and *Love and Marriage* favorably, praising Key for many qualities, while indicating, respectfully, their differences.[12] When, however, Charlotte perceived herself under direct attack by Key, the responses sharpened.

A few commentators discussed the "debate." Jessie Taft (1882–1960), though preferring Key's "broad philosophical attitude" and her "lack of dogmatism" and "sex antagonism," concluded that only experience will tell whether children should be trained by a corps of specialists or whether all mothers should be trained as specialists.[13] *Current Opinion*, however, leaned toward Charlotte, concluding that Key was "profoundly conservative, even reactionary in all that pertains to motherhood."[14]

Charlotte also fired a critical broadside at Ida Tarbell (1857–1944), one of the most influential muckrakers of the Progressive Era, whose *The History of the Standard Oil Company* (1904) was one of the landmark exposes of corporate power in the United States. The occasion was a series of articles Tarbell wrote for *The American Magazine* during the first six months of 1912: "The Uneasy Woman," "Making a Man of Herself," "The Business of Being A Woman," "Homeless Daughters," "Irresponsible Women and the Friendless Child," and "Woman and Democracy."[15] Women, Tarbell counselled, should go back to "the business of being a woman"—that is to bearing and rearing children. A woman could not succeed in man's arena, she continued, and the effort led to the loss of what was strongest in her nature, "her power of emotion, her 'affectability.' "[16]

Charlotte devoted four *Forerunner* pieces to the first four articles, even though they were "pitiful stuff" and of "negligible value," because "the author is so widely known and respected that her name carries weight if her words do not." Woman's "main business," Charlotte concluded, "is being human, a phase of her life of which Miss Tarbell in this series of ineffectual papers takes no cognizance whatever."[17] Charlotte also spoke publicly against Tarbell, on April 15, 1912, along with Beatrice Forbes-Robertson Hale (b. 1883), Anna Howard Shaw (1847–1919), and Rheta Childe Dorr.[18]

Charlotte also found fault with socialist editor Josephine Conger-Kaneko's critique of Tarbell's articles. When Conger-Kaneko wrote that the mental processes of men and women were frequently "very unlike" and that people were male and female before they evolved into human beings, Charlotte responded that it was not a question of human qualities antedating sex qualities, that people "are far more distinctly human than male and female." Conger-Kaneko, misunderstanding Charlotte's point, replied that equal opportunity should not necessitate eliminating "sex lines, sex differences in men and women."[19]

In terms of public recognition, the years 1912–1914 probably were the apex of Charlotte's career. A series of lectures she delivered in 1914, in New York and London, received extensive coverage from the *New York Times,* usually a full-column's worth, studded with copious quotations from her speeches. On a few occasions, there would be a short editorial comment on what she said. In February and March 1914, she delivered a series of six lectures, "The Larger Feminism," at the College Hall of the Hotel Astor. The audience averaged about 200, and the *Times'* accounts ranged from the objective to the sarcastic. In April, she delivered a second series of lectures, also at the Hotel Astor, on "Our Male Civilization." George Middleton who attended the lectures, said that the *Times* coverage "caused wide comment. It was almost the first time any serious publicity had been given" to her.[20]

World War I represented a great divide for Charlotte. By the time it ended, *The Forerunner* had ceased to publish, she had become alienated from a number of reform activists, and she did not seem to fit comfortably into the organizations or parties that developed after 1914. She began as a critic of the European war but ended as a supporter of United States entry into it, thus maintaining her long-standing belief that wars, though wasteful and the products of male aggression, could also be vehicles of social progress. For example, she had termed the Spanish-American War (1898) "a great international effort to establish freedom and justice among a weaker people," and hailed Japan's pending victory over Russia in 1904 as something that would advance not only Japan's ends but those of the world.[21]

But in 1914, she decried United States hostilities with Mexico and the war in Europe. At the end of April, she joined speakers denouncing the United States seizure of Vera Cruz,* saying: "The present war is unworthy of our civilization. It is ridiculous. . . . Who makes war? Why, the working people do the killing, they do the dying, and they do the paying for it. And those who send them forth to war never go themselves. They only reap the profit."[22]

When Europe became embroiled in general war that summer, she helped promote the Woman's Peace Parade—a march of women in mourning—for August 29. She noted that such a march would have a small effect on the war, "But the effect on women is the important thing. If this is taken up, as it should be, throughout the country: if thousands of women feel this international misfortune so deeply that they are willing to come out and make funeral marches because of it the result will be a tremendous strengthening of their public spirit and also of their feeling of collective power. Everything that makes for solidarity among women is good."[23] She spoke at several mass antiwar meetings in 1914 and 1915 and played a prominent role at the founding congress of the Woman's Peace Party, in January 1915.[24]

As the war spread and casualties mounted, Charlotte regularly commented on its positive effects. The peace movement would grow, she argued, and socialism, education, and the influence of women would be strengthened as forces working against future wars.[25] She foresaw a

---

* As part of his campaign to topple the regime of Mexican President Victoriana Huerta (1854–1916), President Woodrow Wilson (1856–1924; President of the United States, 1913–1921) had stationed warships off the Atlantic Coast of Mexico. On April 10, in Tampico, some United States sailors were arrested. Though they were immediately released with an apology, Wilson demanded a formal salute to the American flag. When the Mexicans refused to comply, and Wilson learned that a German arms shipment had arrived in Vera Cruz, he ordered warships to shell and Marines to seize the city. War was avoided when Argentina, Brazil, and Chile mediated the conflict.

spirit of "world motherhood" rising from the blood-soaked fields of
Europe that would replace the past's "history of men's fights" with the
future's "history of women's services."[26] She called on "war-maids and
war-widows" to develop their "sense of collectivity," take care of one
another, and unite to gain political and economic power.[27] She also
urged the peace movement to add a positive element to its campaign
—not to be simply against war but for the establishment of a world
federation, a federated government of the nations of the earth: "the
only reliable means by which to harmonize interests, to adjudicate race
conflicts, and to maintain national integrity."[28]

Once the United States entered the war, Charlotte, mainly because
of her growing antipathy toward Germany, broke ranks with the
pacifists. By 1916, she was debunking German "Kultur" and labeling
Germany "a very Frankenstein among the nations."[29] Zona Gale wrote
that she and others who knew her were surprised by Charlotte's
Germanophobia and considered it "an utter contradiction of [her]
thought."[30] George Middleton said that the war ended her friendship
with him and his wife, because "Charlotte had little tolerance for those
who had opposed our entrance into it."[31]

Gilman did not support the rights of conscientious objectors and
dissidents, nor did she defend those jailed for their antiwar activities. In
fact, she believed that those groups who had resisted the war, such as
the Intercollegiate Socialist Society, had "fallen into deserved disrepute"
as a result.[32]

Although Charlotte served on the National Advisory Council of the
Congressional Union, a militant suffrage organization, and on the Executive Committee of its successor, the National Woman's Party, she was
beginning to lose touch with the various movements that had once
embraced her thinking, if not her person. While they narrowed their
focus and tactics, she retained her broad strategy and broader vision.
Sometimes, as on the question of how women should vote in the
presidential election of 1916, she offered conflicting advice.

In fact, her concluding comment on women and the 1916 election
was the last article on the last page of the final issue of *The Forerunner*.
Its small reader base had not repaid expenses, and it had not attracted
more readers, Charlotte believed, because she was so "universal a
heretic. . . . There were some who were with me on one point and

some on two, but when it came to five or more distinct heresies, to a magazine which even ridiculed Fashion, and held blazing before its readers a heaven on earth which they did not in the least want—it narrowed the subscription list."[33]

Writings

Statements of Purposes of The Forerunner

"As to Purposes"*

What is The Forerunner? It is a monthly magazine, publishing stories short and serial, article and essay; drama, verse, satire and sermon; dialogue, fable and fantasy, comment and review. It is written entirely by Charlotte Perkins Gilman.

What is it For? It is to stimulate thought; to arouse hope, courage and impatience; to offer practical suggestions and solutions, to voice the strong assurance of better living, here, now, in our own hands to make.

What is it About? It is about people, principles, and the questions of every-day life; the personal and public problems of to-day. It gives a clear, consistent view of human life and how to live it.

Is it a Woman's Magazine? It will treat all three phases of our existence—male, female and human. It will discuss Man, in his true place in life; Woman, the Unknown Power; the Child, the most important citizen.

Is it a Socialist Magazine? It is a magazine for humanity, and humanity is social. It holds that Socialism, the economic theory, is part of our gradual Socialization, and that the duty of conscious humanity is to promote Socialization.

Why is it Published? It is published to express ideas which need a special medium; and in the belief that there are enough persons interested in those ideas to justify the undertaking.

* *The Forerunner*, 1 (December 1909), p. 33.

"A Summary of Purpose" *

As this seven years of work draws to a close it seems worth while to attempt a synopsis of the general purpose and main features of the undertaking.

The form chosen, this small monthly, was selected as a steady compelling demand on the author to produce and go on producing, regularly.

The subject matter, for the most part, is not to be regarded as "literature," but as an attempt to set forth certain views of life which seemed to the author of real importance to human welfare.

Many have asked why this matter was not presented through the medium of established publications. * * * Why did not John Wesley† preach in the established church?

Our magazines, useful, valuable, amusing and instructive, all depend on pleasing (a) as large a subscription list as they can reach; and (b) their advertising paymasters. (Perhaps the a and b should be transposed.) The larger the subscription list, the more "average" it becomes. The average reader does not care for the sort of stuff carried in The Forerunner. Neither does the big advertiser approve of such far-reaching social iconoclasm.

When we return to the "reform publications," we find they necessarily appeal to a special audience, an audience wedded to that particular "movement" and having a slight opinion of most others. The Equal Suffrage papers, for instance, can hardly offer to their readers matter quite outside of that great cause, and often considered by them as unnecessary or even dangerous.

One of the great suffrage leaders once said to me: "I think that after all, your work will be a help to the movement. What you ask for is so much worse than what we ask for that they will give us the ballot to stave off further demands."

* *The Forerunner,* 7 (November 1916), pp. 286–290.
† When the Church of England closed its door to the evangelical preaching of George Whitefield (1714–1770), he began to preach outdoors. John Wesley (1703–1791), his friend and the developer of a more rigorous version of worship (Methodism) than that offered by the Church of England, followed Whitefield's example. Both drew huge crowds.

These "so much worse" demands of mine are for the economic independence of women, the expert care of children in addition to that of their mothers and the professionalizing of "domestic industry."

The Socialist papers, again, have small use for a presentation quite outside of and beyond that great movement. Being known as a Suffragist and a Socialist has sometimes stood in the way of other work in more conservative quarters, but it has not provided a satisfying means of expression through the publications of either party.

The variety, the breadth, the depth of social alteration suggested in The Forerunner inevitably narrow the circle of readers. Those agreeing on some counts violently disagree on others; fewer and fewer become those sufficiently interested in all to enjoy the whole output—or most of it.

On the subject of sex, for instance, the old school disliked any frank expression on the matter, considering it indelicate, if not immoral, to advocate the woman's right to her own body and to decision as to when she should become a mother; while that still older school who cover their reversion to primitive promiscuity by the term "The New Morality," even more sharply objected to the position that sex union is intended primarily for parentage and that we to-day are over-sexed and grossly over indulgent.

Thus, being too specific for the "average reader," and not specific enough for the reform devotee, there remained but a limited market for my work, editors picking and choosing with intelligent care among such parts of it as they were willing to print.

Therefore, as a "Social Invention," feeling that the ideas were valuable, I determined to present them at my own expense, if necessary—and it was necessary. In these seven years I have ["]freed my mind" of those things which seemed most pressingly important, with the serene freedom of expression indispensable to right work.

The matter so produced is now available in the bound volumes, as long as they hold out, and selections can be reprinted in later years. At any rate the work is done, and it has been set before—counting the seven years—some thirty-five thousand people. For each year the estimated readers were five to seven thousand; and to reach that number monthly, was a privilege, indeed.

What, in essence, is the nature of the social philosophy thus set forth? It may be summarized under several heads.

A. As to Human Life in general:

That Human Life, i.e., Social Life, is organic; that it is as "natural" as any lower form, is governed by natural law and has at work upon it the same Lifting Force, often called God, which has developed all life forms, has brought us so far on our way, and is still pushing upward in us.

B. As to Pain and Sin:

That our visible difficulties and distresses are not inherent, not necessary, but merely due to our misconceptions, and may be easily and swiftly outlived as soon as we understand them.

C. As to Religion:

That the main error in all religions is in their demand for a fixed and absolute belief, a habit paralyzing to the human mind.

D. As to God:

That the force called God is the truest thing there is; a ceaselessly acting force, to which we are all welcome, always. There is no anger in it, no punishment, no need to be praised and placated or importuned with prayers.

It is There—for us to use, always; Love, Power, Peace—the Push of the Universe. It calls for no beseeching, and no worship, only for full use. In living in accordance with this ever present force we live naturally and follow the laws of social evolution.

E. As to Children:

That the critical period of babyhood and early childhood is precisely the most important in our whole lives.

That at present this period is incompetently managed by mothers and servants.

That babies and little children should be placed in the most carefully prepared cultural conditions, and in the care of the highest grade of specially talented, trained and experienced teachers.

That such conditions and such care require the grouping of little children in specially arranged houses during those hours of the daytime the mother is at work.

F. As to Education:

That our earlier and still current system of education produces poor results and works irreparable injury; that the brain power of the race will be greatly enlarged as soon as we learn how to allow full growth to the child mind, and assist in the free development of special aptitudes.

Further, that our rapidly spreading systems of continuous education, university extension, evening schools, lectures, moving pictures, etc., should be carried out beyond any limitations we now see; that the whole people should be educated to their full capacity their lives long.

That our school systems should include much travel, all children being shown their world, at least by sample, and taught to love it; and also they should be given a full acquaintance with the rudiments of all industry, to know and love that, too.

That our doctrines of "obedience" and of continually "forcing yourself to do what you don't like" are not educational, but essentially degrading.

G. As to Our Brains:

That the human Brain, or mind, rather, is prevented from clear perceptions of the facts and principles of social life by the persistence of a vast mass of ancient misconception and falsehood, which is artificially preserved and forced upon each new person by education, both special and social.

That with the definite removal of these ancient errors the mind will swiftly open to the valuable discoveries of later science.

That the main function of the brain is to govern action and that our general inability so to use it is due to the deplorable influence of early domestic education, wherein the child is constantly forced to unchosen behavior; his own choices and decisions becoming largely disassociated with their normal resultant inactivity.

H. As to Marriage:

That monogamous marriage is the best for humanity as for many of the higher animals and birds; and that its permanence and happiness will be established by the normal progress of women.

I. As to Women:

That the female of *genus homo* is over-developed in sex and under-developed as a human being; and that this condition acts as a check upon all further social progress:

That she is by nature "the race type" rather than the male; and as he is also over sexed, his exclusive management of human affairs is self-limited, and has kept society "marking time" in many vitally important lines in spite of our rapid advance in others.

That the humanizing of women will automatically remove a large share of our pain, disease and "sin"; bringing with it a standard of health, beauty, power and personal happiness hitherto undreamed of.

That this humanizing involves the entrance of women upon full social relation, not only politically but economically; and their complete independence of masculine "support."

J. As to the Home:

That a private home, in a detachable house with its own garden, is desirable for nearly all families, and for many individuals.

That for the individual, the normal minimum of decent comfort is two rooms and a bath;

That the enjoyment of a home, by family or individual, does not imply the performance of any labor therein;

That what we call "domestic industry" is a relic of pre-social time and should be wholly discarded wherever possible;

That the legitimate performance of this industry should be by professionals; the preparation of food, for instance, becoming an honored and well paid business and the consumer purchasing it cooked instead of raw;

Such cleaning as remained in a kitchenless house could be easily done by trained workers coming in by the hour.

(This does NOT involve the faintest degree of "co-operation" —that deadly mistake so often and so foolishly repeated. Neither does it involve a "community kitchen," merely a natural business development such as gives us bakeries and laundries.)

That such a method of supplying our personal needs would give to woman the opportunity for specializing industry, would reduce the expense of living by more than half, and greatly improve our standard of health and comfort.

That we need thorough scientific inquiries into the whole matter of improved methods of living with experiment stations and elaborate research.

K. As to Dress:

That dress is a form of social expression of the highest importance; that at present the dress of both men and women largely fails of its function, while that of women is pitiful, grotesque and injurious along many lines.

That the clothing of women, and their slavish submission to the constant changes dictated to them by tradesmen, seriously affects the race, owing to the close connection between soul, body and dress.

No noble body can endure in the costume of an idiot pet monkey, no noble soul can exist in such a contemptible exterior.

L. As to Economics:

That we are wrong in holding as the base of our economic science, that "the impulse to labor is to gratify desire," meaning when examined further "to obtain something wherewith to gratify desire."

That in reality human work is social, that the causative demand is social, and the compelling force is social[;] human work is a manifestation of social energy, bearing no immediate relation to the supplying of the individual need.

That in order to promote and improve human work we have to so develop young human beings as to bring out all their special powers and to provide full opportunity of expression for them, at the same time keeping them well nourished and well educated; and also expelling from the race mind the mass of accumulated falsehood and scorn as to "labor."

That under such condition, the output of humanity from the highest form of art to the lowest grade of labor, will both be improved and increased, and all human life become happier.

That the major difficulty in our understanding all these problems is our individualistic misconception; we try to manage social economics in lines of personal interest, necessarily conflicting. Not until we see that every form of industry is a contribution to society, and administer them on that basis, can we have either peace or prosperity in economics.

M. As to Socialism:

That the real principle of Socialism is that above mentioned, the social administration of social functions—meaning all human work. Socialism consists in "The ownership and management of all natural monopolies and the machinery of production and distribution"; that is not only justice, but enormous gain to the world.

That the socialist official propaganda has unfortunately placed its heaviest emphasis on the theories of "economic determinism" and "class consciousness" and the "class struggle," and the disputes thus aroused have done much to prevent general acceptance of the essential principles.

N. As to Art:

That art, in all its forms, represents a high grade of social service, of extreme value; but that art, like economics, is prevented by individualism and is even considered by many artists as a mere means of self-expression.

That the world suffers and starves for lack of beauty, while the artist is engaged in exhibiting to us his own interior—which is not always beautiful.

O. As to the Individual:

That each of us is not only a separate animal, but a vital part of the organic social life, empowered by that mighty social spirit, and only fully happy when freely discharging social energy in legitimate social service. This means in action simply to be doing one's own special work for the common advantage, but in feeling, it should involve full consciousness of the purpose, and wide knowledge of the interrelated importance of that work.

Further, that the individual may and should use the splendid powers given by the social organization, to develop body and mind to their highest capacity and should live, not only in the personal safety and comfort a highly developed society should assure its members, but in the boundless range of full consciousness; having our full history in mind, and looking forward to the glorious possibilities which are in our hands to achieve.

P. As to Progress:

That the world is much farther along in fact than in feeling and thought; the ideas in our minds following slowly and reluctantly after the event and our emotions long ages behind our ideas.

That when we disconnect our minds from antiquity and recognize the facts of our present degree of gain and of the practically unbounded power we possess to make further gains, mankind will cover in a few generations more advance than has been made in a thousand years.

A constant free responsible motherhood can cleanse the world of its worst disease in three generations; by exercising its natural right of choice among fathers for the coming race.

The new standardization of food, possible only with the widest professionalization, together with wide spread knowledge of food values and hygienic living, will at the same time rid us of another group of diseases.

The elimination of alcohol will take care of most of those remaining.

Each of us remains confronted with the personal problem. Our dawning social consciousness finds us bound, suffering, thwarted, starved, crippled in many ways. The more we see the possible joy of human living, the more painful become present conditions — if unchangeable.

But they are changeable.

The personal relief is this: so thoroughly to grasp the larger social issues as to overlook the personal difficulties — as a wounded soldier rejoices in the victory even though he may not live to taste its fruits.

We are now in painful conditions. We can change them. We will. But in the mean time, suffering remains to most of us, and is to be borne by looking outside of and beyond it.

There is nothing to prevent humanity developing a type as beautiful, as strong, as intellectually able as any in the past; and with a far wider vision, a vast increase of knowledge, a measureless gain in power; and the spirit of love which belongs to a conscious world.

The Man-Made World; or, Our Androcentric Culture

Chapter XII. Politics and Warfare*

I go to my old dictionary, and find; "Politics, 1. The science of government; that part of ethics which has to do with the regulation and government of a nation or state, the preservation

* *The Forerunner*, 1 (October 1910), pp. 21–25; reprinted New York: Charlton, 1911, pp. 208–226.

of its safety, peace and prosperity; the defence of its existence and rights against foreign control or conquest; the augmentation of its strength and resources, and the protection of its citizens in their rights; with the preservation and improvement of their morals. 2. The management of political parties; the advancement of candidates to office; in a bad sense, artful or dishonest management to secure the success of political measures or party schemes, political trickery."

From present day experience we might add, 3. Politics, practical; The art of organizing and handling men in large numbers, manipulating votes, and, in especial, appropriating public wealth.

We can easily see that the "science of government may be divided into "pure" and "applied" like other sciences, but that it is "a part of ethics" will be news to many minds.

Yet why not? Ethics is the science of conduct, and politics is merely one field of conduct; a very common one. Its connection with warfare in this chapter is perfectly legitimate in view of the history of politics on the one hand, and the imperative modern issues which are to-day opposed to this established combination.

There are many to-day who hold that politics need not be at all connected with warfare; and others who hold that politics is warfare from start to finish.

In order to dissociate the two ideas completely, let us give a paraphrase of the above definition, applying it to domestic management—that part of ethics which has to do with the regulation and government of a family; the preservation of its safety, peace and prosperity; the defense of its existence and rights against any stranger's interference or control; the augmentation of its strength and resources, and the protection of its members in their rights; with the preservation and improvement of their morals.

All this is simple enough, and in no way masculine; neither is it feminine, save in this; that the tendency to care for, defend and manage a group, is in its origin maternal.

In every human sense, however, politics has left its maternal base far in the background; and as a field of study and action is as well adapted to men as to women. There is no reason whatever why men should not develop great ability in this department of ethics, and gradually learn how to preserve the safety, peace and prosperity of their nation; together with those other services as to resources, protection of citizens, and improvement of morals.

Men, as human beings, are capable of the noblest devotion and efficiency in these matters, and have often shown them; but their devotion and efficiency have been marred in this, as in so many other fields, by the constant obtrusion of an ultra-masculine tendency.

In warfare *per se,* we find maleness in its absurdest extremes. Here is to be studied the whole gamut of basic masculinity, from the initial instinct of combat, through every form of glorious ostentation, with the loudest possible accompaniment of noise.

Primitive warfare had for its climax the possession of the primitive prize, the female. Without dogmatising on so remote a period, it may be suggested as a fair hypothesis that this was the very origin of our organized raids. We certainly find war before there was property in land, or any other property to tempt aggressors. Women, however, there were always, and when a specially androcentric tribe had reduced its supply of women by cruel treatment, or they were not born in sufficient numbers, owing to hard conditions, men must needs go farther afield after other women. Then, since the men of the other tribes naturally objected to losing their main labor supply and comfort, there was war.

Thus based on the sex impulse, it gave full range to the combative instinct, and further to that thirst for vocal exultation so exquisitely male. The proud bellowings of the conquering stag, as he trampled on his prostrate rival, found higher expression in the "triumphs" of the old days, when the conquering warrior returned to his home, with victims chained to his chariot wheels, and trumpets braying.

When property became an appreciable factor in life, warfare took on a new significance. What was at first mere destruction, in the effort to defend or obtain some hunting ground or pasture; and, always, to secure the female; now coalesced with the acquis-itive instinct, and the long black ages of predatory warfare closed in upon the world.

Where the earliest form exterminated, the later enslaved, and took tribute; and for century upon century the "gentleman adventurer," i.e., the primitive male, greatly preferred to acquire wealth by the simple old process of taking it, to any form of productive industry.

We have been much misled as to warfare by our androcentric literature. With a history which recorded nothing else; a literature which praised and an art which exalted it; a religion which called its central power "the God of Battles"—never the God of Workshops, mind you!—with a whole complex social structure man-prejudiced from center to circumference, and giving highest praise and honor to the Soldier; it is still hard for us to see what warfare really is in human life.

Some day we shall have new histories written, histories of world progress, showing the slow uprising, the development, the interservice of the nations; showing the faint beautiful dawn of the larger spirit of world-consciousness, and all its benefiting growth.

We shall see people softening, learning, rising; see life lengthen with the possession of herds, and widen in rich prosperity with agriculture. Then industry, blossoming, fruiting, spreading wide; art, giving light and joy; the intellect developing with companionship and human intercourse; the whole spreading tree of social progress, the trunk of which is specialized industry, and the branches of which comprise every least and greatest line of human activity and enjoyment. This growing tree, springing up wherever conditions of peace and prosperity gave it a chance, we shall see continually hewed down to the very root by war.

To the later historian will appear throughout the ages, like some Hideous Fate, some Curse, some predetermined check, to drag down all our hope and joy and set life forever at its first steps over again, this Red Plague of War.

The instinct of combat, between males, worked advantageously so long as it did not injure the female or the young. It is a perfectly natural instinct, and therefore perfectly right, in its place; but its place is in a pre-patriarchal era. So long as the animal mother was free and competent to care for herself and her young;

then it was an advantage to have "the best man win": that is the best stag or lion; and to have the vanquished die, or live in sulky celibacy, was no disadvantage to any one but himself.

Humanity is on a stage above this plan. The best man in the social structure is not always the huskiest. When a fresh horde of ultra-male savages swarmed down upon a prosperous young civilization, killed off the more civilized males and appropriated the more civilized females; they did, no doubt, bring in a fresh physical impulse to the race; but they destroyed the civilization.

The reproduction of perfectly good savages is not the main business of humanity. Its business is to grow, socially; to develop, to improve; and warfare, at its best, retards human progress; at its worst, obliterates it.

Combat is not a social process at all; it is a physical process, a subsidiary sex process, purely masculine, intended to improve the species by the elimination of the unfit. Amusingly enough, or absurdly enough; when applied to society, it eliminates the fit, and leaves the unfit to perpetuate the race!

We require, to do our organized fighting, a picked lot of vigorous young males, the fittest we can find. The too old or too young; the sick, crippled, defective; are all left behind, to marry and be fathers; while the pick of the country, physically, is sent off to oppose the pick of another country, and kill—kill—kill!

Observe the result on the population! In the first place the balance is broken—there are not enough men to go around, at home; many women are left unmated. In primitive warfare, where women were promptly enslaved, or, at the best, polygamously married, this did not greatly matter—to the population; but as civilization advances and monogamy obtains, whatever eugenic benefits may once have sprung from warfare are completely lost, and all its injuries remain.

In what we innocently call "civilized warfare" (we might as well speak of "civilized cannibalism!"), this steady elimination of the fit leaves an ever lowering standard of parentage at home. It makes a widening margin of what we call "surplus women," meaning more than enough to be monogamously married; and these women, not being economically independent, drag steadily upon the remaining men, postponing marriage, and increasing its burdens.

The birth rate is lowered in quantity by the lack of husbands, and lowered in quality both by the destruction of superior stock, and by the wide dissemination of those diseases which invariably accompany the wifelessness of the segregated males who are [s]old off to perform our military functions.

The external horrors and wastes of warfare we are all familiar with: A. It arrests industry and all progress. B. It destroys the fruits of industry and progress. C. It weakens, hurts and kills the combatants. D. It lowers the standard of the non-combatants. Even the conquering nation is heavily injured; the conquered sometimes exterminated, or at least absorbed by the victor.

This masculine selective process, when applied to nations, does not produce the same result as when applied to single opposing animals. When little Greece was overcome it did not prove that the victors were superior, nor promote human interests in any way; it injured them.

The "stern arbitrament of war" may prove which of two peoples is the better fighter, but it does not prove it therefore the fittest to survive.

Beyond all these more or less obvious evils, comes a further result, not enough recognized; the psychic effects of [the] military standard of thought and feeling.

Remember that an androcentric culture has always exempted its own essential activities from the restraints of ethics,—"All's fair in love and war!" Deceit, trickery, lying, every kind of skulking underhand effort to get information; ceaseless endeavor to outwit and overcome "the enemy"; these, with cruelty and destruction are characteristic of the military process; as well as the much prized virtues of courage, endurance and loyalty, personal and public.

Also classed as virtue, and unquestionably such from the military point of view, is that prime factor in making and keeping an army, obedience.

See how the effect of this artificial maintenance of early mental attitudes acts on later development. True human progress requires elements quite other than these. If successful warfare made one nation unquestionably master of the earth, its social progress would not be promoted by that event. The rude hordes of Genghis Khan [1162?-1227] swarmed over Asia and into Europe, but remained rude hordes; conquest is not civilization, nor any part of it.

When the northern tribes-men overwhelmed the Roman culture they paralyzed progress for a thousand years or so; set back the clock by that much. So long as all Europe was at war, so long the arts and sciences sat still, or struggled in hid corners to keep their light alive.

When warfare itself ceases, the physical, social and psychic results do not cease. Our whole culture is still hag-ridden by military ideals.

Peace congresses have begun to meet, peace societies write and talk, but the monuments to soldiers and sailors (naval sailors of course), still go up, and the tin soldier remains a popular toy. We do not see boxes of tin carpenters by any chance; tin farmers, weavers, shoemakers; we do not write our "boys' books" about the real benefactors and servers of society; the adventurer and destroyer remains the idol of an androcentric culture.

In politics the military ideal, the military processes, are so predominant as to almost monopolize "that part of ethics."

The science of government, the plain wholesome business of managing a community for its own good; doing its work, advancing its prosperity, improving its morals—this is frankly understood and accepted as A Fight from start to finish. Marshall [sic] your forces and try to get in, this is the political campaign. When you are in, fight to stay in, and to keep the other fellow out. Fight for your own hand, like an animal; fight for your master like any hired bravo; fight always for some desired "victory"—and "to the victors belong the spoils."

This is not by any means the true nature of politics. It is not even a fair picture of politics to-day; in which man, the human being, is doing noble work for humanity; but it is the effect of man, the male, on politics.

Life, to the "male mind" (we have heard enough of the

"female mind" to use the analogue!) *is* a fight, and his ancient military institutions and processes keep up the delusion.

As a matter of fact life is growth. Growth comes naturally, by multiplication of cells, and requires three factors to promote it; nourishment, use, rest. Combat is a minor incident of life; belonging to low levels, and not of a developing influence socially.

The science of politics, in a civilized community, should have by this time a fine accumulation of simplified knowledge for diffusion in public schools; a store of practical experience in how to promote social advancement most rapidly, a progressive economy and ease of administration, a simplicity in theory and visible benefit in practice, such as should make every child an eager and serviceable citizen.

What do we find, here in America, in the field of "politics"?

We find first a party system which is the technical arrangement to carry on a fight. It is perfectly conceivable that a flourishing democratic government [could] be carried on *without any parties at all;* public functionaries being elected on their merits, and each proposed measure judged on its merits; though this sounds impossible to the androcentric mind.

"There has never been a democracy without factions and parties!" is protested.

There has never been a democracy, so far,—only an androcracy.

A group composed of males alone, naturally divides, opposes, fights; even a male church, under the most rigid rule, has its secret undercurrents of antagonism.

"It is the human heart!" is again protested. No, not essentially the human heart, but the male heart. This is so well recognized by men in general, that, to their minds, in this mingled field of politics and warfare, women have no place.

In "civilized warfare" they are, it is true, allowed to trail along and practice their feminine function of nursing; but this is no part of war proper, it is rather the beginning of the end of war. Sometime it will strike our "funny spot," these strenuous efforts to hurt and destroy, and these accompanying efforts to heal and save.

But in our politics there is not even provision for a nursing corps; women are absolutely excluded.

"They cannot play the game!" cries the practical politician. There is loud talk of the defilement, the "dirty pool" and its resultant darkening of fair reputations, the total unfitness of lovely woman to take part in "the rough and tumble of politics."

In other words men have made a human institution into an ultra-masculine performance; and, quite rightly, feel that women could not take part in politics *as men do*. That it is not necessary to fulfill this human custom in so masculine a way does not occur to them. Few men can overlook the limitations of their sex and see the truth; that this business of taking care of our common affairs is not only equally open to women and men, but that women are distinctly needed in it.

Anyone will admit that a government wholly in the hands of women would be helped by the assistance of men; that a gynae-cocracy must, of its own nature, be one-sided. Yet it is hard to win reluctant admission of the opposite fact; that an androcracy must of its own nature be one-sided also, and would be greatly improved by the participation of the other sex.

The inextricable confusion of politics and warfare is part of the stumbling block in the minds of men. As they see it, a nation is primarily a fighting organization; and its principal business is offensive and defensive warfare; therefore the ultimatum with which they oppose the demand for political equality—"women cannot fight, therefore they cannot vote."

Fighting, when all is said, is to them the real business of life; not to be able to fight is to be quite out of the running; and ability to solve our growing mass of public problems; questions of health, of education, of morals, of economics; weighs naught against the ability to kill.

This naive assumption of supreme value in a process never of the first importance[,] and increasingly injurious as society progresses, would be laughable if it were not for its evil effects. It acts and reacts upon us to our hurt. Positively, we see the ill effects already touched on; the evils not only of active war; but of the spirit and methods of war; idealized, inculcated and practiced in other social processes. It tends to make each man-managed nation an actual or potential fighting organization, and to give us, instead of civilized peace, that "balance of power" which is like the counted time in the prize ring—only a rest between combats.

It leaves the weaker nations to be "conquered" and "annexed" just as they used to be; with "preferential tariffs" instead of tribute. It forces upon each the burden of armament; upon many the dreaded conscription; and continually lowers the world's resources in money and in life.

Similarly in politics, it adds to the legitimate expenses of governing the illegitimate expenses of fighting; and must needs have a "spoils system" by which to pay its mercenaries.

In carrying out the public policies the wheels of state are continually clogged by the "opposition"; always an opposition on one side or the other; and this slow wiggling uneven progress, through shorn victories and haggling concessions, is held to be the proper and only political method.

"Women do not understand politics," we are told; "Women do not care for politics"; "Women are unfitted for politics."

It is frankly inconceivable, from the androcentric view-point, that nations can live in peace together, and be friendly and serviceable as persons are. It is inconceivable also, that, in the management of a nation, honesty, efficiency, wisdom, experience and love could work out good results without any element of combat.

The "ultimate resort" is still to arms. "The will of the majority" is only respected on account of the guns of the majority. We have but a partial civilization, heavily modified to sex—the male sex.

"Should Women Use Violence?" *

When the militant branch of the women suffragists of England began their career of "violence" by thrusting themselves into the House of Commons, waving flags, shouting, chaining themselves to grills, and getting themselves arrested, there was as much if not

* *Pictorial Review,* 14 (November 1912), pp. 11 and 78–79.

more condemnation aroused than we now hear for their later "outrages." [. . .]*

If the objection to the behavior of the militant suffragists is against violence *per se,* it can be held only by the strictest non-resistants. That is, it can be held logically only by them. If the objection is that the position of women in England does not call for violence, to answer that requires an intimate knowledge of English conditions. If it is, however, the commonly advanced one that women should never use violence, it becomes open ground for discussion.

The non-resistants hold an indisputable position—if their premise is granted. If human beings should never on any account resist evil, or anything else, then we must unhesitatingly condemn these misguided women for their campaign. But if we hold this ground we must as unhesitatingly condemn the soldiers of all time, including both sides in our Civil War, and our hitherto revered forefathers in the American Revolution, as well as every rebellion against tyranny and every fight for liberty in all history. There are very few who sincerely and thoroughly hold this position—not enough to call for serious argument. Most of us believe that violence is right—when justified. The other two objections are more open to discussion: Are women ever justified in using violence? Are these English women justified?

Let us quote on the side of those who condemn all violence on the part of women, the extremely urgent remarks of Sir Almroth Wright, M.D., on the subject. This gentleman attained a sudden burst of notoriety, immediately after the first [sic] window breaking affair in London, by a long letter to the *Times* of that city.† His general ground was the usual androcentric one that

* The Women's Social and Political Union (1903), deeply angry with the lack of response of the Liberal Party after its electoral victory in 1906, began to invite arrest by the place and manner of its demonstrations: picketing the houses of the government's chief ministers and heckling them when they spoke in public. When tried, the women chose prison over fines. In 1909, after laying siege to the House of Commons and breaking many windows, several hundred were arrested. When they went on a hunger strike, they were force fed. There was a lull during the debates over the government's "Conciliation Bill," but when it was tabled, in November 1910, new demonstrations were organized. Peaceful parades, during the summer of 1911, did not seem to advance the cause, so, in March 1912, a new window-smashing campaign began.

† Sir Almroth E. Wright (1861–1947) was an eminent bacteriologist and immunologist. His letter, nearly three full columns in length, was entitled "Sir Almroth Wright on

women are females and nothing else, to which he added the views
of one whose business deals mainly with sick women. The whole
mass of women who are most active in the woman's movement
he waved aside as hysterical spinsters or "perverts." Normal
women, from his standpoint, care only for marriage, housekeeping
and child care. All others are therefore abnormal—a point easily
established. But this medical man went even farther and stated
that all women were more or less crazy, just on account of being
women, saying, "No doctor can ever lose sight of the fact that the
mind of a woman is always threatened with danger from the
reverberations of her physiological emergencies."

In his whole long, perfervid letter nothing rouses him to more
passionate eloquence, however, than what he calls "the essential
point in the relation of women to violence." Under pressure of
the fierce emotion raised by this outrage against nature, he pro-
claims that there is an ethical law which forbids women ever to
use violence. Lest he be pressed too hard to show his revelation
or quote authority, he explains that his law "is not an ordinance
of man; it is not written in the statutes of any state; it has not
been enunciated by any human lawgiver. it belongs to those
unwritten and irreversible commandments of religion which we
suddenly and mysteriously become aware of when we see them
violated." This is sheer sentiment and emotion; absolutely unscientific, foundationless, beyond proof. It consists merely in saying, "I feel this way," or, more generally, "Men feel this way."
But what if they do? Is a popular emotional reaction of one sex an
unwritten and irreversible commandment of religion?

Freely granting that there is among men a general prejudice
against any use of violence by women, and granting that most
women have accepted this masculine prejudice as docilely as they
have so many others, we have proved nothing more than a popular
prejudice. Nothing is established to show it to be either wise or
right, much less to give it that mysterious sanction invoked by Sir
Almroth. As a matter of fact, if we admit violence to be ever

Militant Hysteria" (Times), March 28, 1912, pp. 7–8). It was reprinted in the book he
wrote on the subject, The Unexpurgated Case Against Woman Suffrage (London: Constable,
1913), pp. 77–86.

justified, may not a mother give battle in defense of her children? May not a maiden fight in defense of her honor? May not the women stand beside the men, wherever it is necessary, in common defense of home or country?

That females are not by nature as belligerent and combative as males is true enough; but the hen faces the hawk as fiercely as the cock faces his rival—and the hawk is more dangerous. Among all birds and beasts where fighting is part of the business of life, where the care of the family calls for killing, the female kills as readily as the male—and no one blames her for it. It is not "unfeminine" for the lioness or the osprey to use violence. Even a hen sparrow will peck if you put your hand in the nest.

When and where and how arose this masculine theory that women should never use violence? Does it find any explanation in the fact that of all male creatures man is the one who uses most violence against the female?

Another popular masculine myth assumes that man is woman's natural protector, though, as a matter of fact, he is often the worst danger she can hope to meet. This flowery piece of verbiage is handed down the ages as solemnly as its companion—that wherever there is evil *cherchez la femme*. One look at the heaped-up evils of the world ought to silence that last idiocy forever. The three greatest evils in history are war, intemperance and prostitution, and it takes a very masculine mind indeed to blame women for these, or for gambling, prize-fighting, business arson, a venal press, selling bad meat to soldiers or felonious assault upon little girls.

Yet with all these evils in his mind—we assume that he gave some thought to them—Sir Almroth Wright, insisting upon his mystic prohibition of any violence on the part of woman, says that for her "to violate any ordinance of that code is more dishonorable than to transgress every statutory law." Not any, please note, but "every." A woman is less to blame for theft, forgery and all the list of crimes and vices our statutes seek to check than for using violence—against man!

This is the kernel of the nut. Our natural protector has used what violence he pleased, throughout our gloomy history, toward the woman he assumed to have been "given him," for may not a man do what he will with his own? Not only by using his own physical force against hers to compel her to his will, but with the help of the accumulating forces of civilization—law, religion, education, public opinion—he has restrained, coerced, condemned and executed women in private and in public. Her relative lack of fighting strength or inclination, her periods of extra incapacity when bearing the burdens of maternity, her gentler natural tendencies, her acquired patience and submission under unbroken ages of tyranny, her lack of education and of experience and her comparative moneylessness—these ought, you would think, to have protected her protector sufficiently.

But some deep seated terror lurks within him, as shown in Kipling's plaintive, reiterant poem, "The Female of the Species Is More Deadly Than the Male [1911]."* In spite of all the heaped-up disabilities mentioned, the age-long habit of endurance and the general condition of dependence, there remained a possibility that sometime, somewhere, somehow, women *might* "hit back." At the first sign of it out rushes the inspired lawgiver from that Sinai, *The London Times,* and enunciates this hitherto unknown commandment—"unwritten, unassailable, irreversible." He is not so secure as he thinks; it is no longer unwritten, for he has written it, and has so become the laughing stock of the century. It is not unassailable, but is being assailed by many ready pens that call in vain for him to prove his words. As to its being irreversible, if he means that it never can be applied to men, he is quite right. If he means, however, that it cannot be laughed at, set aside and forgotten, he is quite wrong.

The deep seated popular feeling against feminine violence is based not on a distinction of sex so much as a distinction in status. Women must not "rebel" against their owners and masters Their submissiveness is that of the child, or of the servant who stands mute under reproof because it is not "her place" to "answer back." The sense of outrage felt by Sir Almroth Wright, M.D., is analogous to what he would experience if his child, being spanked,

---

* Rudyard Kipling's Verse: Inclusive Edition, 1885–1918 (Garden City, N.Y.: Doubleday, Page, 1922), pp. 418–421.

should leap at him with a razor; or his cook, being reprimanded, should knock him down with a gridiron.

Women are expected to put up with whatever is done to them. They may wheedle, beg and tease, maneuver and use tricks and falsehoods. They may with no blame whatever play upon the major weakness of their masters—this we call "feminine influence;" but they must on no account hit back—this is *lèse-majesté.*

In plain fact there is no reason whatever why the female of genus *homo* should not use violence whenever it is necessary, as much as the female of genus *canis, felis, cervus,* or any other. If the dangerous negroes of the black belt knew that every white woman carried a revolver and used it with skill and effect there would be less lynching needed. If would be better that one woman should shoot than that a hundred men should burn and otherwise suffer torture. Ever since small firearms were invented, women have been safe, or should have been safe from assault. Even back of that, a knife in the garter was protection from "an Austrian lover."* Girls of to-day taught ju-jutsu [sic] or even a little plain skill in wrestling and boxing, are far safer from the attacks of casual "protectors" than they once were. [. . .]

If [the militant suffragists'] cause is a just one and their course wisely chosen, there is no reason whatever why they should be "feminine" or "ladylike" in this field of conduct. These adjectives have no weight whatever outside the processes of sex. A woman should be feminine in her capacity of sweetheart, wife and mother, as the lover, husband and father should be masculine; but in the whole range of human activities, in all of our life above the sex line, there is no need to be either masculine or feminine. An astronomer, an artist, a shoemaker, a cook, may be by chance either a male or female; but there is no call for sex qualities in the work. You do not have to be "masculine" or "feminine" as an administrator, inventor, discoverer or executive; if you are, it is apt to interfere with your task. It was distinctly unfeminine and unladylike for Jeanne d'Arc [1412–1431] to take to plate armor and cross-saddle riding; but she is not blamed for it—in later history. She was at the time.

* Rapist?

(The last question, are these women justified in their particular acts of violence at this time, is the most difficult one for an
American writer to answer.)

It is impossible to put yourself in the place of women of
another country confronted with a different opponent; under
different conditions, and having a different history to look back
upon. The specific weight of their grounds of complaint, the
irritating effect of the quality of opposition they have met, the
relative value of the methods of attack chosen—these are things
impossible for an outside to judge discriminatingly. It is true that
among English women, even among English suffragists, there is
condemnation of the proceedings of the militant branch; but even
that resolves itself into a question of judgment, as in a difference
in military policy among generals.

The outside observer should be cautioned to mingle many
grains of salt with the reports given by newspapers. Even where
the intention is honest and unbiased and where some measure of
discriminating ability is added to the intention, we must remember
that the whole weight of the world's prejudice is against the
rebellious woman. When the struggling suffragettes struck a policeman the world rang with the outrage. That the policeman used
not only cruel violence but gross indecency in making his arrests
made no impression—was not reported. When a slim, enthusiastic girl or a nervous, high-keyed little woman arose to question
the speaker in a public meeting, a common English custom, this
insolence was reported across the ocean. That several men at once
should seize, beat, throw down and drag out the interrupter made
no impression—was not reported. [. . .]

To those who think women have no other uses but those of
femininity, no other legitimate hopes, desires or duties, the whole
woman's movement is abnormal.

By those who agree that common justice, equality before the
law and personal freedom are good for women as for men, some
parts of the woman's movement are welcomed and approved.

By those who feel that the most important step in the world's
development to-day lies in the *humanizing of women,* the whole

movement is recognized as good, though in its minor and local efforts it may often err.

It would be impossible to expect as great a movement as this, involving a change of status for half of the human race, and carried on for the most part by a small number of the subjected class, to avoid all mistakes. Whether the special bit of heroism which has set that gallant band of English women to breaking windows and trying to shake the Premier* is wholly mistaken, no present-day observer can say. But we can give them credit for immeasurable courage.

"Our Brains and What Ails Them."

Chapter VIII: What Education Does to Us†

[. . .] Human life is identical with social life; one may enjoy all of what we call "the necessities of life" and yet not live at all— humanly speaking; as in the case of a warm, well-fed idiot. But education, when it cut loose from action; when it confined itself to knowing things and despised doing things; really cut itself off from Life.

The brain's ultimate use is that of a transmitter—a transmitter of power into action. Living consists of doing things; to know them is merely a preliminary. Where the brain is developed as a container, and not used as a transmitter, it becomes abnormal. In this abnormality it has developed one ultra-ridiculous perversion of function; a thing so incredibly absurd that it would be impossible to any creature but the human, with our enormous system of mutual support which allows for such a margin of usefulness— and mischief. The human brain, forcibly developed through so many ages as a container, has produced on the one hand a morbid passion for learning, in which the sufferer seeks continually to stuff himself with information and is never satisfied; and on the other, being pushed to it by its innate capacity for transmitting, develops a kind of vicious circle, or spiral, rather, in which good,

* Prime Minister Herbert Asquith (1852–1928).
† *The Forerunner,* 3 (August 1912), pp. 217–221.

useful, human brains spend their youth in acquiring a quantity of knowledge for the sole purpose of teaching it to others—that they may teach it to others—forever and ever, none of this knowledge ever touching the earth as it were. Such education never "comes out" at all; it merely flows on from mind to mind, like endless generations of unborn children.

These peculiar developments in education find their origin in the early priesthoods, based on the adventitious value attached to what they considered right belief, and on the very practical value of the knowledge of certain arts and mysteries which they for so long monopolized. This does not involve blame for any individuals or for any particular religion. Social functions have their laws of growth like any other life processes, and are as liable to eccentricity and disease. As in the physical organism health requires the normal use of every part, and neglect or misuse invites disease, exactly so in the organic life of society, unless a given social process is properly used it tends to become deformed and diseased.

Religion, for instance, is a distinctly social development, but for its normal use it must be felt and practiced by all; it cannot be followed as a profession, by a few, and its benefits extended to others, as in dentistry or architecture. Owing, however, to the initial mistake of making religion a trade, a means of support, this universal psychic process became instead a limited economic process, with the necessary morbid results of such confusion of function. A slight study of religious history clearly shows the more conspicuous effects of this; the inevitable corruption of religion as it became economically prosperous and powerful, and the constant pushing forth of healthy sprouts of true religion, always in courageous poverty, always pressing out from the priestly cult to reach the whole people.

We are not here following these broad results, but wish merely to indicate how the professional priesthood seized upon the mental faculties as their stronghold, and strove to monopolize the brains of the world and the training of them.

If only the beginning of mental culture, as developed by men fed on sacrifices and free to think, could have been put in circulation at once; made a social gain instead of a class gain; we should have had a very different history. But, following lines of class power and class aggrandizement, the priests and scholars remained one for many ages, and when the irresistible social demand tore education from the cloisters, it was so heavily clericalized that our few brief centuries of partial liberty have by no means freed us from its influence.

We are generally familiar with the main lines of modern growth in education—the steps toward knowledge applied in action of the manual training system; the development of powers of observation and reasoning by the laboratory system; and at last, a movement among that sub-clerical set of subjects, our teachers, for freedom and dignity in the performance of their office.

Education is perhaps the most valuable of social functions, if one can so differentiate in organic values; yet it is even among us in the United States to-day so heavily encumbered with vestigial rudiments, with ancient prejudices, with the slow, stiff, creaking disability of unused powers, that it leaves plenty of room for free discussion and suggestions of further improvement.

We have to consider, in a study of results of education; first, the superficial effect of the information acquired; and second, the deep and lasting effects of the methods of acquirement upon the brain. Here we have a system of brain handling now practically universal among us—or at least we strive to make it so—in which every child is submitted to a certain process; as far as possible to the same process.

What, if we could see it, is the effect of this process on the childish brain?

There is some marked error in our process; some trouble of the gravest importance—this is widely felt; and education has almost as many healthy revolutionaries as religion.

As a perfectly natural social process this great function is accompanied by the normal organic stimulus of desire, and rewarded by the pleasure of fulfillment of function. Wherever we find it working normally we find both these phenomena: every healthy mind dearly loves both to teach and to learn. Since "teaching" and "learning" have become weighed down with many technical associations, I hasten to explain that "learning," as here used, means the receipt of new impressions, and "teaching," the transference of superior knowledge. A normal brain, from ravenous infancy to hale old age, eagerly enjoys new impressions, and as eagerly enjoys the sensation of knowing more than the other fellow and being able to "tell him how."

If education were normal we would find it a wide, free, subtly adjusted system of transference of knowledge wherein each and all could delightedly bring their minds to be fed, life-long; and wherein those most gifted as teachers: i. e., most enjoying the active side of that transference, could delightedly do the feeding.

In place of this we find a singularly complete perversion of function. Learning, that process of life-long joy, has become a prison sentence; rigid confinement of body; forcible feeding of brain; during the years which suffer most under such treatment —childhood. And teaching, noblest of human arts, exquisite pleasure of touching brain to brain and feeling the current of power pour through; pleasure as of a nursing mother; pleasure as of an artist and benefactor; personal delight in the process and glorious conviction of its immense social value—this we have made a nerve-exhausting treadmill, acting to most injure the best teachers and tending to maintain duller and less able minds in that office.

In the mechanical field of life we are continually making progress, developing newer, quicker, easier, cheaper, better ways of doing things. In religion, as shown in the previous chapter, there has been ceaseless effort to maintain the oldest possible methods and beliefs; and in education, the after effects of religion are still painfully visible.

For instance, one of the very oldest religious concepts maintains that there is virtue in pain and difficulty. The underlying truth lies far, far back—the savage's hardening processes by which he schooled himself to bear hardship, effort and torture— the inert race mind retaining the associate sense of virtue in those processes long after they ceased to be useful. Running to unchecked excess in that fenceless field of mental activity detached from life, this became the doctrine of asceticism, an almost universal tenet of early religions. There is no extreme to which this morbid tendency has not cheerfully gone—death being nothing to it; celibacy a trifle; imprisonment for life welcome; and the bitterest tortures accepted triumphantly.

Nothing could better prove the dangerous nature of brain processes detached from their natural relation to life. This alone would have led to the prompt extinction of humanity, but for the overwhelming healthiness of the average mind, which would not accept it. But, with our social power of keeping alive the useless and injurious; and with the tremendous grip of that organized mentality which for so long found its only expression through the church, we have maintained throughout the ages a body of doctrines revered and accepted as doctrines even when mercifully withheld from expression; and of these none is more mischievous than this deep-seated racial error of the virtue of suffering.

Our present beliefs are not, for the most part, new inventions. If you look carefully at your beliefs you find them to rest on other beliefs, older, less defensible; and because the group of concepts covered by religion was not to be studied and thought about it has remained intact for a longer time than any other groups— unless it be those concerning sex.

Transmitted from the church to the school, this ancient error finds its continuing result in our common belief that it is good for the children to have a hard time there. Because some fifty thousand years ago the little savage, doomed to hunger and thirst, to cold and pain, was fitted for it by forced endurance of these evils, therefore—consider the stretch of that "therefore"!—our children must be made to undergo the "discipline" of the school that they may the better bear "the discipline of life." Now take that long-attenuated "therefore" which has stretched all down the ages without a leg to stand on and look at this end of it—for once.

Will anyone show how the arbitrary dreariness of our "system of education" fits for life—for Human Life, to-day?

Children in school must sit in fixed seats at regular distances in large groups for long hours. When, out of school, will they ever be required to do this? In church, you say. Exactly. That is where the idea came from. They must sit there in decorous silence and unnatural quiet because congregations must so sit, in order that they may be preached to. Now education is not preaching.

In school, children are required to continually use their minds in learning and remembering statements oral and written. When, out of school, is this required of people?

In school, children are continually required to regurgitate what they have learned, to "pass examinations" at stated intervals — to see if they know what they know. When, out of school, is this required of people?

"But," it will be earnestly advanced, "we have to take this period of their lives to fill their minds with knowledge they will need afterward and have not time to acquire."

Now will any man, in any business whatever, or any woman, in a business or out of it, stand up and explain how much of what they learned in school they ever use in life? Take any group of a hundred middle-aged people and put them through an examination as to what they learned when they were in school. Precious little could they recite to-day of what was so glib upon their tongues at ten or twelve. And of what they do remember, what is the use in life?

Our "therefore" does not fit.

The things we teach are selected according to standards centuries behind us and the methods we use are those of the black, forgotten past. Our study here is not so much to account for this, nor to suggest improvements, but to show its effect upon the brain.

As to matter: the child learns things necessary and unnecessary, without regard to real social values, and in so doing accustoms the mind to false perspective and relation. Still worse, he is thus arbitrarily accustomed to dissociate learning from doing, and shows the same silly pride in "knowing" this or that which distinguishes the "scholars' of the dark ages, or the suffering candidates for a mandarinship* in the dynasty of Ming [1368–1644].

Some necessary, some valuable, some beautiful things he learns;

* The nine highest ranks of public office in imperial China.

but much that is none of these, and never to distinguish between them.

Far more important, is the manner of his education. The most glaring first effect is that of forcible feeding. No words can exaggerate the outrage and injury which is thus perpetrated upon the brain as an organ. The appetite of the brain is as necessary to the healthful acquirement of knowledge as the appetite of the stomach to the healthful acquirement of food. If the brain is normal, not over used and exhausted, it keeps that appetite for life.

Our education, seizing upon the child mind, forces it, under various penalties to "pay attention" and to receive, among its limp, reluctant cells, information for which it has no desire; in receiving which it takes no pleasure; the retention of which is as arbitrary an act as the holding of pebbles in the mouth. An enormous share of the dull indifference of the average mind to any knowledge, of its case-hardened callosity to efforts to impress it, is directly due to this abominable mishandling of the brain in childhood.

As if it were not enough to force into the mind what it does not want we then add that incredible use of the stomach pump —the examination. This is more foreign to any natural function of the brain than the similar act is to the stomach. The stomach, being poisoned or over-full, tends to relieve itself that way. The brain has no such muscles. Its only safety is in forgetting. Most mercifully we do forget most of our education, but education does all it can to prevent it. Over and over the child is required to forcibly bring out what we forcibly put in. The result on the brain as an organ is to make of it a worn and withered wallet, a mere bag, to be stuffed and turned inside out at pleasure. By so far as this process is effective do we lose our most precious mental capacities; that eager questing appetite for knowledge, that subtle and reliable arrangement and correlation of ideas, their easy retention and prompt reappearance when wanted, which distinguish the normal brain. It is common knowledge that our most useful minds are by no means identical with those best educated. Too much is lost in the process.

One other gross evil marks our educative process—the competitive system. Anything more foreign than this to real brain culture it would be hard to find. The competitive instinct is wholly androcentric, being in origin, a sex-characteristic of the male. Through his monopoly of all specialized professions he has inevitably infected them with this spirit.

As a masculine sex-instinct competition is healthy, right and proper. By means of it males compete for the favor of females, to the improvement of the species. As a social instinct it is wholly out of place, and therefore mischievous. In economics it detracts from wealth rather than adds to it. In all trades and professions it degrades, and in the higher social functions, the arts, the sciences, in religion, in education, its evil results are most evident.

We use this sex-instinct as an incentive to spur the flagging energies of little children. We have, by making it an integral part of education sought to develop it in girls as well as boys, though grossly foreign to their natures, and made it a common force in life. This is absolute social injury. As well might we set children to compete in eating as to compete in learning. Brains differ. *In their difference lies their social value.*

When we can muster strength enough to really let go of the worst and oldest mistakes of our ancestors, and let our brains grow; when we are strong-minded enough and clear-minded enough to see what education might be to us; then we shall enter a period of mental growth which it is good to contemplate.

Think of a magnificent body of specialists who loved teaching better than any work, and were free to teach. Think of the ceaseless effort from generation to generation, to so simplify, classify, and relate necessary knowledge as to make it absorbable with the least effort. Think of the delicate, varied arts with which such knowledge might be arranged, like a great tempting garden before the child mind. Think of the careful study to distinguish those priceless social benefits—the variations in brains; and to cultivate them. Think of every little young brain, fed and never forced, exercised and never tired, growing in freedom and eager joy, and each bringing to the problems of life its special complement of power and individual capacity.

In those days teachers will not be brow-beaten by cheapjack politicians; "feminization" will be no more dreaded then [sic] "masculinization"; and people will learn throughout life—and enjoy it.

Chapter IX: The Effect of the Position of Woman on the Race Mind*

[. . .] The brain is the organ of humanity, the essential base of social life, the means and measure of its existence. Social life is as imperative in its instincts and appetites as any other form of life. The brain, its dominating organ, cries for use, for exercise, and suffers without it like a man in prison. If one wishes to gather a sense of pain to last throughout life, cast one shuddering look down the ages at the condition of women's brains. Each girl born with as much brain as her brother. Each woman, throughout her entire life, denied the use of it, suffering her life long the gnawing of an unappeasable appetite—a wholly natural and righteous appetite, the strongest appetite in human life—that of the soul, as we call it; the psychic demand for association, specialization and interchange.

None of these things for her. Personally she was kept alive and well or ill-treated as it happened; but kept alive at least long enough for reproduction, else the race perished. Maternally she was encouraged, yes forced, to full activity. But for the whole range of faculties and interests which distinguish the civilized man from the savage, none were for her save a few partial and perverse activities like those of what we designate with such exquisite absurdity—"Society."

As to the results of this deprivation, history is luminous and loud. The demand of a healthy brain for the information denied it we have called "feminine curiosity." The uneasiness of a brain so starved on the larger side, so over-developed on the lesser, we have called "feminine unrest." Whatever morbid results appeared from this wholly morbid condition we unhesitatingly set down to the peculiarities of sex, and having produced a paradoxical, contradictory, sub-human, extra-human creature, we regarded it with fond pride and sagely remarked: "Woman is an enigma." If we

---

* *The Forerunner*, 3 (September 1912), pp. 247–251.

had done this to some outside creation, producing our amusing monstrosity in tree or flower, the results would have been less injurious. The deadly work was done upon the human race—and the most important half for its effect upon the whole—the mother.

These were women. Men had to live with them to some degree. Children were born of them; children were reared by them—the earliest years of education were left to the uneducated. That transmission of thought and feeling from mind to mind which is so essential to the human life was denied to half of it.

To be human we must congregate—associate—exchange. Women must not. They must remain in the original pre-human relation, that of the family, in its separate dwelling. How they have seeped and leaked out of their isolation whenever possible. How they have gathered together, irresistibly, at the well, in the market place, in the ball-room, in the church. Human beings *must* associate, must exchange, must engage in collective activities. It is the imperative governing condition of human life. Women have done what they could at it—under criticism.

And the men? Being human they had to combine. Being male they had to compete. History becomes more luminous—and louder. Men had to get together, specialize, produce and exchange, and they have done so freely, splendidly; building the world we have so long—shall we say enjoyed?

But they were males; preponderantly males; and their maleness has been grievously in the way of their humanness. Fight they must; the masculine instinct to overcome and to destroy competitors; and our smooth fruitful human progress has been visibly jarred by this untoward complication. If the women had been there, human too—but they were not. The women were at home, being females.

So the human brain has grown, by normal use and exercise, in the male; and been stunted, denied normal use and exercise in the female; and the more normal brain has been injured by the unavoidable contact with the less normal, and the race-brain—

the common inheritance of us all—has been steadily robbed and weakened by the injury to the mother-half.

This is the effect of the position of women on the brain. Let us follow it more in detail; first personally, upon the woman's mind; then reactively, upon the man's; and then, through inheritance, association, and direct education, upon the child's.

The "feminine mind" to which we so feelingly allude, in which we point out such deep-seated ineradicable differences from the male mind, is not a sex-mind, but a class-mind. Its mysterious peculiarities are by no means due to the female sex, but are due to the artificial environment with which that sex has been surrounded. "Homekeeping youths have ever homely wits." The one bald fact that women have been kept shut up, confined to the house, in varying degrees of imprisonment, while men have been free to move, both locally and abroad, is enough to explain most of that "subtle, baffling, wonderful" difference.

If men had been arbitrarily divided into two classes; if half of them had been given the range of all the trades, crafts, arts and sciences, all education, all experience, and achievement, and the other half shut up at home, never allowed out alone, and taken under escort to only a small part of life's attractions; confined exclusively to a few primitive industries; denied education as well as experience, we would find mysterious, subtle, baffling differences between the two classes.

Of later years, in some countries, education in the technical sense has been gradually extended to women; and they have shown a singularly human capacity for absorbing it. Even in the ages behind us, wherever women were given education, no baffling differences in brains prevented their receiving it as readily as their brothers. When our modern colleges refused admission to women, the old objection was that their minds were incapable of competing with those of the young men. Now an objection to co-education is that it puts too great a strain upon the young man to compete with the woman.

Education, in so far as it consists in learning from books and lectures, presents no difficulties to the "feminine mind." The difference which does present itself, in varying degree, and which is not steadily diminishing, is in the *attitude toward life*.

"The feminine mind," we say, is more submissive, less critical, less argumentative, less experimental; it lacks initiative; and then we proudly repeat that "no mind of the highest order has appeared among women." A favorite clincher, added to this, is that even in music, where women have had every advantage and encouragement, we have no leading feminine composer.

There is no question whatever as to the statements given, but questions many and searching as to the underlying facts, and especially as to definitions. Remember that the whole measure of merit and honor in the world is masculine; the judges are masculine; and that all our human achievements, so far, are heavily masculinized. We have made our disparaging distinctions as to "the female mind," but it has never occurred to us to consider "the male mind" and its limitations.

It is true that the brain is not a sex-distinction; either of man or woman; but it is also true that as an organ developed by use it is distinctly modified by the special activities of the user. If the lifelong activities of the individual are sharply differentiated along sex lines, then the brain is reactively affected. Men have the advantage of the whole range of human experience to develope the human brain; but they have the disadvantage of being more heavily modified to sex, by nature, than the woman.

The female of the species is more nearly the race type; the male is more especially the sex-type. This we have never seen because of the universal assumption that the dominant masculine tastes, abilities and instincts were human. They are not in the least human; they are merely masculine, distinguishing all male creatures, human or not. The dominant masculine characteristics are Desire, Combat, and Self-Expression. These have heavily colored all human life, in every department; and in their associative reaction have modified the race-mind male-wards. This over-developed "male mind" naturally considers any divergent action shown by the other sex as "female"; whereas it may not be female at all, but merely human.

When all the honors of the world were given to Military

Conquerors and the adored Climax of such Superiority was found in that megalomaniac destroyer, Napoleon [1769–1821]—of course no female name could be rated so high. When we honor constructive industry as much as warfare we shall have more female heroes. When we honor illimitable endurance as much as combativeness; when we recognize the anti-social quality of the ultra-male belligerence, and the social value of the adaptable, persistent serviceableness we have hitherto considered "female," we shall put up other monuments than those to soldiers. After a few centuries of full human usefulness on the part of the women, we shall have not only new achievements to measure, but new standards of measurement.

This will give a new view of "the feminine mind." It will be seen that those qualities in which it differs from "the male mind" are not necessarily female ones; that she is nearer the norm than he; that he often does the differing, branching off widely from essential human qualities in the direction of mere masculinity.

When all this [is] said, and appreciated, it remains true that the majority of women to date, have not succeeded in developing a degree of brain power other that that produced by their conditions; and have not succeeded in wringing from a male world any recognition of admiration for anything in particular except their feminine qualities—which were all that the male world wanted of them. It is not feminine qualities which distinguish the minds of women so sharply; it is the quality of domestic labor; they are heavily modified by kitchen service, by parlor imprisonment. The major lack in the minds of women is in experience. Beginning with childhood, when the boy is allowed to be out on the platform asking questions, and the girl is compelled to sit still, pulling her offensively short skirts over inoffensively long legs, the boy knows more about things than the girl possibly can. He knows more streets, more places, more people, more processes, more "life." This difference increases with their growth. It is quite true, blessedly true, that this is all changing today; that our girls are rapidly losing that fine know-nothing "bloom," which gave such disproportionate and gratifying superiority to any "male mind;" that "bloom" which is brushed off so soon by exercise, which disappears so quickly in the light of knowledge. This makes us wonder if, after all, it was bloom—or perhaps mould.

But heretofore, and still to a great extent, this is the major disability of the "feminine mind"—mere lack of information and experience. It remains a heavy handicap even now. The judgment of women is narrowed because they do not know the premises. Our tardy allowance of school and college education does not give knowledge of life.

The next great lack is in responsibility. Suppose that life required an assured skill in the art of sailing. Suppose that in the first instance girls were never allowed in boats, nor taught anything about them. Suppose, secondly, they were occasionally "taken sailing," but never allowed to touch rope or tiller. Suppose, thirdly, they were really taught sailing—by the use of models, but though they could pass oral examinations, they were never allowed to sail a boat. To be human today, in a civilized country, requires the trained intelligence of big business men (not the malefactors, but the real workers) and that intelligence is not developed except by doing big business.

If Andrew Carnegie had passed his life between kitchen, bedroom, and parlor, he might have been esteemed and beloved by those who profited by his services, but would not be a planter of libraries and a promoter of world peace.

A girl may lead her brother in school and college, and then continue to amass "culture" for the rest of her life, but that does not develope the human faculties of the brain. Our humanity requires those basic conditions, Association, Specialization, Interchange. The acquisition of knowledge for private consumption is not a social function. Suppose her brother, after his valedictory address, spent the rest of his life as a private housekeeper; would his "education" suffice to occupy and exercise his mind?

We quote in blissful acquiescence [Alfred] Tennyson's [1809–1892] dictum: "For woman is not undeveloped man, but diverse."* If he had said "female is not undeveloped male, but diverse," which is what he meant, and what we all mean, he would have

---

* "The Princess: Part Seventh," lines 258–259, in *The Complete Poetical Works of Tennyson* (Boston: Houghton Mifflin, 1898), p. 159.

been quite correct. But if by man he meant "human," he is exactly wrong. Women are undeveloped human beings, that is what ails them; and their brains are more severely affected than their bodies.

It is bad enough to see the bodies of women so excessively modified to sex that they almost lose the power of locomotion, but it is worse to see their minds so excessively modified by the narrow range of exercise allowed them that they live in a sort of prehistoric state of sub-social domesticity. If we could see it, if it could be expressed to us pictorially, it would be as if Mr. Horse was mated to Mrs. Eohippus—the same species, but a trifle behind the times. If we did mate our horses thus, it would have a curious effect on the strain of trotters.

It has a curious effect on humanity. Men are always being bewildered, puzzled, enraged, by the unaccountable discrepancies they discover between their minds and women's. they have explained it all by [the] simple sweeping attribute of sex—women were that way—because they were peculiar. Why the female of genus homo should be so mysterious while the female of other species was so easily comprehensible they did not ask. And they did not concern themselves much about this abysmal difference between their minds, because it was not their minds that they married. So long as white men cheerfully, though temporarily, mate with African and Indian, Hawaiian and Filipino, we cannot expect them to be very critical about their wives' brains. The brains of women are less developed humanly, but their taste in selection is certainly higher than man's.

The brain difference remains a serious race disadvantage, however, whether men object to it or not.

If white men continually married their Semgambian* transients, and reared families by them, the race mind would be markedly affected. Even the scant association of home life, from which most men escape as far as possible, has its benumbing and belittling effect on the minds of men. "Women talk about such

* The correct term is Senegambian, a derogatory term for blacks. It derives from the Province of Senegambia, a merger of the former French colonies of Senegal and Gambia by the United Kingdom in 1765. The province was returned to France in 1783.

little things!" said one disgusted man. He thought it was because they were women. What does he talk about? He "talks shop"— his business, whatever it is; and he "talks politics"—the world business, as far as he touches it. He talks of his experience and his responsibilities. So does she. But her experience is identical with that of her million sisters for all the years, sex experience and household experience. The mental effects of the first she cannot share with him; the mental effects of the second he flees from.

The wider-experienced, more-socially developed man seeks woman as a female—and avoids her as a friend and companion.

"On Ellen Key and the Woman Movement" *

That great Swedish thinker and lover, Ellen Key, in her book on "The Woman Movement," translated by M. B. Borthwick, and published here by G. P. Putnam's Sons [New York, 1912], has voiced with power and beauty her conception of woman's place in life.

In the course of her book she gives special attention, and opposition, to what she names "the amaternal theory," using the Greek prefix, as in the word "asexual," and in this opposition my name and work is mentioned.

When lecturing in Europe in 1904 and 1905 I was told that Ellen Key considered my work as in strong antithesis to hers, but I was unable to see why, as I found myself in full agreement with so much, so very much of her teaching. Neither in "The Century of the Child," nor in "Love and Marriage" did I find much antithesis made clear, but in this book it comes out so strongly that a definite discussion is possible. Certain things are brought forward in her treatment of the woman movement which emphasize the difference between the European and the American woman's attitude toward life. She speaks continually and insistently of the development of personality, of individuality, among modern women, and seems to miss entirely the attitude of social service which fills our country with earnest women who seek freedom

* *The Forerunner*, 4 (February 1913), pp. 35–38.

and power, not for themselves, but in order to benefit the community.

Self-culture, self-expression, personal liberty, are desired and attained, but the moving spirit of our thousand woman's clubs and summer schools is the stir of newborn social conscience. That this is so is proven by the attitude of our humorists, satirists, and pen-mercenaries generally, who when the wish to ridicule the "advanced women," represent them as engaged in futile or mischievous attempts at charity, reform, education.

What Ellen Key looks forward to as "social motherliness" is already at work in the American woman; not yet with smooth efficiency, it is true, but in the right direction.

The position so strongly and repeatedly defined by the Swedish feminist is this:

The object of our life is the improvement of human beings; the improvement of human beings is best attained by the right birth and rearing of children. To this end we need the full development of the individual character of both men and women through education, association, freedom, work and love. To this end also we need the consecration of the individual mother to her children.

Now I am not primarily "a feminist," but a humanist. My interest in the position of woman, in the child, in the home is altogether with a view to their influence upon human life, happiness and progress.

My position is this:

The object of our life is the improvement of social relations; the improvement of social relations is best attained by the right performance of social functions, i.e., all forms of human work which benefit society. To this end we need the full development of individual service in both men and women, through education, association, freedom, work and love—human love. To this end also we need a social motherhood.

The vital points of difference between the two views are these:

She speaks of the whole range of enlarging social activity on the part of women as a means of earning a personal livelihood, or of self-expression, allowing for a special field of elevating or reformation efforts as "social service," and she assumes that the best education of the child requires the continuous devotion of the individual mother.

I hold that the enlarging range of social activity on the part of women is a social duty, not a personal one, and that the best education of a child requires the devotion of specialists besides that of the mother.

I will make one quotation to show the difference in the first point:

"For the universally human characteristics, forced to remain latent in the primitive division of labor because the father was obliged to exercise all his strength in one direction and the mother in another, can now, through the facilities of culture in the struggle for existence, be developed on both sides: woman can develop the latent quality which became active in man as 'manliness'; man can develop the latent quality which became active in woman as 'womanliness.' " [Pp. 218–219.] She goes on with the usual division of human qualities into male and female ones.

Now I hold that "the universal human characteristics" have no sex connotation whatever. Sex distinction we share with all the higher animals, and even our own special and advantageous development in sex qualities is not at all the same thing as our development in human qualities.

The improvement of agriculture, industry, commerce, art, education, religion—these things have nothing whatever to do with "manliness" or "womanliness," with "fatherhood" or "motherhood."

Ellen Key, with the rest of the world, fails to recognize that the distinction of species is far larger and more important than the distinction of sex. Our humanness is a quality common to both sexes, and the evil of the previous position of women is that they were confined to the exercise of sex faculties only—however nobly developed, and denied the exercise of the human ones.

The reason that women need the fullest freedom in human development—and this means not merely education but action

—is twofold: it is needed because women are half the people of the world and the world needs their service *as people,* not only as women; and secondly—here I think Ellen Key agrees to a certain extent—that women as women, i.e., as mothers, need full human development in order to transmit it to their children.

Doing human work is what develops human character. Human work is specialized activity in some social function—any art, craft, trade or profession that serves society.

What society most lacks to-day is the capacity of individuals to feel and think *collectively,* to grasp social values, to recognize, care for, and serve social needs, to see in the common business of life, not personal expression or personal aggrandizement, but social service. The reason we lack this capacity is that half the world has been denied the means to develop it. Women, in specializing as human beings in some trade or profession, are serving both the individual and the collective needs of their children; they help make a better world, and they make better children.

Here we approach the second point of difference, an unbridgeable chasm.

If Ellen Key—with the whole world behind her—is right, then I am absolutely and utterly, foolishly and mischievously wrong. The mass of authority, the intensity of feeling, the duration of a conviction, are, however, no faintest proof of its continuing value. The whole world was always against the proposal of any new idea.

The old assumption is that the interests of the child are best served by the continuous and exclusive devotion of the individual mother.

The new assumption is that the interests of the child are best served by the additional love and care, teaching and example, of other persons, specialists in child culture. Note the word "additionally"; I have never once, in writing, or from platform or pulpit, denied the right and duty or the joy and pride of every normal woman to be a mother, to bear her children, to suckle her children, to provide—assisted by the father—the best conditions for their offspring. What I do deny, absolutely, is that the individual mother is, or ever can be, all sufficient as an educator of humanity.

The individual animal mother is so sufficient because animals do not specialize as we do. One conspicuous quality of humanity is in its profound personal distinctions. A kitten or a cub is a kitten or a cub—and may be efficiently care[d] for by its mother; but each child varies from the other, and from its parents, in ever-widening degree, and for the understanding and right handling of this human quality our children need not only love, but the widest experience.

This is forever denied the mother.

Not only are some women far better fitted for child care by their natural talents than other women; not only are some women far better fitted for it by opportunities of training; but this remains the hopeless impossibility: so long as each woman takes all the care of her children herself, no woman on earth can ever have the *requisite experience*. This is final.

The human child needs first and always the mother's love, but he needs in ever increasing addition to this the love and care and service of those socially specialized to this great end, giving their lives to it; mothers personally, whenever possible, but mothers socially, for life.

Let me repeat; this does not exclude the personal mother; it does not rob the child of his mother's love, but it gives him also another love, wider and infinitely more experienced.

That woman who loves children more than anything else in the world, who gladly consecrates her life to their care and service, who studies all the little that is now known of child-culture and begins to lay the foundations of a real science in that noble field, who cares for children, teaches children, year after year her life long—she will be one who will "understand" where even mother love falls short. Mother love does not give human understanding. Ellen Key beautifies and extols an ideal Mother who is all-wise and unfailing in intelligent tendencies.

Not all women are such—nor ever can be. The woman who is should spread the wings of her great love over more children than her own, and the less competent thankfully accept her help.

Another minor point of difference is in the assumption, always made, that when a woman has a profession she will therefore be unable to give love and care to her home and family. This assumption rests of course on another—that the home must always be a group of undifferentiated industries as it has been for so long, and that the woman must do both kinds of work at once.

When there is no work done at home the constant presence of the wife there becomes absurd, and when, at last, we make fit places for little children to learn life in, with fit persons to teach them, the constant presence of the mother is also unnecessary.

For the necessary time required for the work of the world, father, mother and child, may be out of the home, and yet when father, mother and child return—it is home indeed.

To Ellen Key the thought and purpose, the enthusiasm and devotion a woman puts into her work is taken from her home, her husband, her child, and she holds, again with the whole world behind her, that it is good for husband, home and child to have the entire devotion of a woman's life. Against this stands the new ideal, the human ideal—that for every one of us the main devotion of life should be to Humanity; that we should so live and *work* as to uplift and improve social conditions—and so benefit every individual, young and old.

Against the growth of this higher emotion, this social passion, there is no single deterrent influence more sinister, more powerful, than the persistence of this ancient root-form of society, this man-headed, woman-absorbing, child-restricting, self-serving home.

We need a larger love.

"Education for Motherhood" *

In the July and August *Atlantic [Monthly]* the great Swedish feminist, Ellen Key, has an essay in two detachments, on "Education for Motherhood." [Pp. 48–56 and 191–197.]

In the first of these she once more exhibits either persistent refusal, or incapacity, to fairly state the views of those who hold that the right rearing of babies and small children requires the

* *The Forerunner*, 4 (October 1913), pp. 259–262.

assistance of specially trained experts, and of an environment beyond that of the average home.

Her error is the same as that of the ordinary unthinking person: she assumes that the additional special care and additional special environment suggested, are not *additional,* but *alternative*— that if that baby has a "baby-garden" to go to, and a "baby-gardener" to care for him, he therefore becomes practically an exile and an orphan.

In her resumé of the abhorred theory, in the opening of this article, she makes sweeping summary of the proposed changes, as "the rearing and education of children outside the home," the parents to "be supplanted by trained and 'born' educators," and adds that "the children would stand in a visiting relation to the individual home." Further she says that believers in this proposed system hold that "The child's need of the mother and the mother's need of the child is a prejudice which must vanish with all other superstitions from lower stages of culture, if the mothers are to be co-equal with men, community members, capable of work, and if the children are to be well-reared for the social vocations which must soon determine the trend of all lives."

"This program," she continues, "rests on three unproved and undemonstrable assumptions: first, that woman's mental and spiritual work in the home, the creating of a home atmosphere, the management of the housekeeping, and the upbringing of children, is of no 'productive value'; secondly, that parents are incapable of acquiring proficiency as educators unless they are 'born' educators; thirdly, that nature amply provides such 'born' educators, so that the many thousands of institutions—with a professional mother for about every twenty children—could be supplied with with them in sufficient quantity and of excellent quality."

So sure is Miss Key that she has rightly defined the theory she opposes that she says: "Of the real outcome of this plan a prominent American woman gave me a touching illustration. As sole support of her son she had been compelled to send him to a boarding school where many little motherless boys were brought up. When she went to visit her boy, the other boys fought with him for a place on her lap, so hungry were they for a moment's sensation of motherly affection."

Before trying to make clear a disagreement it is well to establish all common ground as far as possible, and since Miss Key gives my name as the person responsible for the theory, I will frankly call it mine for the purposes of this argument, though I am not its inventor by thousands of years.

I quite agree with Miss Key as to the ill effects of a mother working outside the home *while no better provisions is made for her children than she could make by remaining in it*. This I have said and written for long years.

Also we agree in the need of a transformed society. She says in this article: "But without such radical social transformation a renaissance of the family life is not even conceivable." This transformed society which, to her mind, will so pay or pension mothers that they may stay at home, will, to my mind, so reduce the hours of labor that the mother need not be away from home more than four hours a day, and further, with the industrial activity of women always counted upon, will so arrange the conditions of labor that the home and the work will not be far apart.

Again I quite agree with Miss Key in her definition of the "wise educator," never one who is "educating" from morning to night. "She is one who, unconsciously to the children, brings to them the chief sustenance and creates the supreme conditions for their growth. Primarily she is the one who, through the serenity and wisdom of her own nature, is dew and sunshine to growing souls. She is one who understands how to demand in just measure, and to give at the right moment. She is one whose desire is law, whose smile is reward, whose disapproval is punishment, whose caress is benediction." But I flatly disagree with the idea that every mother, meaning, generally, every woman, is—or ever can be—such a benign prodigy.

I agree again, most sincerely, with all the deep universal need of "the child for the mother and the mother for the child." I deny, however, that this need exists in one unbroken, unrelaxing strain, every hour of the day and night. The child does need the mother, the mother does need the child; but both are better off for certain breaks in their companionship. When the baby is asleep, when the children are at school, when they are all in bed at night, then even the motherliest mother can breathe a little more freely, and refresh her mind by other occupations.

Both Miss Key and myself agree in demanding a higher standard of education for young children.

The great disagreement between us is in her assumption that this high standard may be attained by every woman—in one year's study.

In the second instalment of her article she lays down her definite proposition of education for motherhood. Women are to give a year to social service as men do in their military training. Motherhood is here classified as social service. (Here let me stop to smile at this instance of our general attempt to keep women in the same old restrictions. With new education and new growth they are rising and pushing, the world over, saying: "We are tired of everlasting confinement to the kitchen, nursery and parlor, to this one identical round of duties for every woman on earth. We differ, as men differ. We want some variety in action. We want to get out of this eternal domestic service and take part in social service." And those who so long to stop this natural growth, cry to them: "Go back—go back where you were before! That is social service!")

To return to Miss Key's position; Boys and girls are to go to school until fifteen. Then both boys and girls are to study their professions for five years. Then the year of social service, which for the boys is military, and for the girls, training for motherhood.

And what is this training?

For five years they have been learning some profession,—it is hard to see what for, unless they expect to take it up after the age of fifty perhaps. Then in one year they are to study this:

1. "A theoretic course in natural economics, hygienic and fundamental aesthetic principles for the planning of a home and the running of a household. (Sewing and cooking she assumes to have been learned in school.)

2. "A theoretic course in hygienic psychology and education

for normal children, with some directions for the recognition of abnormalities.

3. "A theoretic course in the physical and psychical duties of a mother before the birth of a child, and the fundamental principles of eugenics."

"To these theoretic courses must be added practical training in the care of children; which should embrace knowledge of the child's proper nourishment, clothing and sleep; its physical exercise, play, and other occupations, and its care in case of accident."

There! This is what our prospective mothers are to learn, our young women, all of them, in the space of one year! Five have been allowed them to learn that unaccountable profession which is not to be practised for some thirty years—if ever; one is allowed to cover this slight field.

And how, where, of whom, are they to learn these manifold arts and sciences?

Here we come to something so funny that I chuckle as I read it, as I copy it accurately from Miss Key's words:

"Children's asylums, day-nurseries, and hospitals, and mother-homes (where mothers with children would find refuge for longer or shorter periods) would give opportunity for such training, led by the teachers."

Has anyone so little sense of logic and sense of humor as not to laugh at this?

In the first half of her article, with a rich profusion of fine language and exalted sentiment, she strives to show the great superiority of "the home" to the carefully planned "baby-garden," attended by the little ones from near-by homes, presided over by those "born educators" she so persistently scoffs at; and similarly to show the superiority of "the mother" to this ridiculed "born educator" (who would be a mother herself most often, but having an extra degree of love for children as children, besides her instinctive love for her own as her own). In the second article, having recognized the glaring fact that motherhood *per se* does not prove competence, that the right care of children does require some definite knowledge as well as all those sacred emotions, she plans this elaborate course of study, crowded into one year's space, crammed into the head of every girl regardless of aptitude; and then, for this instruction, takes her flock to the very worst forms of child grouping—those despised "institutions" in which we now make shift to give some social care to the poorest, weakest, lowest kind of children!

My opponent, without knowing it, thus concedes my whole case.

"Motherhood" in itself does not confer knowledge or capacity; if it did there would be no need of study or training.

For the study and training necessary we are told to go not to "the home," not to the "mother," but to the very institutions whose deadly effects have been so bitterly enlarged upon in the previous pages.

On reading the first half of this article I took down "Women and Economics" and looked carefully to see if by any chance there was in it anywhere a justification for this perverse misrepresentation. No. Wherever I have referred to the hope of better methods in baby culture I have always taken pains to state that the mother would not be "separated from the child" any more than now when our children, slightly older, go to kindergarten and school.

Miss Key evidently has no objection to that degree of separation, as she clearly allows for school going to the age of fifteen.

By what logical right then does she consider a few hours spent outside the home, by a baby, as more devastating in its influence than the same hours spent, later, in school? By what logical right does she heap scorn on the idea that about one woman in twenty is a "born educator," and then claim that twenty women out of twenty are competent for that work—at least after a year's training; and then, for that training, send them to the despised specialists, not indeed "born" but merely hired, ordinary functionaries of hospitals and asylums?

Once more, wearily but patiently, I will state my position:

Motherhood is a physical and psychical relation, common to all females, highest in ours.

Education is a function having its pre-human beginnings in motherhood, but now a social process, second to none in high importance.

Any normal woman can be a mother, as any normal man can be a father; but every woman cannot be an educator any more than every man can be a musician.

Every normal woman should be a mother, bearing children, nursing them herself, loving them all she is able, teaching them all she is able, and providing for them such care as she cannot herself furnish. (In this last great department of child care the father should assist. At present he does it all—that is, he provides such schooling and special instructions as the child gets.)

Every child should grow up in its own home, with its own family, in a separate house, with its own garden when possible.

But—here is the Great Divergence: Every child, as a member of society, is entitled to social care and provision quite outside of and beyond the family care and provision. As we, collectively, establish great universities, colleges and schools, for our children, so we should prepare child gardens, numerous and convenient, where all our little ones could have their special guardians, special playgrounds, special care and special educational environment— beyond that of the home.

What scarlet headline capitals must I use to show that going to such a place for part of the day does NOT deprive a child of home and mother? What detailed and repeated description can reach the public mind and convince it that a neighboring baby-garden with a small group of happy, well-loved little ones is NOT an orphan asylum nor an infant hospital?

The story of the little boys and the visiting mother is an excellent illustration, not at all of the baby-garden theory, but of Miss Key's misunderstanding. Here a mother is compelled to send her little son to a boarding school. No such arrangement is involved in my position, which assumes only that the baby shall be in the baby-garden while the mother is doing her four hours' work, and shall be at home when she is.

No one calls a child in the kindergarten a homeless exile, robbed of his mother's love; why consider the baby as such? Is it incapacity to understand which perpetuates this misrepresentation, or conscious unfairness?

Miss Key may sneer at the "born educator," but it remains

true that the special genius for child care is not common to all women, and is found in some. It is not as rare as the genius of the great artist or musician, but quite frequent enough to provide for little ones a grade of training far higher than the present, and to provide for the women who possess it a life of fruitful joy.

Given, first, the kind of woman who really enjoys the care and guidance of little children enough to give her life to it; given, second, not one year's crammed confusion of "education for motherhood," but many years of wide study, and of careful preliminary practise; given, third, a place which is meant to provide peace, beauty and unconscious education for the opening soul; given, fourth, a long succession of grouped little ones to observe and learn from—and we shall at last begin to lay the foundations of the real science of baby culture.

Then indeed there will be some "education for motherhood." All mothers, in daily contact with higher methods, may begin to improve their own. The standards of child culture will rise from year to year by the purely natural process of observation and experience.

No unpractised individual theorist can teach mothers sufficiently. No one mother, enriched only by her own experience with her own children, can teach other mothers sufficiently.

The accumulated learning of doctors, nurses, and pedagogs can give us information on their specific lines, but how to rear a baby not only in physical health, but in soul-health, with the maximum of development and the minimum of nerve-waste, can never be taught until it is learned, and can never be learned until serious, life-long, study and practise is given to it.

There are two inexorable limitations to the work of the individual mother, which I once more repeat.

One is this: Even if every mother had the talent—which they have not; even if every mother took the exhaustive course of training requisite—which they will not; still, so long as each mother takes all the care of her own children, no one can ever have the requisite *experience*.

You do not want doctor or dentist or dressmaker to *begin on you.* You expect of them previous practise—under the eyes of experts, the more the better.

In all other human work we have the benefit of the accumulated progressive experience of the ages. Only the culture of babies —most important of all work—is left to that eternal amateur— the mother.

The other paradox is this: Suppose we have an individual mother possessed of all three requisites, talent, training, *and* experience; that is, a woman who had fitted for the position of baby-gardener and held it long, but who finally decides to withdraw from that position and consecrate her services to her own baby at home.

Such ceaseless focussing of professional ability upon one child, or a few, is too intense an atmosphere for little ones to unfold in. The mother-and-child relation should be kept wholesomely unstrained, and the teacher-and-child relation also. To share with many other little ones the wise supervision of the teacher for part of the day, and to return fresh and eager to the love of an as fresh and eager mother, is far more healthful.

Any mother who is capable of giving all that a child needs, and keeps such unusual power exclusively for her own, is a social traitor.

"The New Mothers of a New World" *

The time has come for some clear statement of the larger hope, the deeper purposes, underlying the world-wide movement among women. [. . .]

There is need of some broad platform, some high and definite purpose, to coordinate all this activity, to give form and direction to the movement.

Such a platform is here advanced, not in the least as requiring adherence from all—that would be an impossibility. It will be disputed by many, opposed condemned, hotly repudiated. Neither does it involve any criticism of the spontaneous and varied phases

* *The Forerunner,* 4 (June 1913), pp. 145–149.

of woman's progress, from the small local gathering for mutual improvement to the great international associations for world improvement. It recognizes the pre-eminent claim for political freedom, now so strong and successful, the claim for economic freedom, even more basic, the demand for education, for freedom in all the fuller needs of life.

This platform is offered to the thinker, the sociologist, the perplexed student of the "unrest" of women, as a basic explanation of the whole movement, and a justification of its results. [. . .]

[The New Mothers of the New World] will be grown women —not mere girls, the half-child, ignorant creatures, so readily coerced—full-grown women, wise, strong, wholly independent, strong in personal freedom, and stronger in that new union the world has never seen, the union of motherhood.

They will study their world, their nations, this mysterious field of politics which should cover only the judicious caring for the people, this abstruse science of economics which is merely the best method of caring for the people, this whole field of social study, the study of which means learning how to make and rear the best people, and secure the best development of all human power.

And these New Mothers will say:

"We are tired of men's wars. We are tired of men's quarrels. We are tired of men's competition. We are tired of men's crimes and vices and the diseases they bring upon us, of this whole world full of noise, confusion, enmity and bloodshed.

"The pressure of population shall cease.

"We will marry only clean men, fit to be fathers. The other may still be serviceable citizens, if they are able, but they shall not be fathers. We will breed a better stock on earth by proper selection—that is a mother's duty!

"We will bear children less in numbers and greater in vigor, beauty and intelligence. We will learn to rear them in health and joy and strong intelligence—we, together, who have so seldom been able to do so alone.

"We will rebuild our nations. They shall be clean-blooded, clear-brained, broad-minded. We will not teach our children the history of their fathers' wars that they may forever hate one another, but we will teach them the advantages of union, association, interchange.

"We will work together, the women of the race, for a higher human type, ours to make, for universal peace, for a socialized economic system that shall make prosperity for us all, for such growth in industry, art and science, in health and beauty and happiness, as the world has never seen.

"We will be the New Mothers of a New World."

A new standard is rising—the woman's standard. It is based not on personal selfishness but on the high claims of motherhood, motherhood as a social service instead of man-service. This new motherhood shines before us like a sunrise. Women as world builders, women recognizing the need of stronger, nobler people and producing them, women saying to men—"You have had your day—you have worked your will—you have filled the world with warfare, with drunkenness, with vice and disease. You have wasted women's lives like water, and the children of the world have been sacrificed to your sins. Now we will have a new world, new-born, new-built, a mother-world as well as a father-world, a world in which we shall not be ashamed or afraid to plant our children." [. . .]

"Birth Control" *

The time will come when every nation must face the question, "How many people can live comfortably, healthfully, happily, upon this land?" That is the ultimate reason why we must learn that "the pressure of population" is not an unavoidable fate, but a result of our own irresponsible indulgence.

This time is still a long way off. At present the main reasons advanced in advocacy of the conscious limitation of offspring are these: the economic pressure which often makes it difficult, if not impossible, to rear large families without degradation of the stock from injurious conditions; the injury to women of a continuous repetition of maternity, especially when combined with hard work

* *The Forerunner,* 6 (July 1915), pp. 177–180.

and lack of comfort; and back of these, less freely stated, a desire for "safe" and free indulgence of the sex instinct without this natural consequence.

Of the first reason it may be said that the economic pressure is our own making and may be removed when we choose. That a race of our intelligence should sink into conditions so miserable that it is difficult to raise healthy children; and then, instead of changing those miserable conditions, should weakly renounce parentage, is not creditable to that intelligence. While we have not come within centuries of "the limit of subsistence"; while there is land enough and water enough to feed a vast population as yet unapproached; it is contemptible for us to accept mere local and temporary injustice as if it were a natural condition. That the more ignorant masses should do this would not be strange; but they are not the main culprits. So far they have faced the evils around them with nature's process—the less chance of a living, the more young ones.

Wiser people, more far-seeing, with a higher standard of living to keep up, have accepted their restrictions as final, and sought to limit their own numbers as to maintain that standard for the few.

If we would apply our reasoning power and united force to secure a fair standard of living for all of us, we could go on enjoying our families for many centuries.

In the meantime, accepting our present limitations, we do have to face the very practical and personal problem—how many children ought a woman to have whose husband's wages average $600 a year[?] That is the average for millions, even in our country.

Face this fairly: $2.00 a day for all but the fifty-two Sundays, say three holidays, and a most modest allowance of ten days' unemployment—less than $12.00 a week the year around, with rent and food prices what they are now. How many children *ought* a woman to have under these circumstances?

Then, either for this woman, overworked and underfed; or for the professor's wife, also overworked in the demands of her environment; and, though having enough to eat, also underfed in the rest and relaxation she needs; we must face the limitations of physical strength.

Here again, in a large sense, our position is pusillanimous.

Maternity is a natural process. It should benefit and not injure the mother. That women have allowed themselves to sink into a condition where they are unfit to perform the very functions for which their bodies are specially constructed, is no credit to their intelligence. Instead of accepting the limitations and saying: "We are not strong enough to bear children," the wise and noble thing to do is to say: "Our condition of health is shameful. We must become strong and clean again that we may function naturally as mothers."

In spite of this, the practical and personal problem confronts the individual mother: "I have had three children in three years. I am a wreck already. If I have another I may die or become a hopeless invalid. Is it not my duty for the sake of those I have, to refuse to have more?"

The third reason, by no means so outspoken, but far more universal than the others, is at once the strongest force urging us toward birth control, and the strongest ground of opposition to it.

The prejudice against the prevention of conception and the publication of knowledge as to the proper methods, is based partly on religious conviction, and partly on an objection to the third reason above given. The religious objection is neither more nor less difficult to meet than others of the same class. A wider enlightenment steadily tends to disabuse our minds of unthinking credulity as to ancient traditions. We are beginning at last to have a higher opinion of God than we used to entertain. The modern mind will not credit an Infinite Wisdom, an Infinite Love, with motives and commands unworthy of the love and wisdom of a mere earthly father. Still, for those who hold this objection, and upon whom it is enforced by their Church, it is a very serious one.

The other is still more serious; so much so that no one can rightly judge the question without squarely facing this, its biological base—what is sex union for. No one can deny its original purpose through all the millions of years of pre-human life on earth. But when human life is under consideration there are two opinions.

The first holds that the human species is sui generis in this regard; that we differ from all other animals in this process; that it has, for us, both a biological use quite aside from reproduction, and a psychological use entirely beyond that.

The second is to the effect that for our race, as for others, this is a biological process for the perpetuation of the species, and that its continuous indulgence with no regard to reproduction or in direct exclusion of reproduction indicates an abnormal development peculiar to our species.

The first opinion is held by practically everyone; the second by a mere handful. To those who have watched the growth of ideas in the human mind this disproportion proves nothing whatever. Of course a few people are as likely to be wrong as a great many people. Of course a small minority of people have held views as absurd as those of large majorities. Nevertheless it remains true that every advance in all human history has been begun by the ideas of a few, even of one perhaps, and opposed with cheerful unanimity by all the rest of the world.

An idea must be discussed on its merits, not measured by the numbers of people who "believe" this, or "think" that, or "feel" so and so. Especially as to feeling. The emotional responses of the mass of people are invariably reactionary. "Feelings" which belong to a more advanced state are always hard to find. Even in one's own mind, the intellectual perception comes first, the settled conviction later, and the appropriate emotional response later still.

One may be fairly forced by sheer reason and logic to admit the justice and expedience of equal suffrage for men and women; one may accept this as a strong belief and act accordingly. Yet the swift warm sense of approval for what is still called a "womanly woman," the cold aversion to what we have for long assumed to be "unwomanly," remain.

Because of these simple and common phenomena we must not be swayed too much in our judgment on this question as to the true use and purpose and the legitimate limits of the sex function, by the overwhelming mass of sentiment on the side of continuous indulgence.

For clear discussion it will be well to state definitely the thesis here advanced, which is:

That with the human species as with others the normal purpose of sex-union is reproduction;

That its continuous repetition, wholly disassociated with this use, results in a disproportionate development of the preliminary sex emotions and functional capacities, to the detriment of the parental emotions and capacities, and to the grave injury of the higher processes of human development;

That our present standard of "normal indulgence" is abnormal; this by no means in the sense of any individual abnormality, but in the sense of a whole race thus developed by thousands of generations of over-indulgence;

That, when the human species, gradually modifying its conduct by the adoption of changed ideas, becomes normal in this regard, it will show a very different scale of emotional and functional demand; the element of sex-desire greatly reduced in proportion to the higher development of parental activities worthy of our race; and of a whole range of social emotions and functions now impossible because of the proportionate predominance of this one process and its emotions;

That this change will necessarily be a slow one; and involves, not the pious struggles of a convicted sinner against a sin, but the wise gradual efforts of a conscious race to so change its habits, to so modify itself, as to breed out the tendency to excessive indulgence, and allow the re-assumption of normal habits;

That the resultant status is not of an emasculate or e-feminate race; or of one violently repressing its desires; but rather that of a race whose entire standard has changed; in physical inclination, in emotion, and in idea; so that the impulse to that form of sex-expression comes only in a yearly season, as with other species of the same gestative period.

The opposing thesis is so universally held as hardly to need statement, but may be fairly put in this way:

That it is "natural" for the human species to continually indulge sex-emotion and its physical expression, with no regard whatever to reproduction.

That this indulgence has "a higher function" in no way associated with so crude a purpose as bringing forth children, but is (a) an expression of pure and lofty affection; (b) a concomitant of all noble creative work; (c) a physical necessity to maintain the health of men—some say also of women.

This position is reinforced not only by the originally strong sex instinct in all animals, and by the excessive force of that instinct in the human race; but by the world's accumulated psychology on the subject—its pictures, statues, stories, poems, music, drama, even its religions, all of which have been elaborated by the sex which has the most to gain and the least to lose by upholding such a standard.

Without expecting to make much impression upon such a measureless mass of instinct, sentiment, habit, and tradition, we may offer this much consideration of the above position.

First, as to the use of the word "natural." The forces of nature tend to preserve life—under any conditions. Up to the last limits of possibility, the form, size, and structure, habits and feelings of a living species, will change and change and change again in order that it may live. Anything will be sacrificed—so that the one main necessity is maintained—that the creature be not extinct. "Nature," in the sense of creatures below mankind, often failed in this effort, and many species did become extinct. Our human conditions, which are natural too, but not in this special sense, are so favorable that human life is maintained where less able creatures would die.

It is quite possible for a part of society to so conduct itself as would inevitably cause its own destruction if it were not meanwhile fed and clothed and sheltered by another part. It is possible for quite a small fraction of society to promote ideas, theories and habits which would corrupt and degrade the whole if they were not offset by other tendencies. In the specific matter in question the one absolute condition of life was merely this: that enough women reached the bearing age and produced enough children to maintain the race in existence.

The condition of said race might be as low as that of the fellaheen of Egypt, of the Australian savage, of the Bushman of Africa. No matter—if they still live, "Nature" seems to be satisfied.

Moreover, we may say that so universal a habit as the use of alcohol is "natural," meaning that it is easily adopted by all races and classes of men. To call a thing "natural" in that sense does not show it to be advantageous.

As to the "higher function," we should be clear in our minds about the relation between the "height" of the function and its frequence. It may be advanced, similarly, that eating with us has a "higher function," being used as a form of hospitality, a medium of entertainment, of aesthetic as well as gustatory pleasure. All that may be true of the preparation, service, and consumption of food which is perfectly suited to the needs of the body, and for which one has a genuine appetite. One would hardly seek to justify a ceaseless gluttony, or even an erratic consumption of unnecessary food, on those grounds.

It remains further to be discussed in detail whether noble and lofty affection may not be otherwise expressed; whether it is true that the highest creative work, or the most, or even any great part, is associated with our present degree of indulgence on this line; and whether that claim of "physical necessity" really holds good for either sex.

It may be shown that a person, to-day, is in better health if free to gratify his present degree of desire; but that is not the real point at issue, which is—is it normal for the human race to have this degree of desire?

Against the visible sum of our noble achievements, which may be urged as justification of our peculiarities, may be set the as visible sum of our shameful diseases, sufferings, poverty, crime degeneracy. As a race we do not show such an exceptionally high average of health and happiness in the sex relation as to indicate a "higher" method. Rather, on the contrary, the morbid phenomena with which this area of life is associated, plainly show some wrong condition.

Upon which general bias, returning to the subject of birth control, it is advanced:

That the normal sex relation is a periodic one, related to the reproductive process;

That the resultant "natural" product of a child a year is being

gradually reduced by the action of that biological law—"reproduction is in inverse proportion to industrialization";

That when we are all reared in suitable conditions for the
highest individual development, we shall only crave this indulgence for a brief annual period, and that, with no efforts at
"prevention," our average birth rate will be but two or three to a
family;

That, in the meantime, under specially hard conditions, it is
right for a woman to refuse to bear more than that, or possibly to
bear any;

That for reputable physicians or other competent persons to
teach proper methods of such restrictions, is quite right.

As for needing a "safe," free and unlimited indulgence in the
exercises of this function, I hold that to be an abnormal condition.

"Maternity Benefits and Reformers" *

One of the saddest obstacles in the way of legitimate social
progress is seen when some of the noblest workers in one line
oppose a movement of advance in others.

The American Association for Labor Legislation,† through its
committee on Social Insurance, has prepared the tentative draft of
an act on Health Insurance, carefully drawn, and largely in accordance with the best measures now advocated and used in so many
other countries, as England, Germany, Hungary, Italy, France,
Switzerland and Russia.

In this act there was recognition of the great need of maternity benefits, and Section 15 provides as follows: "Maternity
Benefits shall consist of:

All necessary medical, surgical and obstetrical aid, materials
and appliances, which shall be given insured women and the wives
of insured men;

A weekly maternity benefit, payable to insured women, equal

---

* *The Forerunner,* 7 (March 1916), pp. 65–66.
† Inspired by Richard Ely and directed by John R. Commons (1862–1945) of the
University of Wisconsin, it was an organization of state and federal government officials,
university professors, and social reformers, founded in 1906, to investigate labor conditions and propose corrective legislation.

to the regular sick benefit, of the insured, for a period of eight weeks, of which at least six shall be subsequent to delivery, on condition that the beneficiary abstain from gainful employment during period of payment."

In the remarks preparatory to the act, we are told that in our country we have a standing sick list of three million persons at any one time; that each of our thirty million wage earners loses on an average about nine days a year from sickness, with a total wage loss of $500,000,000, and a cost for medical treatment of $180,000,000. This is a total cost of $680,000,000, well over half a billion, coming out of the class which can least afford to lose it, as well as the interruption of industry that affects us all; and it is found that in some 75 per cent. of applications for aid, made to the New York Charity Organization Society, sickness was responsible for the distress. Few reasonable persons will object to the general plan of health insurance; why should anyone object to it for women? And if they do not object to it for other forms of temporary disability in women, why should the maternity benefit be objected to? It would seem as if there would be but three possible reasons; a desire to prevent maternity, to penalize maternity, or to prevent mothers from undertaking gainful occupations.

As the really good and in many ways wise people who are so valiantly opposing the maternity benefit cannot be suspected of the first two, it appears that their one desire is to prevent mothers from working; that is, from working at anything for which they are paid.

A more pitiful misconception of the best lines of social advance by those apparently well qualified to judge has seldom been offered. It is on a par with the opposition to "teacher mothers" —which frankly admits its object to be to prevent mothers from holding their positions as teachers.

All this foolish and wasted effort ignores one of the largest and most vitally important movements of the day—the specialization of women. Women are irresistibly pushing forward into all manner of "gainful occupations," first unprovided for spinsters and widows who "had to work"; then the growing multitude of young girls who worked to help their families and for their own freedom; then married women, to meet family wants and to preserve their own integrity; then, more and more, mothers.

This is the most important feature of the whole movement. Young girls are not women. Spinsters and widows are more or less unfortunate exceptions. The term "woman" should connote wifehood and motherhood. Until "mothers" earn their livings "women" will not.

The first steps of working motherhood, usually enforced by extreme poverty, bring the woman and the child in contact with some of our worst conditions; and we, in our dull social conscience, seeing evil fall upon mother and baby, seek only to push them back where they came from — instead of striving to make conditions fit for them.

What we must recognize is this:

Women; wives and mothers; are becoming a permanent half of the world workers. In their interest we shall inevitably change the brutal and foolish hardships now surrounding labor into such decent and healthful conditions as shall be no injury to any one. That children should be forced to work for their livings is an unnatural outrage, wholly injurious. That adult women should do it, is in no way harmful, if the hours and conditions of labor are suitable; and they never will be made suitable until overwhelming numbers of working women compel them.

Now since maternity is not "a preventable illness" — unless we wish the race to die out, but merely a temporary disability in which the woman discontinues one form of social service to practice another; there is even more reason for providing for it than for the "occupational diseases," which can largely be prevented; or the general diseases which attack us indiscriminately.

The efforts of any army to nurse back to health its fighting units, and to keep them in health — until they are killed! — should be paralleled by the efforts of a peaceful state to preserve the health of its workers, and to nurse them when disabled.

The theory that women must at all costs be kept in the home grows feebler daily. They will not stay there — they have definitely come out. By coming out, by bringing the mothers of the world into industry, we shall at last make the conditions of our workers what they ought to be. When these conditions are right, in hours of labor, in surroundings, in payment, then we shall have less sickness, and less need of health insurance; but with things as they are now, such insurance is wise and right, and most assuredly so for mothers.

"Do We Want a Political Party for Women?" *

Now that we have women voters by the million,† and, so far, no river has blazed up and no sky fallen, some people are urging a separate party, that this large vote may make itself felt. There seems to be a feeling that women, as such, could exercise a powerful influence in politics, all by themselves.

But why should they? How could they? Have they any new theory of government to advance? Any special invention in economics or politics to stand for? Do they want class privileges for themselves, or even class justice as a separate thing?

Great political parties stand on great issues, and the issues must be distinctive enough to warrant the new machinery. What new step are women proposing which can not be taken in the companionship of the present voting population?

The only issues on which men and women night conceivably line up in opposition are those connected with marriage and divorce laws, social purity, and like matters. Here, not only are the women far from united, but there are men in plenty, good men and true, standing shoulder to shoulder with good women in every step of this advance.

Those who want a separate party for women seem to imagine them as a distinct race, or a class whose interests are diametrically opposed to those of men. They are not. Women are folks, just folks, like the rest of us. Their whole claim to the ballot rests on their being human creatures, not on being females.

* *The Forerunner,* 6 (November 1915), pp. 285–286.
† Women could vote in twelve states: Arizona, California, Colorado, Idaho, Illinois, Kansas, Montana, Nevada, Oregon, Utah, Washington, and Wyoming.

A female vote is as unnecessary as a male vote. We want the votes of earnest, conscientious, well informed citizens, whether in skirts or trousers.

Even if women had a huge list of special grievances to be righted by the ballot; even if they could conceivably all unite and agree both on the grievances and the measures of redress; even if women, voting as a party, against men as a party—and men outnumber women in this country by 2,691,978, by the census of 1910—even if the miraculous solidarity of the women outnumbered the natural divisions among men; and even if this minority of women could enforce their decisions upon this majority of men —granting all that, *then* what are the women to vote for?

Is all their demand for political freedom merely a wish to free themselves, and does their interest in politics cease with their own advantage?

By no means. The wise and understanding majority of suffragists have never advocated a woman's party, or even a woman's platform. Their claim to the ballot is on general human grounds; their interest is in the great principles of freedom, justice, and progress. It is by no means the suffragists who assume the rights of women to be opposed to the rights of men. They are, in all the extra-domestic fields, largely identical; and in the family relation they are inextricably connected. Nothing can be good for women which works injustice to man; just as it has never been good for man to work injustice upon women.

We do not want any Woman's Party, and we never shall, unless temporarily there should be a solid massing of men against some just and necessary claim of women. Even then, why a party? The party method is not a real necessity of democratic government. It is a convenient form under which men have taken sides in order to concentrate for some special struggle, and the evils of "party politics" are too conspicuous to need recounting.

It will be a good thing for our country when either men or women, or both men and women join their forces on great issues, immediate issues, electing to office men pledged and competent to remedy existing wrong, and to work for the common good.

We must try to learn that the party system is only a method, and by no means a blameless one, and that an intelligent democracy could elect its representatives without any party tag on them, if it chose.

"The National Woman's Party" *

While Europe's agony goes on relentlessly and some are moved to despair of human progress, one great quiet step forward is being made by the voting women of America.

At the initiative of the Congressional Union,† that active body of suffragists who would have this question of political justice settled once for all by Federal Amendment, a convention was called in Chicago during the same week as the Republican and Progressive, and a new party formed, "The National Woman's Party"; headquarters at Lafayette Square, Washington, D.C.

The party has but one plank, the enfranchisement of women. Its membership is from the "free States," where women already hold the ballot; its purpose, to use the voting power of these enfranchised women to free the others; its method, clear, simple, dignified and efficient, is that common to all democracies, the promise of support to the administration which favors its platform and withdrawal of support from that which opposes it. [. . .]

The importance of this new party can hardly be overestimated. It marks the passing forever, I hope, of the isolated helplessness of women. Among their many artificial disabilities none has been more mischievous in preventing progress than this isolation. [. . .]

It has been flatly denied that women would ever organize as women, some holding that as a sex they were unable to stick together, and others that their interests could not be dissociated from those of men.

This new party disposes of both these views; it is an organiza-

* *The Forerunner,* 7 (August 1916), pp. 214–215.
† Formed in April 1913 by Alice Paul (1885–1977) and Lucy Burns, to wage an all-out campaign for a federal constitutional suffrage amendment.

tion of women, uniting to aid other women; and while its purpose is not in reality against the interests of men, it is but too visibly against their present willingness. [. . .]

The best thing that can be hoped for the new party is that it will be joined in overwhelming numbers by the voting women, pledging themselves to stand firmly together and to vote as one against the party which denies them justice, and then to have one or the other of our leading groups see the wisdom of the proposition and the power of that massed vote, and work to pass the needed Federal amendment. Best of all if it could be done at once by the party in power, now, this summer, saving all the long labor and waste of continued work.

The worst that can be feared is that the two great parties adopt so identical an attitude toward the measure as shall leave nothing to choose between them.

What should be done in that case?

There are still more than three months before [the] election. If in that time the Democratic administration should refuse to advance this measure, to distinguish sharply from the Republican position, then it would be quite fair to oust the the Democrats, not on the ground that the Republicans were better, but that full opportunity was given for a change of heart before [the] election, and that it was not made.

If this is done, successfully, and [is] clearly attributable to the women's votes, they will have established their effectiveness so thoroughly that no subsequent administration will lightly oppose them, and the Republicans, though now indifferent, will see the light before another election.

Meantime, even if this year's effort fails, the women will have developed their organization, and, because of this first effort, be in a far better position to use their power for good hereafter.

"The Present Election" *

This is written in the closing days of October, 1916. [. . .] As a member of the Congressional Union I should work against the

* *The Forerunner,* 7 (December 1916), p. 336.

Democratic Administration — as a matter of principle; but I know other conscientious Women's National Party workers who wish to turn the Western States against [President Woodrow] Wilson, and yet hope he will be elected! To extend the suffrage to women in the majority of our states, is a more important thing than the change in administration pending; yet of the two parties the Democratic is far closer to the spirit of our people, and to those lines of work which mean social progress. One man, a believer in Woman suffrage, said he thought the other issues before the country were of more immediate importance. I asked him if he would feel so if men were not yet enfranchised?

"A Word with the Pacifists on How to End this War" *

It is announced that the purpose of the Ford Peace Expedition† is now accomplished: namely, the establishment of a Neutral Conference for Continual Mediation, with delegates from six nations, the United States, Switzerland, Holland, Denmark, Norway and Sweden.

That is one line of pacifist effort.

Mr. [William Howard] Taft [1857–1930; President of the United States, 1909–1913], by virtue of his headship, and President Wilson, because of his speech before it, represent the League to Enforce Peace,‡ a lasting peace, by the strong arm. The Presi-

---

* *Philadelphia Public Ledger,* July 18, 1916, pp. 6–7.

† When the Woman's Peace Party failed to convince President Wilson to convene a conference of neutral nations to mediate the war, Jane Addams, among others, proposed an alternative, unofficial conference representing the people of the neutral countries. Rosika Schwimmer (1877–1948), the Hungarian suffrage and peace advocate, persuaded Henry Ford (1863–1947) to underwrite its expenses. Ford chartered a ship, *S. S. Oscar II,* to transport the United States delegates to Europe. Over fifty people sailed in December 1915 to Christiana, Norway. Ignored by the neutral governments, ridiculed by the press, and abandoned by Ford, the delegates from the neutral countries met in Stockholm and established the Neutral Conference for Continuous Mediation. Charlotte termed Ford's act "a generous effort" and "nobly purposed," and she accused the press of holding it up to "malicious ridicule." "The Ford Party and the Newspapers," *The Forerunner,* 7 (March 1916), pp. 73–75.

‡ President A. Lawrence Lowell (1856–1943) of Harvard, chairman of the executive committee of the World Peace Foundation, used its facilities and money to found the League to Enforce Peace, in 1915. Its goal was to plan a postwar program for the United States, a league of nations. It made no effort to end the present war, and, when the United States entered the war in 1917, the League tied itself closely to Wilson. Former

dent has of late begun the preparation of the American public mind for the new international arrangements which ought to be made, if necessary by means of a "disentangling alliance," when the European war is over. That is another line.

Other ardent pacifists oppose this method because it presupposes force, and peace should be attained by peaceful methods only.

Extreme fervor of moral conviction is not always accompanied by clear discriminating reasoning power. This is a pity, because the lack of logic is so apt to prejudice observers against that justice and nobility of the cause advanced.

We pacifists, whose basic contention is so wholly right, and whose purpose is so wholly noble, are not free from the above weakness. Our most prominent error is in talking about three things at once when we talk of peace.

The first thing is so big and beautiful that it outshines all others, namely Peace—the largest of P's.

Surely there is no one, save some Prussian war worshiper, or some Oriental, like that gallant Hindu prince who is quoted as saying: "All war is beautiful, but this war is heavenly," * who will not agree that peace is the necessary condition for human life and progress, and war the worst, or at least one of the worst, of evils.

But such views as this may be dismissed in two sentences— as for instance, these:

Peace is the best thing for humanity.

War is the worst thing for humanity.

Then if your hearers disagree you may argue those points; if the hearers agree—it is time to go on and say something.

The next point in the discussion is one of pressing practical importance—how to stop this war.

Upon this subject there is much to be said, and more to be learned. It would have been well indeed if our minds could have saved all the energy spent on the first indisputable topic, and spent it on this most disputable one.

United States President William Howard Taft was its president; Lowell chaired its executive committee. It was funded by business corporations.

* Unable to identify.

The third field under discussion is more important yet, namely: How can we establish and maintain world peace?

Upon those last two points the pacifists might divide, according to their special powers and sympathies, and do great work for either purpose—as indeed they are doing. But what should not be done is to turn the blazing ardor of conviction belonging to "peace" upon the field of intricate and necessary diplomacy involved in stopping the war, or upon that long upward road of international action we must laboriously first build and then walk on to reach the final goal of a federated world.

The truth is that it is a great deal easier to feel impassioned feelings than to think reasonable thoughts, and alas! it is also easier to criticise and condemn than to convince. Especially is it easy, pitifully easy, to split the world into two opposing camps, to see no shades but black and white, to set sheep on one side and goats on the other, and let never an apologetic hybrid run between.

If one does not wholly agree with the urgent advocate of preparedness—"you are a pacifist!" he sneers; if one does not wholly agree with the ultra dove upholder—"You are a militarist!" is the retort.

Being thus safely and finally labeled, the controversy can go on in beautiful simplicity, all the hatred of Prussian "frightfulness" being now directed upon the citizen who thinks our army should be larger, and all the scorn of white-feathered poltroonery being turned upon the citizen who thinks it should not.

This is not only unreasonable; it is unpeaceful.

I am a pacifist, of settled conviction, meaning by that first the recognition that a condition of peace is a primary essential to all human growth, and that war is an absolute injury to that growth; further, in holding that this war should be stopped now—should have been stopped as soon as it began—yes, and before it began; still, further, and most strongly, in seeing the immediate practical necessity for the beginnings of world-federation.

But believing in these things and working for them does not involve a further faith in the doctrine of nonresistance. One may be a wholly peaceful citizen, quite gunless and knifeless, yet fight valiantly if it becomes necessary. There ought to be an extremely clear distinction made between pacifism and nonresistance.

There are those who hold the extreme Tolstoyan* view, who out-Quaker the Quakers† in their refusal to fight, and they, of course, have a right to their conscientious objections. But one may be the firmest upholder of the value of peace, the strongest condemner of the evils of war, and yet fight—when it is necessary.

An antelope is a peaceful animal, yet it will fight a rattlesnake and kill it most successfully by jumping on it with sharp close-gathered little hoofs. The famous "embattled farmers" of our own past were peaceful enough—till the Redcoats became dangerous. Even a hen will fight for her chickens.

The need of peace is so great, so instant, so permanent, that all who are working for it should strive for every element of fairness, for just allowance to their opponents, and for the utmost clearness and discrimination in their own views.

As for their main ground, that peace is good and war is bad, that subject was overtalked by the fall of 1914. A great and obvious truth requires the most careful handling lest its obviousness become absolutely repugnant to the mind. Overstatement and repetition, together with an exalted enthusiasm, are not, to say the least, wholly convincing.

"To My Real Readers" ‡

[...] Be sure that Humanity is moving on; doing well. We may well doubt and criticize the conscious behavior of individuals; but if our progress depended wholly on our understanding and assistance we might almost despair of it, especially in the slow

* Lev Nikolaevich Tolstoy (1828–1910), following a spiritual crisis, formulated five commandments, based on his interpretation of Christ's teachings, to guide him, including: "resist not him that is evil" and "be good to the just and unjust." He assigned the income from his last novel, Resurrection (1879) to the Dukhobors, a Russian pacifist sect.
† The Religious Society of Friends, established in England in 1652, took a definite stand against war in 1659. In the United States, however, Quakers participated in the War for Independence, the Civil War, and World War I. Beginning with World War II, the question of military service was left to the individual conscience.
‡ The Forerunner, 7 (December 1916), pp. 326–328.

black early ages. But since we have been pushed and lifted up to our present stage in spite of universal ignorance and active opposition, we may now, in our stubborn social consciousness and well directed efforts to "assist nature" feel strong assurance of immediate gains.

Don't worry about God.

God is *there* working all the time, not angry or jealous or any of those things the limited intelligence of those ancient Hebrews discredited Him with, but a steady lifting force, always to be relied on, bearing no grudge against the last and highest form of creation —Humanity.

Don't talk of "A Supreme Being," but of "The Underlying Force." To think of God in terms of personality discredits Him. "He" postulates sex. A man-shaped deity involves internal organs —and processes. Spirit is Force, not personality.

Cast out of your mind the trailing, sticky remnants of early misbelief. God is *right there*. No matter what you have done—it makes no difference to God—only to you. As soon as you reach out to that Force and use it, you find it ready.

"God is a Force to give way to—

God is a thing you have to *Do* —"

Do you not see the pathetic egotism of those early Hebrews in imagining their special God, of whom they were the special children—all the rest of the world airily waved aside as inferior —as so intimately concerned over their little sin and didoes? Fussing because they didn't "worship" Him enough or with the exact kind and amount of sacrifice, irritable to a degree, raging most unbecomingly when they misbehaved. We never shall have a decent uplifting religion till we first dissociate it from the utterly derogatory ideas we have been taught were "sacred," and second associate it with the rest of the laws of the universe.

Everything that is true about God and Jesus will keep, will bear examination, will agree with everything else that is true. It's a mighty weak religion that will not bear discussion.

As to Jesus—do Him justice. Here is personality. Here is a man, and the son of man. If you care anything at all about Him take Him seriously. If you think what we can gather of His teachings, as filtered down to us through many minds, and as heavily infected with the earlier Hebrew theories, are true, then practice them. But to ignore the extremely practical rules of behavior He taught, and yet to expect to climb into heaven on His shoulders, is ungentlemanly!

There is no more pathetic instance of our perverse misunderstanding of the essential truth of religion than the colossal mistake of Christianity—ignoring the life of Christ and fixing all their attention on His death. He, two thousand years ago, saw and proclaimed the unity of human life, saw the divine spirit *in humanity*—pointed it out to us, told us that the love of God was to be shown in love of mankind; and that love meant service. He foresaw it, foretold it, tried to make us see it. We couldn't then. We can now.

We know more. We have covered the earth with people and knit it together by a thousand ties. We now have definite knowledge of this unity and are rapidly learning the interdependence which goes with it.

Let us be thankful that this early dawn did shine upon the world; let us give all due reverence and gratitude to the God-filled soul who saw so clearly and who died for the faith that was in Him—as many a martyr has done since.

But as for the Truth so taught—if we see it and feel it we should *use it,* put it in practice. We best honor [Benjamin] Franklin [1706–1790] and [Samuel F. B.] Morse [1791–1872] by using the telegraph, or [William F.] Channing, [Francis] Blake [1850–1913] and the other eager scientists who invented the telephone as much as Alexander [Graham] Bell [1847–1922] did by using the telephone—not by worshipping them. This whole business of "worshipping" is merely an ancient habit. It is of no use to the worshipper or the worshippee. Jesus is better honored by a quite unconscious fulfilment of the truth He taught than by the most ardent genuflections.

Try to have a vivid sense of the splendor of Human Life. Our miserable present conditions, our poverty and wealth with their attendant crimes and diseases, our morbid sex-conditions with their hideous fruit, our petty, silly, tedious lives—all these are quite unnecessary and out of date, and may be swept away as soon as we choose.

It is not that we have to wait to build the home. The home is built—and we don't know enough to occupy it. We have now every condition necessary to the kind of life we ought to have. All that ails us is false ideas. Once we wake up and see things as they are we can make over our material and social conditions in a lifetime and rebuild a clear, clean-minded race in three generations.

Women ought to feel a glorious new pride in their sex, now that it is shown to be the main trunk of the tree of life. They ought to feel an unbounded hope and power in their ability to remake the race and to help manage it on better terms than ever before. And they ought also to burn with shame, deep scorching shame, at the pitiful limitations with which so many of them are still contented.

They have no longer the excuse of ignorance. They have no longer the excuse of helplessness. Our intelligent, educated American women who are not informed of their real duty in life—and doing it—have no excuse.

The immediate hope of the world is in women; humanity "groaneth and travailleth" for its mother. She'd better hurry.

It's a little hard on men to-day. Being the sex to which pride is a natural emotion; having had that natural pride of sex swollen and aggravated by long ages of illegitimate mastery, it is hard indeed for men to "climb down." Yet enough remains for them to be honestly proud of. They and they alone have built the world as we know it. Women, though the beginners of industry, and the faithful servants of the world, also occasional contributors of useful inventions, have it is true kept on replenishing the earth with new people, but have done scarcely nothing toward race-improvement. In their degenerate position as dependents they could not even fulfil their essential duty of race choice—but were chosen by the sex not fitted for that responsibility, and so have helplessly assisted in transmitting inferior types.

But men, even handicapped by their sex, obscurely suffering from their abnormal position as masters, saddled with unnecessary burdens and crushed by the conditions they themselves produced and maintained, yet have built the world—so far.

They have grown to a stage of Humanness where they are now able to overlook the once all important sex distinction.

The age of men will stand long in history; following the earlier and far longer Age of Women. Now we are coming to the age of Humanity. It is time. •

There is no real loss confronting men. They are all going to gain infinitely more than they lose. In the common glory of a smoothly working humanity all the discord and recrimination of the exaggerated sexes will be forgotten.

One generation of children, reared under new conditions, will contentedly accept "their world," and not regret ours.

Chapter Five

· · · · ·

The Last Years,
1917–1935

Victory in Europe, the Red Scare, the Nineteenth Amendment, and an extended period of social and economic disruption divided the woman's movement and stilled most of its radical voices in these years. The collective push for social reform legislation, however, continued through 1924. Eight women's organizations founded, in 1920, the Women's Joint Congressional Committee to serve as a clearinghouse for federal legislation in the areas of prohibition, public school education, protection of infants, physical education, protection of women in industry, peace through international arms reduction, and full citizenship rights for women. However, when only six states ratified the child-labor amendment to the Constitution, passed by Congress in June 1924, that signaled the end of the progressive phase of reform feminism. Battered by red-baiting, frustrated by adverse court decisions, and fragmented over the Equal Rights Amendment, social reform feminism became defensive and disunified.[1] The collective, feminist consciousness of women in organizations waned; their interests became narrower and more individualistic. By the 1930s, all voluntary organizations were finding it difficult to raise money, and the most active women's groups were those campaigning against war.

Charlotte's days of influence declined markedly after she closed *The Forerunner*. Although she remained in demand, through 1924, as a name to grace executive boards and letterheads (League of Women Voters, Women's Meeting on League of Nations, Fifteenth International Congress Against Alcoholism, e.g.), her voice no longer commanded the allegiance of young female activists.

She had little to say in her autobiography of the impact the war had on her, save that she now had "a new sense of the difference in races and the use of nations in social evolution."[2] She supported the League of Nations and heaped contumely on the Russian Revolution, calling Bolshevism a "Jewish-Russian nightmare" and a "Russian Tyranny."[3] It angered her, she wrote the socialist William English Walling (1877–1936), how feebly "people have allowed Bolshevism to completely overshadow and discredit genuine Socialism!! . . . I do think that the movement toward socialization . . . has been set back for *years*— maybe fifty years!"[4]

Several of her articles and lectures dealt with her new attitudes toward race. Whereas during the early years of the twentieth century she had criticized those warning of "race suicide" in the face of incoming millions of immigrants, indeed celebrating "the mingling of peoples that goes to make up our own people,"[5] in the twenties she registered her foreboding. Her extended residence in New York City and the war altered her thinking about races and convinced her that it was social folly not to discriminate. She wrote in her autobiography: "I brought to the city a large, undiscriminating love of Humanity, without a shadow of race-prejudice or preference. I had much to learn": that there was a "deep, wide lasting vital difference between races"; that race-consciousness in the world was "rising and moving more portentously than ever"; and that the "study of the world must now turn on an understanding of races and their relative degree of advancement," so that the world would be divided fairly—not on the basis of " 'the pressure of the population.' "[6]

Only four of her articles appeared in print during 1917 and 1918, because, she wrote: "I had said all I had to say."[7] But at the end of 1918 she negotiated a contract to write a series of short commentaries for the *New York Tribune* syndicate, and, from March 1919 through April 1920, she turned them out almost daily. She also undertook a six-week trip, lecturing with one of the smaller Chautauquas.* But, she wrote,

* The Chautauqua Assembly was established in Ohio, in 1874, to train Sunday-school teachers during the summer months. Like the Lyceum idea (1825–1860), it expanded into a nationwide network of forums for speeches on self-improvement and popular-culture.

"As a Chautauqua lecturer I was as much a failure as in the pleasant platitudes of newspaper syndicates." She was, she concluded, "a teacher ... and what is required in this work is an entertainer."[8] Though she continued to propose lecture series and draft articles for periodicals, the engagements and manuscript acceptances decreased during the 1920s.

She remained on the Woman Party's National Executive Committee, arguing in vain for a broad-based organization that would represent women's "mass power."[9] She participated in the Woman's Committee for Political Action, founded in spring 1923, to rally to progressivism "all women who put principles before parties or candidates," but lost interest when it surrendered its independence, linked itself to the Conference on Progressive Political Action, and collapsed itself into the campaign to elect Wisconsin Senator Robert La Follette (1855–1925) President.[10] She then ceased to be a partisan of any particular woman's political organization. She praised the work of all the political interest groups that had emerged in the wake of the Nineteenth Amendment and were lobbying legislatures for laws favorable to women and children. In fact, during a time when the League of Women Voters* and the National Women's Party were at loggerheads over the Equal Rights Amendment, Charlotte praised each of them and did not take a forthright position on the ERA.[11]

She and her husband had moved to Norwich Town, Connecticut, in 1922, where she wrote what would be her last published book, *His Religion and Hers* (1923). It was the best-written, most cogent manuscript since *The Home*. It has a flow that many of the intervening works lack. But then it was a subject she had been thinking about most of her life. In late 1898 she had written Houghton: "I am immensely interested in finding sound sociology as I see it in the teachings of Christ; because I have long felt that our next advance must come through development of existing religious feeling and not in contradiction to it."[12]

She argued, in the book, that religion, as presently practiced, did not guide humans toward their divine purpose, their main social duty, "race improvement." They would have to be taught, therefore, to replace "the remote, uncertain, contradictory views concerning a book-derived God" with a "sense of social responsibility, a social conscience,

* Formed in 1919, by members of the National American Woman Suffrage Association.

hope and purpose for society, knowledge of the laws of social evolution, lives governed and guided in accordance with those laws." [13]

It was reviewed in over two-dozen periodicals, and the large majority of them were positive. A British edition appeared in 1924.

She wrote articles on town planning, monogamy, the educational value of motion pictures (as stimulators of children's imagination), and young people's "obsession" with sex. She feared that the sex impulse was becoming pathological, and she placed much blame on Sigmund Freud (1856–1939). Psychoanalysis, she wrote, was an obstacle to the advance of women, "a resurgence of phallic worship" in solemn phraseology.*[14]

Though she regularly praised advances women were making, she just as regularly criticized the behavior of young women, seeing in them "an unchecked indulgence in appetite and impulse; a coarseness and looseness in speech, dress, manner, and habit of life; and a wholesale resistance to any restraint more worthy of a fractious young male than a reasonable being." They were, she continued, unconcerned with the race-cleansing practice of "rigidly selective motherhood" and preoccupied with "mastering birth control and acquiring 'experience.' " [15]

Nevertheless, she softened her position on birth control, having come to believe that there was more of a threat to the world from population pressure—"a basic and permanent cause of war"—than indulgence in recreational sex.[16] And when the Ways and Means Committee of the United States House of Representatives held hearings, in May 1932, on a bill to allow doctors, hospitals, and clinics to use the mails to transmit contraceptive information to each other and their patients, Charlotte testified in support, telling the congressmen:

> I wish any of you would for the moment use your imagination and think of what it is to the woman, either by coercion or compulsion or persuasion to have forced upon her, as it were, another life within her to carry, to bear, to bring forth, to nurse, when she does not want to. When she does want to she is free to. There is nothing to prevent her. The whole thing hinges on that; the woman who does not want more children must not be made to bear them.[17]

* It is not clear if she actually read any of Freud's books. An undated reading list (probably composed in 1925) includes his *A General Introduction to Psychoanalysis* (first translated into English in 1920). Gilman papers, folder 22.

In May 1924 she took an inventory of her accomplishments and concluded she was "now happy, comfortable, taken care of by Houghton. . . . But!—To reestablish myself and set the books going—must do some fresh distinctive work—now."[18] But she could not place a detective story, *Unpunished,* nor a rewritten version of *Social Ethics,* and she wrote Grace, in July 1929: "I'm getting desperate to have something printed."[19] Lecture and speech engagements were now few and far between. She wrote Alice Stone Blackwell, in December 1930: "I greatly miss my audience—no lectures wanted any more, and books not taken."[20] All her books were now out of print, and when the International Congress of Women adopted a list of the hundred best books written by American women during the last century, none of her books were on it.[21]

In 1932, doctors found an inoperable cancer growing in her breast. She had always believed that human beings should not have to suffer from chronic pain, torment, and misery. "Sickness is a morbid condition, an evil condition," she had written. "It generates a miserable self-consciousness and irritability. A sick body is a heavy strain upon the mind, and injures its natural working."[22] Convinced that there should be as much dignity in death as in life, she began to store chloroform for the day she could no longer stand the pain.

Houghton died in May 1934, and at the end of August Charlotte returned to Pasadena, where Katharine was living, to spend her final days. On August 15, 1935 she wrote Edward Ross: "I've had the best-behaved cancer you ever saw—no pain at all. But in June I had shingles, which is a devilish disease, and now 'complications' have set in, nephritis and dropsy, and a fairly laughable weakness; so I'm going to go peacefully to sleep with my beloved chloroform. I'm getting fed up with sheer weakness."[23]

Two days later she died from an overdose of chloroform. In her suicide note, she wrote:

> Human life consists in mutual service. No grief, pain, misfortune or "broken heart" is excuse for cutting off one's life while any power of service remains.

> But when all usefulness is over, when one is assured of an unavoidable and imminent death, it is the simplest of human rights to choose a quick and easy death in place of a slow and horrible one.

Public opinion is changing on this subject. The time is approaching, when we shall consider it abhorrent to our civilization to allow a human being to lie in prolonged agony which we should mercifully end in any other creature.

Believing this choice to be of social service in promoting wiser views on this question, I have preferred chloroform to cancer.[24]

Carrie Chapman Catt defended the decision, arguing that Charlotte had not taken her life, she had only cut it short by a very brief period, thereby avoiding trouble to her daughter and pain to herself.[25] And Florence Finch Kelly (1858–1939), reviewing Charlotte's autobiography the following year, wrote: "There is no denying to Mrs. Gilman and her work the quality of greatness."[26]

Charlotte Perkins Stetson Gilman had experienced, felt, or seen many of the social obstacles blocking equality for and intimacy between the sexes. She had overcome the obstacles in her own path and then used her experience and her fine mind to develop theories to explain and reforms to overcome obstacles in the path of human progress. Though in historical perspective it can be seen that her thinking did not altogether transcend the intellectual, gender, and cultural limits of her era, and that she could be utopian, hortatory, and insensitive to racial concerns, she remains a shining example of the power of creative thinking, clear writing, and force of will.

Writings

"The New Generation of Women" *

Clearly and strongly defined among the distinctive features of our times stands the change in the status of women. Within scarcely more than a century from the first stir among advanced thinkers there has arisen in gathering force what has been known as "the woman's movement," more recently called "feminism," with results so swift and startling as to arouse alarm among the more conservative.

The very suddenness of this change, as well as the close

* Current History, 18 (August 1923), pp. 731–737.

intimacy of the relations involved, account for much that is unwelcome; but it is only within the last few years that any conspicuous new evils could be pointed out in the behavior of women. A survey of the whole field, however, together with recognition of contributory causes which have nothing to do with the woman's movement, reduces our anxiety over local misconduct.

For a long time the movement was rightly called a revolt. Women lived under conditions of such glaring injustice that at first they demanded only "women's rights," such as equality before the law, equal opportunity in education, equal pay for equal work and an equal share in democracy.

Over the whole world, in proportion to its civilization, this stir is felt; the women of China have made swift advance, the women of Turkey are leaving off their veils, the women of Europe and America are showing in education, in industry, in the professions, in political ability, capacities which used to be thought quite beyond them.

The World War was a strong factor in the immediate past, calling upon women for unusual activities. The result of those activities astonished the world. But the war also brought other forces into play, acting both on men and women and leading to other results in many ways unfortunate.

Before going into these it is desirable to consider the results of the woman's movement as a whole, using our own country as a fair sample of the most progressive nations. We must distinguish sharply between the general progress of the age, common to both men and women, and the special gain or loss of women in comparison with men.

Woman's Advance in Education

In education, for instance, the improvement is marked and rapid. In school, college and university, in popular literature and lectures, this improvement gives reason for mental progress in both sexes; but the gain of women is far greater in proportion. From being an almost uneducated class, supposed to have inferior brains, they have moved forward to such easy equality, in many cases to such superiority, that some now hold that the same courses of our college curricula, earlier considered beyond the powers of "the feminine mind," are now "too feminine."

This sudden advance in education must be further distinguished by its having been made under heavy opposition. A most interesting record could be made of this fact, as proving the weight of masculine prejudice, which so long placed every obstacle in the way of feminine progress.

There can be no longer any reasonable doubt as to the equality of the woman's mind with the man's in ability to learn. Whether this is accompanied by an equal ability to invent, to create, to make new steps in the world's advance, cannot be so swiftly established, on account of the conditional disadvantages of women. The man, married or single, is free to concentrate upon his specialty, and is, indeed, required to; while the woman if she is married carries upon her shoulders that group of primitive industries which we call "housework," in addition to the cares and untrained labors of child-culture. Motherhood itself would take some years from her professional life, though motherhood is not a disability, but a special power. A year's vacation should be taken with each baby.

The single woman, on the other hand, while freed from these complications, has not, as has the man, a home and a "help-mate" to strengthen and comfort her while she works. She is robbed of normal functioning as a mother and of the pleasures of family life; celibacy is an unnatural state for either sex.

But after allowing for all this, it may fairly be said that so far the woman's mind does not manifest in the same degree the qualities of individual initiative and of creative power that we are accustomed to consider peculiar to the man's. That some instances do exist, however, shows it is not a sex distinction. Perhaps another century or so must pass, with great development in "the belated trades" of the household and an ennobling specialization in child-culture, before it can be authoritatively stated that there is any essential difference in mental qualities; whether, in short, there is sex-distinction in the brain.

If the question arises as to whether there is any general revolt or protest by women against their previous status, this may be heartily answered in the affirmative. There are two lines of proof to be offered—one, the achievements established by women in so many lines of work, in so many new habits and customs of dress and behavior; the other in that inexorable record of passing events, current literature. The short story or novel gives a picture of its times. The blushing, weeping, swooning maiden of the past is wholly gone. Instead of fainting on Reginald's breast and crying "My preserver!" the heroine of today quite frequently preserves him.

Our previous judgments of women are being most rudely reversed in many directions. Women used to be called "conservative," especially in matters of religion, but now every new cult has its flocks of feminine followers, and the most widespread of them all has a woman prophet.* Here, at least, is no lack of initiative.

Too much must not be demanded, in measure of progress, from this newly emancipated class. They emerge from ages of domestic seclusion into a world already established and carried on by men—in short, into "a running concern." They cannot change it at once, even as far as they desire to, and much of their immediate behavior is mere reaction.

Mental and Physical Development

Their most advantageous steps, considered personally, are those of mental and physical development. Mentally, these steps are long and swift. We now see women in the learned professions, including the ministry; women in business; with ever-widening range; women editing magazines and papers, and writing to such an extent that literature bids fair to be called a "feminine profession."

In physical culture the change is as marked, Definite gymnastic training, that high art by which the ancient Greeks produced the most beautiful bodies the world has ever seen, is but a recent growth in our country. Its application to girls was long resisted, as was every other new advance for them. Yet now every girls' school and college has its physical training department; the girls' camps teach all manner of feats of strength and skill, even to

---

* She is probably referring to Aimee Semple McPherson (1890–1944), who founded the International Church of the Foursquare Gospel.

"hurling the javelin," and the outdoor sports of our young people are shared by both sexes.

There still remain critics and opponents of such training, people who believe in some mysterious disability in the female which unfits her for more than the lightest activities. These critics have never found it unfeminine for a woman to spend her days over a washtub, nor have they noticed that the sturdy peasant women of Europe work in the fields as well as in the house, and are none the less mothers of large families. Neither have they once looked at the other species of females and observed that a mare can run as well as a stallion, a lioness fight as well as a lion.

As a large general fact, it is exactly as good for girls to have physical training as it is for boys, and exactly as bad for either of them to have wrong training or to overdo it. We may even admit that girls, lacking the earlier rough-and-tumble play of boys and plunging into new exercises with more nerve than muscle, might more easily go too far and hurt themselves. But against every instance of some school or college girl being so hurt we may bring up the list of promising young men who are being crippled and even killed at football, who are dilating their hearts at rowing or running, breaking their fingers at baseball, and succumbing to the too-frequent early breakdown of the athlete.

No one contends that the sad record of injury and death to boys and men proves that physical culture is bad for them; it proves only unreasonable excess. Meantime the history of our women's colleges shows most favorable results from suitable physical training. A strong, active, well-muscled body is a blessing to a woman as much as to a man.

Moreover, it is only through true physical culture that we may rebuild the nobler types of beauty shown in the sculpture of the past. Man's admiration of woman has nothing to do with beauty. The Hottentot [Khoikhoi] admires the steatopygous development of his women; most Oriental races admire them fat, and some African tribes fatten them like Strasbourg geese. Women themselves have shown no knowledge of the true shape and proportions of the human figure; few have it yet.

We are but forty years or less from the wasp waist, and,

though the girls of today go corsetless, their concave, slouching attitude of recent years shows that the change was not due to any wisdom on their part. A generation of white-nosed women who wear furs in Summer cannot lay claim to any real progress in the sense of common beauty or the beauty of common sense.

Our best hope for a high standard of human beauty lies in a well-organized system of physical culture, accompanied by the teaching of beauty in our schools, illustrated with picture, statue and story, to make it a familiar ideal. Toward such improvement there is a perceptible advance.

The women of today are able to wear comfortable, beautiful and hygienic clothing if they know enough. There is far more latitude of choice, more freedom from narrow comment, and a clear improvement in a certain standardization of styles, as in the "sport suit," the business suit, and, best of all, the meeting of real athletic needs by the knickerbocker and riding suit. The woman swimmer may buy a rational "swimming dress," even though the beach lounger wears an utterly irrational "bathing dress."

Independence and Vital Living

Behind all these lies the most essential change in the status of women, their growing economic freedom. No matter what other equality might be obtained, so long as one sex was dependent on the other for its food, clothing and shelter, it was not free. Any reference to our census returns for several decades will show how wide and swift is the change in this regard. Girls of today, even well-to-do ones, expect to have some occupation, at least before marriage, and the number of married women who still keep up a "gainful occupation" increases every year, to which additional income their husbands are becoming reconciled. It is true that most of the women who work for their livings are still in the lower grades, but the winning of higher levels goes on constantly, with larger work and better pay.

The general effects of the emergence from earlier conditions it is still too early to measure with convincing accuracy, especially if the observer has not felt the weight of past restrictions. But some of the gains made are sufficiently common and obvious to force recognition. For instance, ten or twenty years have been added to the lives of women, both in active work and in enjoyment. A century ago 15 was a marriageable age, 30 was mature matronhood, and 40 was old age. As to anything over 40—that was sheer senility.

Women live somewhat longer than do men, but their life cycle in men's minds covered in the past only the child-bearing period; they had less childhood, less youth, less maturity and far more of the least desirable period, old age. Save as somebody's mother or grandmother, they ceased to be. Today they have longer childhood, longer youth, and maturity holds on steadily, with health and strength, ambition and enjoyment, well into what used to be mere fireside knitting time. The woman of 50 and onward has a wide free outlook; many have undertaken new trades and professions and carried them on successfully. This is a great and beneficent change of status.

It is early to look for achievements in law-making or law-enforcing. The use of the ballot is still new to women; they are for the most part without any general program of their own, and their special efforts have been mainly directed toward the improvement of conditions affecting women and children. They have, naturally enough, accepted the politics of their fathers, as men usually do, or they have united valiantly in new measures toward certain reforms, as men also do.

Furthermore, it should be remembered that women, even if united, do not outnumber men. In our country there are more men than women so they cannot be expected to introduce any great advance without men's help. The change which is sure to follow upon their entrance into politics will not be clearly shown in history for some generations. It will result from a new sense of the duty of women to the world as mothers—mothers not merely of their own physical children, but world mothers in the sense in which we speak of city fathers, only with their duties more nobly apprehended and more practically fulfilled.

The initial accomplishments already made may be seen, like other signs of recent progress, in that running mirror of events, current fiction. The opening chapter of a popular novel, published within two or three years, describes a vigorous heroine who slips out early in the morning in her pajamas and some sort of wrapper, swims happily in a forest pool, and then climbs a beech tree to enjoy a marmalade sandwich which she had brought with her. As she returns to the house she is met by two grown children, who congratulate her on her forty-third birthday! The problem before this lively lady is how to take up again her study of medicine, in which she had made great advances before marrying. In this she does not succeed, but that she wishes to do it shows the change in women. Happy wifehood, proud motherhood and a comfortable income do not satisfy her; she has also the feelings proper to a human being, and wishes to function socially.* Some story of fifty years or so ahead, perhaps less, will show us women successfully accomplishing both their feminine and their human responsibilities — in spite of Mr. Hutchinson's piteous protests in another current novel.†

At present the new status of women is still more a matter of assertion than of accomplishment; still more easily attained by the single woman or the widow than by the wife and mother. Yet wifehood and motherhood are the normal status of women, and whatever is right in woman's new position must not militate against these essentials.

The difficulties here are peculiar to our times. Women have to overcome very ancient prejudices and deep-seated emotions; they have to establish and hold new relationships without injury to older ones, and they are called upon to do this at a time when domestic service, that common basis of all our home-keeping above a certain grade, is slipping from under our feet. This change of status affects a large class of women, the servants; and another large class, the employers. The servants, as a class, are moving from the limitations of their old grade, our lowest industrial stage, out into a variety of occupations offering possible advance.

Neither the employers nor the servants are conscious of the historic importance of this movement. The servants make the change because they personally prefer the position of an employee to that of a servant; and the employers make no change at all to

---

* Unable to identify.
† Arthur S. Hutchinson, *If Winter Comes* (Boston: Little, Brown, 1922).

meet the new condition, but sit complaining of their discomforts and difficulties in narrow-minded self-pity. Nevertheless this extremely important change of status is going on, and in a generation or so we shall see the labor which we are so fondly convinced must be done by amateurs at home, being done by professionals, and the product furnished to the home with labor employed by the hour.

Women's Abuse of New Freedom

Meanwhile, in this period of uneasy makeshifts, when the old is slipping away from us and the new is not yet clearly apparent, there are certain very conspicuous and undeniably evil features in the behavior of some classes of women. In our great cities especially, and elsewhere among those who imitate the foolishness of great cities, women have shown an unmistakable tendency to imitate the vices of men. In this they are not only as bad as, but worse than, men because anything injurious to the race is more harmful and more reprehensible as it affects the mother.

The behavior of the women in this matter is precisely that of any servile class suddenly set free. Indulgences previously enjoyed by the master and denied to the slave are eagerly seized upon as proof of freedom and equality. It is certainly to be hoped that our race-mothers will soon see not only the danger, but the undignified absurdity of imitating the worst weaknesses of men.

There is, however, much more involved in this present period of indecency than the rising of women. Any student of recent and current history can observe a movement of moral relaxation, a lowering of standards in sex relationship which has been going on for the last half century or so. In England this became more and more visible in the days of, let us say, Aubrey Beardsley [1872–1898] and The Yellow Book, culminating disastrously in the sad end of that scapegoat of the "higher-ups," Oscar Wilde [1854–1900]. In France we see it blossoming freely in [Paul] Verlaine [1844–1896] and [Charles] Baudelaire [1821–1867], in that dallying with the "Fleurs de Mal," which was languidly accepted as the "fin de siècle" movement.* It remained for the German people to

---

* Charles Baudelaire's Les Fleurs de Mal (1857) was a collection of poems on sexual and erotic subjects and cultural decay. Paul Verlaine addressed the same subjects and, by

give us the quintessence of all this in the solemn philosophical sex-mania of Sigmund Freud, now widely poisoning the world.

In the old status of women, now broken and changing under our eyes, they were as a sex quite helplessly under the tutelage and dominance of man; so taught by religion, so held by custom, so forced by law. From this dominance they are now largely free. But so agreeable a mastery was not to be surrendered without a struggle. The real trend of the woman's movement is away from the long abuse of this relationship. It postulates freedom of the woman from that abuse, not freedom to join in it. The misused movement we call "birth control" is intended to protect the mother from enforced childbearing, and has been most beneficial to the crowded poor. But in the present mishandling of that movement it has come to be, as it were, a free ticket for selfish and fruitless indulgence, and an aid in the lamentable misbehavior of our times, affecting both men and women.

That this misbehavior is more marked and more condemned in women is quite right; in all that affects the health and happiness of the race the mother is the more important factor.

The special demand of women for a permanent name of their own is wholly right, and has no faintest bearing on the matter of sex misconduct. In the old days, when women had no social relationship whatever, and were to be distinguished only by which man they belonged to, as with a slave or a dog, it would have seemed absurd for them to claim a permanent name. Any question about them was not "Who is she?" but "Whose is she?"

Now, however, as women enter into one profession after another, really counting in social relationship, it is necessary to know them by name. Moreover, it increasingly often occurs that a woman may make a name for herself perhaps more widely known

---

muting the explicitness of his verse, continued the transition to symbolist poetry. Beardsley, perhaps the greatest drawer of his era, was the art editor of *The Yellow Book,* an avant-garde journal, for one year and illustrated Wilde's *Salomé* (1896) with sensual drawings of women. Wilde, one of the leading writers and wits of the latter part of the nineteenth century, had his career and reputation devastated by a series of trials culminating in his conviction for homosexual offenses in 1895. Charlotte had reviewed the first two issues of *The Yellow Book,* generally favoring the first but displaying hostility toward the second, mainly because of Beardsley's drawings. *The Impress,* October 20, 1894, p. 10, and December 22, 1894, p. 11.

than that of her husband, so that he is disrespectfully spoken of as "Mr. Jane Smith." "Mrs. John Smith" we have not thought ignominious, but "Mr. Jane" we do. So the man whose name is, so to speak, taken away from him, becomes willing that his wife should have one of her own—and leave him his!

The "legitimatizing" of children born out of wedlock is another movement resting on social justice. Whatever punishment society may think just for the man or the woman who offends against the law, there is surely no law against being born. The child has committed no sin, merits no punishment. Moreover, in punishing the real offenders, since the man is usually the wooer, and since in case of a child resulting the mother has to face her responsibility alone, with a condemnation not accorded him, it is quite startlingly unfair to add to her burdens the shame and loss of the unoffending little one. We need not feel that this belated consideration for the child is any mark of greater license among women, but of a higher sense of justice in both men and women.

It is in precisely this appearance of larger human instincts that we may see the best proofs of development in the rising of one-half the world. Their first demand was for justice, the next for freedom, and now they are beginning to shoulder responsibility and to seek to enact laws in the general interests of the community, instead of merely those in the special interests of a sex.

Divorce Increase Symptom of Revolt [sic]

Some, naturally deprecating the commonness of divorce today, feel this as an evil due to the movement of women. That more frequent divorce is so due is largely true, but that is not the evil. The evil lies in the conditions of married life, which used to be borne in silence, with death as the only relief, and which now are held to be causes for divorce. Those most condemning it seem to consider the majority of divorces to be such as are eagerly advertised by a yellow or yellowish press; whereas, in fact, the majority of divorces in America are sought by women over 40, women who have endured whatever they suffered from until the children were grown, and who break an unbearable marriage when they are far from likely to make another one, and when any kind of occupation is hard to find.

With new knowledge of disease and its effect upon children, of the disastrous results of alcoholism through paternity (or maternity), there is a strong and true feeling that it is wrong to maintain a marriage when such conditions obtain. This feeling is a credit to both men and women and tends toward a higher standard of birth.

Home Not Lost, But Changing

There are two main lines of disapproval among those who "view with alarm" the new status of women—one of sentiment, the other of a sound concern for the future of the race. On the sentimental side we are certainly undergoing a rapid and serious change. No poet of our time could describe a wife as did Jean Ingelow:

> Who, waking, guideth as beseems
> Her happy house in order trim,
> And tends her babes, and, sleeping, dreams
> Of them and him.*

That view of marriage which required the absolute absorption of the wife in the husband is not commonly held today, nor is it likely to return. But we lose that utter devotion only to gain a far higher thing—friendship. Sentiment is not lost, but it is changed. Even in the closely allied feeling which deprecates "the passing of the home" we need not fear; it is not being lost, that home, but it is changing.

In our dread of the "new woman" we should not lose sight of the fact that we never were satisfied with the old kind. The records of the world's literature show but too plainly how low an opinion men have always had of women.† The kind of woman

---

* Jean Ingelow, "The Letter L," *Poems by Jean Ingelow* (London: Oxford University Press, 1921), p. 75.

† The low opinion of woman is prominent in all ancient literature, and is clearly expressed in common proverbs. From a "Handbook of Proverbs of All Nations," I may quote the following: "Men are deeds, and women words"; "A man of straw is worth a woman of gold"; "Man, woman and the devil are three degrees of comparison"; "Whoso loseth his wife and a farthing hath great loss in the farthing"; "A dead wife's the best goods in a man's house." There are many more proverbs of a similar trend of cynicism. [Footnote in original. She is probably referring to Henry George Bohn, *A hand-book of proverbs, comprising an entire republication of Ray's collection of English proverbs, with his additions from foreign languages* . . . (London: Bohn, 1855).]

who is gradually taking the place of the old is really a more agreeable and far more competent creature.

In that deeper concern for the race future we have sounder ground for distress, if indeed the new status of women militates against motherhood. But that cannot be shown. This offensive current of licentiousness is not a new thing in the world. Such a period was seen in the reign of Charles II. of England [1630–1685; ruled 1660–1685], in more than one reign in France, under that eminent German Empress Catherine [II] of Russia [1729–1796; ruled 1762–1796], and so on here and there throughout history. There is distinctly nothing new in license and indecency. Women of all ages have been participants or victims in such excesses.

What is new, what does distinguish the women of our times, is such action as that brought by our women's clubs to require medical examination before marriage. This effort to protect the unborn from the worst of diseases requires knowledge, courage, and a high sense of woman's responsibility.

No honest thinker need be alarmed by the new status of women. The laws of nature are apt to have their way. Women are first, last and always mothers, and will so continue. But while motherhood in the past was grievously warped and hindered by various kinds of oppression and injustice, the motherhood of the future will be wiser, stronger, more effective in improving humanity.

We may look over and beyond the physical indecencies of our misguided young people, as well as of the older generation, and the mental indecencies of a sex-sodden psychoanalysis, and see before us the same dutiful and affectionate mother whom we have always loved, with a broader outlook and larger powers.

Motherhood will keep.

"Is America Too Hospitable?" *

There is a question, sneeringly asked by the stranger within our gates: "What is an American?" The American, who knows he is one but has never thought of defining himself, is rather per-

* *The Forum,* 70 (October 1923), pp. 1983–1989.

plexed by the question. A simple answer is here suggested: "Americans are the kind of people who make a nation which every other nationality wants to get into." The sneering stranger then replies: "By no means. It is not your nation we admire,—far from it! It is your great rich country we want to get into."

But Africa is a great rich country, too; why not go there? They do not wish to go there; the country is "undeveloped"; there are savages in it. True, but this country was undeveloped, when we came here, and there were savages in it.

Our swarming immigrants do not wish for a wilderness, nor for enemies. They like an established nation, with free education, free hospitals, free nursing, and more remunerative employment than they can find at home.

The amazing thing is the cheerful willingness with which the American people are giving up their country to other people, so rapidly that they are already reduced to a scant half of the population. No one is to blame but ourselves. The noble spirit of our founders, and their complete ignorance of sociology began the trouble. They honestly imagined that one kind of man was as good as another if he had the same opportunity,—unless his color was different. Consequently they announced, with more than royal magnificence, that this country was "an asylum for the poor and oppressed of all nations."

"F.P.A.'s"* remark on this point is worth remembering,— "Some of us, who are not particularly poor nor oppressed, but who have to live in the asylum, suggest that the more violent inmates be confined in separate wards."

Those high-minded old forefathers of ours were strangely lacking in even the political knowledge of their time, to imagine that "the poor and oppressed" were good stock to build up the country. The more competent, skillful, and daring were able to get on at home. The poor and oppressed were the under dogs, necessarily. A nation largely composed of under dogs is not likely to remain on top.

Never was a nation founded at so high a level of political idealism. However there were three things our generous founders

* Franklin P. Adams (1881–1960), a satiric commentator on society and social foibles.

could not foresee: the development of steam manufacturing, of steam transportation, and of colossal selfishness ready to sacrifice the good of the country to private profit.

Any man who knows enough to recognize that the advantages of another country are better than his own; who is strong enough to break home ties, brave enough to face the unknown, and who has saved enough to pay his passage, is likely to make a good citizen in the land of his choice.

But when we scour Europe for "cheap labor," deliberately seeking poor citizens instead of good ones, baiting them with glowing advertisements, and arranging to be paid from the proceeds of their labor, the resultant flood of low-grade humanity is not immigration at all, but sheer importation, which should be dutiable!

We used fondly to take for granted that the incoming millions loved the country as we did, and felt eager to join it. Some of them do. Enormous numbers do not. It is quite true that we ourselves are a mixed race,—as are all races today,—and that we were once immigrants. All Americans have come from somewhere else. But all persons who come from somewhere else are not therefore Americans. The American blend is from a few closely connected races.

The idealism of our forefathers with its unavoidable ignorance, is more than matched today by our own idealism,—though we have knowledge enough to modify it. With glowing enthusiasm we have seized upon one misplaced metaphor, and call our country now a "melting pot" instead of an asylum. Our country is our home. Any man who wants to turn his home either into an asylum or a melting pot is,—well, he is a person of peculiar tastes.

Why did we ever so stupidly accept that metaphor? A melting pot is a crucible. It has to be carefully made of special material and carefully filled with weighed and measured proportions of such ores as will combine to produce known results. If you put into a melting pot promiscuous shovelfuls of anything that comes handy you do not get out of it anything of value, and you may break the pot.

The blending of races is not a new process. It has been going on ever since the different racial stocks were established and began to fight with one another, killing the men and marrying the women, mixing continually. We have all history to tell us about it, and all political geography to show us the results.

Since genus homo is one species, it is physically possible for all races to interbreed, but not therefore desirable. Some combine well, making a good blend, some do not. We are perfectly familiar in this country with the various blends of black and white, and the wisest of both races prefer the pure stock.

The Eurasian mixture is generally considered unfortunate by most observers. Of European races some seem to mate with better results than others. On the Levant, where there is as complete and longstanding a mongrelization as could be offered for study, the result is not an improved stock.

It is an entire mistake to suppose that the well-ordered World Federation to which we look forward requires the wiping out of national entity, or the physical compounding of racial stocks.

It is also a mistake to suppose that social evolution requires the even march of all races to the same goal. Again we have the open pages behind us to study. The sea-weeds and mosses have not all become oaks and roses, the monads and rotifers have not all become quadrupeds, nor have all the quadrupeds become bipeds and mammals. Evolution selects, and social evolution follows the same law. If you are trying to improve corn you do not wait to bring all the weeds in the garden to the corn level before going on.

Genus canis, like genus homo, can interbreed practically without limit. But if you want a watch-dog you do not mate an Italian greyhound with a hairless pup from Mexico.

If dogs are left to themselves, in some canine "asylum" or "melting pot," they are cheerfully promiscuous, but do not produce a super-dog. On the contrary they tend to revert to the "yaller dog," the jackal type so far behind them.

The present-day idealists have two main grounds of appeal in their defense of unlimited immigration. One is the advantage to us of the special gifts of the imported stock; the other is the advantage to them of the benefits of democracy. This last may be promptly disposed of. Any people on earth who want a democracy and are able to carry it on, can have one at home. There is no power above them which can prevent it. But if they do not want a democracy, or are unable to carry it on, they are a heavy drawback to us.

We are young in our great effort, we have by no means succeeded yet in developing this high form of government in full efficiency, in unimpeachable honesty and wise economy. Democracy moves on by the spread of ideas; majorities must be convinced, converted; a community of intellect is needed. The more kinds of races we have to reach, with all their differing cultures, ideas, tastes, and prejudices, the slower and harder is the task of developing democracy.

It would be far more helpful to the world if we could make such clear advance alone as to set all nations to imitating us, rather than to mix our physical stock and clog the half grown "body politic" with all manner of undemocratic peoples.

Now as to those "gifts" they are to bring us. In an article in *The Survey* some years since, Mr. John Collier, writing "For a New Drama," tells of a "Polish National University" with 1500 students, at Cambridge Springs, Pa., which is "consecrated to the preservation, in this new and deadening world, of those group achievement and group hopes,—one among a hundred streams of group endeavor,—which are our most precious heritage in all this land."*

It is not quite clear whether it is the Polish group which contributes our most precious heritage, or all the hundred. We ourselves, apparently, are only responsible for "this new and deadening world," our "melting pot" a sort of contribution box, enriched from without.

Mr. Collier thinks that "before long the Poles will become self-conscious with reference to drama," and further hopes, "the interdiction against the hyphen notwithstanding, that America may prove to be indeed a free land, and may learn to solicit as well as tolerate this impulse of group creativeness which is inarticulately manifest in the half-formed drama of the Poles."

This is a very good expression of a common and serious error.

* *The Survey*, 36 (May 6, 1916), pp. 137–141.

It is true of course that each separate nation has its own "gifts." A nation is a self-supporting group of people long enough associated in one country to form a certain type and to develop a certain culture of its own. It then produces after its kind such contributions to social progress as it may, some nations more, some less. A wandering people, as the Gypsies, is not a nation.

The development of humanity is measured by these national gifts, these steps in commerce and industry, in science, in religion, in literature and music and all the arts, in discoveries and inventions. But this distinctive product is evolved in the privacy of each nation, so to speak, and may then be shared.

The painting and music of Italy appeared in Italy, the art and science of France in France, the inventions and literature of England in England. Separate colonies of different nations in another country are not noted for their "gifts," much less a mixture of heterogeneous peoples of the most contrary genius and tendency. If "the half-formed drama of the Poles" is to become a living thing it will be in Poland, not in Pennsylvania.

The American people, as a racial stock, are mainly of English descent, mingled with the closely allied Teutonic and Scandinavian strains, of which indeed the English are compounded, together with some admixture of the Celt and Gael. The Latin races are represented more in South and Central America, with the French largely segregated in one province in Canada. It may be added, as to such a settlement, that when it came to the world war, this colony of transplanted Frenchmen would fight neither for the country they came from nor the country they came to. It is the French in France who command the honor and admiration of the world.

The American people, as representing a group culture, brought with them from England and Holland and Scandinavia the demand for freedom and the capacity to get it. Owing to their vast and sudden advantages in soil and climate, in mineral wealth and geographic isolation, they made rapid growth and were able to add to their inherited tendencies a flexible progressiveness, an inventive ingenuity, a patience and broad kindliness of disposition which form a distinct national character.

It is precisely this American character which is taken advantage of by the "poor and oppressed." The poorer and more oppressed they are the more they need it. Some great and good citizens have come to us, from various stocks, but this is a question of race mixture. There is no claim here made as to racial superiority. Almost any race is superior to others in some particular. Each has not only a right but a duty to develop its own special powers. The intellect of India or China is far more highly developed than ours in some lines, but if these races possessed this country they would only make another India or China. Indeed if our land were reinforced with a vast population of angels from heaven it would not be America!

One of the sharpest irritants arising from the various alien elements in our national body comes from an intensely self-satisfied group of young foreigners who come here to criticise and improve us. These, being more vocal than the poor and oppressed, are loud in disapproval. They are not content with founding universities for themselves, but enter ours and seek to dominate them.

They openly scorn our national culture, proclaiming the high superiority of their own. They are particularly sarcastic about our recent feeble efforts to digest the indigestible and assimilate the unassimilable, looking over this great country, in which already there are a full half of varied Unamericans. We have whole colonies of them with their own languages, schools, and newspapers, their children growing to maturity without even learning English, merely using this country as a convenience for temporary profit or permanent colonizing. Observe them in the war, taking flight in great numbers to fight for their respective home-lands, or staying here to work us in their interests. Even so long established residents as the Irish remain Irish,—they are not Americans. They would willingly sacrifice the interests of this country, or of the world as a whole, for the sake of Ireland.

Nationals of such pure intensity should bestow their talents on the lands they love. Internationalists, of the sort who wish to belong to none, but mix all racial ingredients into a smooth paste, should select an uninhabited island for their experiment.

These social mixers should study the art of cooking. You may take sugar, butter, eggs, milk, and flour, with dried fruit and flavoring extracts, and by rightly combining these ingredients make cake. You may take meat, bones, onions, tomatoes, with salt, pepper, and fine herbs, and by rightly combining these ingredients make soup. But if you mix sugar and meat, butter and bones, eggs and onions, milk and tomatoes, fine herbs and flavoring extracts, salt, pepper, and dried fruit,—you make neither soup nor cake but something we pay to have removed.

What is an American? The only kind of person on earth who invites all creation to crowd him out of house and home. And even he is beginning dimly to wonder if it is not time to withdraw the invitation.

His Religion and Hers: A Study of the Faith of Our Fathers and the Work of Our Mothers.*

Chapter III: Suggested Causes

[...] What would have been the effect upon religion if it had come to us through the minds of women?

If we are to trace our engrossing interest in death to the constant fighting and killing of early man, to the fact that death was the crisis in his activities, the significant event, rousing him to thought, what other interest are we to look for in the life of woman? What crisis set her mind at work, and what would have been its influence on religion?

The business of primitive woman was to work and to bear children. Her work was regular and repetitive; save for the gradual budding of invention and blossoming of decoration, it had no climax. There was small excitement in this, no thrilling event.

Yet her life held one crisis more impressive, more arousing, far, than man's; her glory was in giving life, not taking it. To her the miracle, the stimulus to thought, was birth.

Had the religions of the world developed through her mind, they would have shown one deep, essential difference, the difference between birth and death. The man was interested in one end

* New York: Century, 1923, pp. 45–53, 248–253, and 270–271.

of life, she in the other. He was moved to faith, fear, and hope for the future; she to love and labor in the present.

To the death-based religion the main question is, "What is going to happen to me after I am dead?"—a posthumous egotism.

To the birth-based religion the main question is, "What must be done for the child who is born?"—an immediate altruism.

Woman was not given to bootless speculation as to where the new soul came from, because of the instant exigencies of its presence. It had come, indeed, but in a small and feeble state, utterly dependent on her love and service. With birth as the major crisis of life, awakening thought leads inevitably to that love and service, to defense and care and teaching, to all the labors that maintain and improve life.

The death-based religions have led to a limitless individualism, a demand for the eternal extension of personality. Such good conduct as they required was to placate the deity or to benefit one's self—to "acquire merit," as the Buddhist frankly puts it. The birth-based religion is necessarily and essentially altruistic, a forgetting of oneself for the good of the child, and tends to develop naturally into love and labor for the widening range of family, state, and world. The first leads our thoughts away from this world about which we know something, into another world about which we know nothing. The first is something to be believed. The second is something to be done. [. . .]

Birth-based religion would steadily hold before our eyes the vision of a splendid race, the duty of upbuilding it. It would tell no story of old sins, of anguish and despair, of passionate pleading for forgiveness for the mischief we have made, but would offer always the sunrise of a fresh hope: "Here is a new baby. Begin again!"

To the mother comes the apprehension of God as something coming; she sees his work, the newborn child, as visibly unfinished and calling for continuous service. The first festival of her religion would be the Birth Day, with gifts and rejoicings, with glad thanksgiving for life. In the [wo]man's religion, the demand for ever-watching love and care, is that of the child, always turning to its mother —

> An infant crying in the night,
> An infant crying for the light,
> And with no language but a cry.

The mother, feeling in herself that love and that care, pours them forth on man, her child. Such recognition and expression of divine power are better than "worship." You cannot worship a force within you; the desire of the mother soul is to give benefit rather than to receive it.

As the thought of God slowly unfolded in the mind of woman, that great Power would have been apprehended as the Life-giver, the Teacher, the Provider, the Protector—not the proud, angry, jealous, vengeful deity men have imagined. She would have seen a God of Service, not a God of Battles. It is no wonder that Christianity was so eagerly adopted by woman. Here was a religion which made no degrading discrimination against her, and the fulfilment of which called for the essentially motherly attributes of love and service.

Women have adhered to all previous religions, of course, having no others; but the new teachings of Jesus were widely accepted by them and widely spread through their efforts. They were not, however, the interpreters, the disputers, the establishers of creeds. They did not gather together to decide whether or not men had souls. They did not devise the hideous idea of hell, the worst thought ever produced by the mind of man. It cannot be attributed to women any more than to Jesus that his wise, tender, practical teaching of right living was twisted and tortured into a theory of right dying.

Believing as they must the doctrines of gloom and terror forced upon them, and sharing in the foolish asceticism of the early Christians, we still find in religious associations of women their irrepressible tendency to love and service. It was not in nunneries that Benedictine and Chartreuse were concocted; we do not see pictures of fat nuns carousing in cellars. No, the convent turns naturally to the school, the sisters as naturally to nursing and teaching; and when, outside of religious orders, we see the first little organizations of women, these are charitable, educational, or to help the sick.

We all know, some of us to our cost, the reformatory impulse in woman. Her instinct for care, for training, for discipline, is a grievous thing if highly developed and focused on too small a group. This is sadly well known to many a man who has to live under the tutelage of his wife's mother after having escaped from his own. The entrance of women upon politics was most dreaded because of that reformatory tendency.

This essentially feminine impulse would have had a strong influence in molding religion, an influence lightened by that vision of a new-born, ever-growing race, open to constant improvement. We cannot improve a dead man; we can, a baby. The mother does not sit down among her mischievous brood and say, "Children are bad by nature," and, "We cannot legislate morality." (As if legislation were not for precisely that purpose!) She would not call the inevitable mistakes of childhood a "problem of evil." [. . .]

Chapter XIII: Natural Development and Effects of Her Religion

[. . .] Our primitive ideas of God, which we insist on maintaining as immovably as possible, have left us in strange difficulties as to human trouble. To a personalized and masculized [sic] deity we attributed all knowledge and all power; to ourselves we attributed nothing but "poor human nature"; and then, having to face the obvious miseries of life, the explanation was sought in some "inscrutable" purpose of God or in some malicious anti-god of awful power. Of late years the somewhat clearer and less reverent mind of man has postulated a god good enough as far as he went but incomplete; a young half-grown deity, doing his best with this world, and likely to improve.

But thought of God aroused by birth leads along a different road, to a different conclusion. The primitive woman had no more knowledge than the primitive man, but she had impulses and feelings quite other than his, and utterly different experiences. Early religion was not built on knowledge but on impulses, feelings, and experiences.

From hers would naturally arise such thoughts as these:

"Here is Life. It comes in installments, not all at once. The old ones die, the new ones come. They do not come ready-made;

they are not finished, they have to be taken care of. It is a pleasure to take care of them, to make new people. Everywhere we see the same process, motherhood carrying on life. The mother tree has seeds which make new trees, the mother birds lay eggs which make new birds, the mother beast brings forth her little one to take her place in time and carry on the line. . . .

"What a wonderful thing is Life! Live everlasting, going on continuously, in steps, the evercoming new ones taking the place of the old worn-out ones—how beautiful! And we cannot stop it if we would; nothing stops it; after the flood has fallen, after the ice is melted, after the forest fire has burnt out, year after year when winter is over, rises Life, always young, re-born—how glorious! . . .

"This grain is large and fine, it grows best in this kind of soil, I will pull out the other things around so that it will grow better. I will get some more and plant it here where it grows best. . . . This seed which I planted and took care of is better than what grew without help. I can make things better by taking care of them. . . .

"I have taught my child all I knew. He is wiser than that other whose mother died; who grew up, indeed, but is not so wise. Teaching is a help in living. Care and teaching makes things better. . . .

"I can make things! I can make pots of clay. I can make baskets of reeds. I can make clothes of skin. I can build a shelter for my little ones. I can soften food with fire—it keeps longer if it is cooked. . . .

"Not only can I make things but I can make them beautiful! With colors, with stitches, with lines on the soft clay, with patterns in the woven reeds, I can make beauty! Beauty! What a pleasure it is to be skilful and make things, and to make them beautiful! I will teach my daughter. . . .

"She has thought of a new pattern, more beautiful than mine. Ah! Life is not only in the animals: it is in the things we make; they grow too! Life, always coming, through motherhood, always growing, always improving through care and teaching! And this new product of life—not babies but things, useful things, made beautiful—what a joy life is! . . .

"What does it all? What is behind it all? Who is the first Mother, Teacher, Server, Maker? What Power under all this pouring flood of Life? What Love behind this ceaseless mother-love? What Goodness to make Life so good, so full of growing Joy?" . . .

Thus would the woman's mind have reached the thought of God.

Chapter XIV: His and Her Religion and Economics

We have indicated something of the kind of faith which is aroused through conscious motherhood, a faith resting firmly on the laws of nature, seeing God work through them.

What lines of action would naturally follow? In what way would they differ from the action encouraged by previous beliefs?

Primarily and essentially they differ in agreeing with natural impulse instead of undertaking a permanent struggle with it. The natural impulses of motherhood are altruistic in origin, and so tend to develop. The services of motherhood are immediately useful, and tend to become increasingly so. Therefore the growth of conduct would lead on into wider social coordination, without having to struggle with inner impulses of a destructive nature.

That group of impulses which, originally normal and useful, have become so injurious to social growth through long over-development, do not so operate through the mother. Free from the agony of fear, the weight of a looming sense of evil, the constant difficulty of struggling against one's own desires, motherhood's beneficent activities tend to widen into rich and peaceful social relationships. [. . .]

To the normal woman there is not the faintest need for any "struggle." She knows that every normal child delights to "work" if the work is the kind he likes; and that if he is properly fed and taught and generally comfortable he has strength for exertion and pride in accomplishment. She knows that work is the expression of power, and that power comes from the nourishment one has had, not from what one is going to have.

The whole feminine attitude toward life differs essentially from the masculine, because of her superior adaptation to the service of others, her rich fund of surplus energy for such service. Her philosophy will so differ, her religion must so differ, and her conduct, based on natural impulses, justified by philosophy and ennobled by religion, will change our social economics at the very root.

The elaborate structure of "political economy" with which men have sought to explain and justify their strange behavior, is much like the other elaborate structures evolved from the detached floating theories of speculative religions. To the mother the gross absurdities of food going to waste in one place and children starving in another cannot be explained away by any number of thick books.

The innate, underlying difference is one of principle. On the one hand, the principle of struggle, conflict, competition, the results of which make our "economic problems." On the other, the principle of growth, of culture, of applying service and nourishment in order to produce improvement.

This difference in principle, once expressed in religion, must tend to change our industrial relations for the better.

"Where Are the Pre-War Radicals?" *

Of the radicals I knew some have remained fixed, as the Single Taxers, still satisfied with their theory but perhaps more tired; some have plunged from Socialism into Communism—a long leap, or from Pacifism to Bolshevism—a longer one; some are sufficiently occupied with Birth Control; other wallow in Freudian psycho-analysis, which has the combined advantages of wide popular appeal in its subject matter, an imposing technology, and profitable use as a business.

There are many who are discouraged by the war and its

* A symposium of twenty-five people, of which two were women (Gilman and Ida Tarbell), including William Allen White (1868–1944), Newton D. Baker (1871–1937), Roger Baldwin (1884–1981), Clarence Darrow (1857–1938), Eugene V. Debs, Morris Hillquit, John Haynes Holmes (1879–1964), Norman Thomas (1884–1968), and Burton K. Wheeler (1882–1975). *The Survey*, 55 (February 1, 1926), p. 564.

effects, who feel that social advance is hopelessly checked, at least for the present, and who have taken refuge in a more personal philosophy. There is something very soothing in the vast reaches of New, or even Old, Thought; wherein we may wander alone and reach prodigious heights of attainment which, even if we cannot prove, at least no one else can disprove.

The group I know the best, Socialists but not Marxians, who see in Socialism a gradually introduced change in business methods working for the good of the whole community, recognize but too clearly how this normal advance is delayed by the Bolshevist performance, and hold their fire for the present.

Some have attained what they worked for, as the Prohibitionists and Equal Suffragists, and if they had no further purposes they are quiet; though hardly contented with the results. The more advantages secured the harder it is to rouse the public to see the need of anything further. Neither does the exercise of power attained give any assurance that "Labor" *per se* is any wiser or more disinterested than "Capital."

For myself there is a definite relief in being free from the work demanded by the various "causes" now won or temporarily in abeyance, and able at last to write and lecture on my own lines of social philosophy. To the average mind a Socialist or Suffragist can be nothing else, talk of nothing else. But now, when the ballot does not free woman from economic dependence, and when economic independence can not be maintained by the wife and mother until her household labor is professionalized, that immense structural and functional change in our economic base, the home, begins to loom large before us.

"Socialist Psychology" *

Social evolution is as natural a process as physical evolution, and follows similar lines.

In the evolution of the physical organism individual cells are drawn into relationship for their common advantage, become fixed and specialized in physical functions, and develop a group-con-

* Unpublished article or lecture, March 5, 1933, typescript, Gilman papers, folder 178.

sciousness governing conduct for the benefit of the organism. In the evolution of the social organism individual human beings are drawn into relationship for their common advantage, become fixed and specialized in their social functions, and develop a group-consciousness governing conduct for the benefit of the society.

We know little of the steps by which free separate cells become fixed and differentiated as bone-cells, lung-cells, liver-cells and so on; or of the slow appearance of a directing consciousness which made the mass an independent body, acting for itself, instead [of] themselves, but we can see going on about us and within us the gradual appearance of that directing consciousness in society.

The psychic unity of a common belief; the physical unity demanded by warfare; the mechanical unity developing as we are netted together by road and streets, by all increasing means of communication and transportation; the growing complexity and interdependence of our economic processes; all contribute to the formation of the social consciousness.

It is most widely felt in time of war, the original stimulant to common action; its most conspicuous expression is in the essential social function of government, which may be studied in every stage of development among the peoples now on earth; and in the more advanced cultures the social consciousness is forcing its way to recognition in the individual mind.

Able to realize a common good, to visualize a future benefit, to feel a common danger; armed with the constructive powers of a democracy or the destructive powers of a mob, we are beginning to take action for what we conceive to be the benefit of society.

Shortly before the French revolution [of 1789] this keen interest in the common good, forced into activity by the conspicuous injustice and incompetence of the existing system, found expression among thinkers in new theories of human relationship, as [Jean-Jacques] Rousseau's [1712–1778] "Social Contract." [1762] Those who interested themselves in such study were called "socialists" precisely as we use the term botanist or entomologist.

The French socialists were warmly humanitarian, and so were the English followers of this line of thought, but the powerful

work of Karl Marx put a definite stamp on the movement, as did
the argumentative Paul [5?-67?] on the spirit of Christianity, or
the rigid [Jean] Calvin [1509–1564] on the Protestant steps to a
freer religion.

Marx unfortunately was no sociologist, even in imagination.
Among all the complicated processes which form and maintain a
society he saw only the economic. In the historic steps by which
our self-seeking individuals are growing into social relationship he
saw only Oppressors and Oppressed, a long story of some men
who were especially selfish and cruel, compelling other men to
work for them and give them all the proceeds of their labor, save
enough for the barest living.

The arithmetical fact that the Oppressors were as one to a
hundred compared to the Oppressed did not seem to him of
importance, save indeed that he saw they were quite able to
overthrow their Oppressors—if they only would!

With his basic theory of economic determinism governing all
that followed, he named the existing system of industry Capitalism, set up in opposition to it his system of Socialism, and taught
that the only step from one to the other was by revolution of the
Oppressed, complete destruction of Capitalism and immediate
substitution of Socialism.

To promote this desired end he strove in all ways to rouse the
Oppressed to the attack. Numbers they had but no sense of unity,
no organization. To develop this he first gave them a name, The
Working Class. Again the arithmetic failed to impress him. To call
almost the whole of humanity a "class" is really somewhat ridiculous.

The benefits promised by the new system they were to introduce after they had removed the old one were beyond the mental
grasp of most of this large Class of his naming. It sounded too
much like heaven. The instincts of the Oppressed were after all
very much like those of the Oppressors, only weaker. The public
gain, in the future, was not a strong appeal to the mass.

In order to waken and inspire action lower impulses were
stirred, envy and hatred, revenge for past sufferings, and all this
was used by socialist propagandists, with the favorite implement

of "calling names." This Working Class was fairly deified and the Capitalists were dubbed "Bourgeosie" [sic] and so damned.

It is one of the minor marvels of our social processes that we can take a common word, or forge an entirely new one and then load it with violent emotion: As seen so conspicuously in Soviet Russia, where even the peasants (meaning Russia by eighty per cent) were made into "Classes" by word of mouth, just marked off arbitrarily according to their relative ability and possessions—Kulak, Seredniak, Bedniak (or something like that)*—and treated accordingly. They did not know they were classes, any more than an ordinary grocer knows that he is a Bourgeois.

The kind of Socialist Psychology thus formed is plain to see in Marx-adoring Russian today. In its deification of the proletariat it takes the attitude of a man worshipping his own meat. True it is that our lives depend on those who do the work of the world, but that work in its most valuable phases is not done by the day-laborer.

The physical body is for the most part composed of "the plain people" doing the simpler kinds of work, but if it had no other constituents, it would not be a very efficient body.

That economic basis of Marxian socialism vitiates it so deeply as to have set against it millions who would gladly have accepted a legitimate socialism, based on sound sociology. Such legitimate socialism rests on quite other considerations, and involves a psychology markedly different.

The picture before us is a fairly simple one, the stuff of which society is being made was in the scattered loose-knit hordes of savages, from which all social forms have risen. They had only the group consciousness of a physical family, enlarging to a tribe, and for long their only social functions were those of occasional group-hunting and group-fishing.

Social evolution has brought us from this to the large close-knit powerful bodies we call national. It has developed the varied and interconnected social functions by which such bodies live, in a greater or less degree according to our stage of progress.

"Humanity" is being developed among us through social evo-

* *Kulaks* were better-off peasants; *seredniaks* middle peasants; and *bedniaks* poor peasants.

lution, and some of the wasteful experiments of successive cultures have shown far more progress than others, are, so to speak, more human. The whole process is similar to those of physical evolution, the same wide variation of types, the repeated failures, the partial successes, and the grad[ual] appearance of more competent bodies, and of higher intelligence.

Social evolution is easier to understand than physical, because its range is so short, comparatively, its protoplasm of scattered savagery is still observable, as in the Bushmen of Africa. We have enough recorded history to give some indication of the upward steps of the arrested forms, and of the wide range of failures, and such an exhibition of present types as should clarify our study.

We find today among what we consider the most "advanced" nations a very general consciousness of social needs and deficiencies, many efforts to improve the minds and to protect the health of the citizens. Military protection, a primal social function, is well developed and civil law seeks to punish crime and ensure justice.

But with all our social progress, all the elaborate organization of law, of government, of education, we are sadly slow in socializing our economic processes. The first groups fought for their hunting grounds. Later groups fought for their grazing grounds, later still for their farming grounds. "A country" was secured to the people, but in that country they were left to their resources and efforts, each man to "make a living" as best he could.

Society stood over the process like a referee at a prize fight, making laws to restrain the predatory instincts which are still so strong in us, administering checks and privileges to somewhat man[age] the wild confusion and to ensure "opportunity" to the combatants.

For combatants they were; living in army-protected peace in their beloved country; and spending arduous lives in, negatively, each man working for himself and family, and, positively, those abler and smarter enriching themselves hugely at the expense of the others. We call it "the struggle for existence." We assume it to be not only natural, unavoidable, but beneficial. We hold that only by freedom in such combat—known as "competition"—can our best qualities be brought out and the best results obtained.

This theory of social economics has resulted in the conditions with which we are so familiar throughout history, leading to both special wealth and general poverty, producing and maintaining an unavoidable proportion of vice, crime and disease, and leading again and again to the downfall of an apparently successful society through the deterioration of the people.

We are now sufficiently socially conscious to recognize the evils of our economic anarchy, and the Marxian socialist thrusts forward his theory of change with fiery vigor. The only large sample offered us of the result of this doctrine is in the experiment in Russia, and so far its methods rouse both horror and contempt, and its results, showing in fourteen years of absolute power incapacity to provide its people even with sufficient food, clothing and shelter, are not so alluring as to win wide approval.

That proletarian dictatorship shows no knowledge of the social organism, no understanding of the laws and processes of social evolution, only the passionate desire to establish the Working Class as all that is needed to make a society, and to manufacture that society out of those materials, at once, by force.

In the face of this ghastly exhibition and our natural revulsion at the very name of socialism, it is not easy to establish the real nature of the economic changes before us, their natural, gradual and steadily beneficial results.

Under all the emotions aroused by names, what are the facts as [to] the economic needs of a healthy society?

A society is composed of human animals and those animals must be maintained in health and happiness if the society is to be so. Here is no difficult problem. Human animals, like others, need pure and sufficient food, protection, shelter, proper exercise, and right conditions for mating and rearing young. These are the absolute basic necessities of social life.

An intelligent conscious society must guarantee such conditions to its members.

Quite beyond these personal necessities come the social necessities, first of which is the maintenance of all those social functions of production and distribution, of transportation and communication in which are ensured at once the widest individual development and our common advantage.

Once recognizing that all human industry is a social process we question if "free competition" is the best method of promoting it. The whole record of the past shows that it is not. The hope of the future is in the socialization of what we have previously considered private activities.

Instead of recoiling in alarm at Russia-blackened visions of forcibly "communized" occupations, look calmly at such well-known social servants as the postman and the school-teacher. These were once private employees, hired by those who could afford it, denied to those who could not. In the normal process of socialization they are now hired by the public, paid by the public, and their services enjoyed by the public—irrespective of personal ability to pay. That is legitimate socialism.

No one is afraid of the socialized functions we already have.

Everyone is afraid of having any more. Why?

We saw long since that a democracy required an educated community, and in the interests of that common advantage we not only provided but enforced such education as we thought best. Our ideals of education are open to improvement, and are indeed improving, but at least we recognize it as a public necessity and provide it.

Certain other things are as necessary, or more so: as steady employment, and all the necessities of life.

These we have thought best assured by competition. They are not. Our anarchic methods of economics visibly do not ensure proper provision for everybody, and as visibly do ensure a dreadful proportion of paupers, defectives, degenerates, vice, crime and disease. These are not natural, society makes them.

When the Boer War [1899–1902] showed to England a decline in the stature of her soldiers, some social consciousness was stirred, and there was instituted a truly English "Commission of Inquiry Into the Causes of the Physical Deterioration of the British Poor"—or a similar title.* One thing clearly standing out from that study is the statement by Charles Booth, in his book on the subject, of the effect of London slums on their inhabitants.†

He showed that when the laboring people came from the

---

* Interdepartmental Committee on Physical Deterioration, 1904.
† Charles Booth, *Life and Labour of the People of London* (1889).

country to London—and the increasing population from a cramped village must go somewhere—the first generation is fairly well-developed and strong; the second generation is smaller, weaker, more sickly; the third generation is largely diseased, defective, degenerate; and *there is no fourth!*

A society which allows poverty, over-crowding, unemployment, ruins its own stock.

The real change of mind before us involves no exaltation of any "class," genuine or artificial; and no obloquy and persecution of any. It calls for no revolution, no swift and sweeping rearrangement of occupation and communization of payment. It needs only the recognition that our work is social service, so to be ensured, honored and paid.

The work a man does, unless he is a private servant, is for the public, the pay is for himself. The public needs the service of schoolteachers; it provides training for them, it examines them for fitness, engages them and pays them. The public needs the services of all kinds of workers, and should similarly train, examine and employ them.

Every human being able and willing to work should be sure of suitable employment with a minimum wage above the poverty level. Those able to work but not willing should be conscripted for civil service precisely as we conscript men for military service. Why not?

As for the unable, the real defectives, observed and measured from infancy, they should be sterilized at an early age, to limit the supply. But it takes a very little capacity to do work that will more than pay for one's living, if proper conditions are provided, and we can steadily reduce the numbers of the wholly unfit.

For the greater part of our life on earth we have lived in physical danger; through savagery, barbarism, and most of our semi-civilization men carried weapons for self-defence. This demanded courage and alertness. Constant vigilance was the price of safety—if any.

In all these ages of anxiety and terror, we naturally exalted the qualities of the successful self-defender, the ingenious and competent warrior. If any prophet had tried to convince us that a time would come when law, police service, and organized military forces would protect us; so that we need no longer rely on our individual weapons, we should have repudiated such a prospect as not only impracticable but undesirable.

"If our safety was ensured by public protection we should have no incentive to fight for ourselves, nothing to develop our fighting qualities," would be the objection. That is the objection now made by those who dread the prospect of economic peace. Because in our economic anarchy only those succeed who can outstrip the others; or who, still worse, exploit the others for their own advantage; we fear that a condition which provided for everyone would weaken our characters and retard progress.

The greatest obstacle to legitimate socialization is this general conviction that the best service and most progress are ensured by competition, and that competition must rest on self-interest. Yet competition in an organized army is as real as in [a] mob of individual attackers and defenders. It is real but of a different [type.] Publicly employed school teachers strive for higher positions and higher pay as do those privately employed; and having as a body large voting powers they are able to protect themselves better than privately employed teachers.

Civil service examination and public employment do not rob us of any useful powers and instincts. The real result, the tremendous effect on our general psychology, is what socialists should have been teaching us all this time, instead of hatching revolutions.

Look at our present mental attitude in this vast field of economics, covering the whole range of trade, craft, art, or profession; all the activities by which we now say we "earn our livings," by which we shall soon say we serve society.

With the vast majority of us the child grows into a world where he sees his father facing a life of hard work for small pay and by no means sure of that; meeting loss through accident and illness; looking forward with dread to old age. His mother, still more helpless, has only the father to depend on, and the family income is reduced, per capita, by each added child.

These conditions he sees repeated all about him. With this vast majority work is something that has to be done if one is to live at all, yet one has no assurance of this vital necessity—it is given or withheld by individual employers, their lives are in his hand.

Meanwhile the small minority, owing to personal qualities, and to special conditions in no way personal, as laws of inheritance, possession of natural resources, and other advantages, are able to acquire for themselves large fortunes and use them to their further protection and advantage.

The special qualities by which individuals grow rich are by [no] means always socially beneficial; sometimes directly injurious. The ability to rob Peter and pay Paul does not increase wealth. Furthermore, even the wealthy are not safe. They struggle to hold their fortunes, to increase them, and frequently fail. The anxiety, the uncertainty, the effort, are not so close to the maintenance of life itself, but they are very real notwithstanding.

Beside this attitude of fear, this everpresent danger, the further results upon our mind are far from beneficial to society. Neither sordid care nor selfish extravagance are good for humanity, nor is it good to consider human work as a mere instrument wherewith to feed one's self, or to use to get ahead of other people.

While we depend on our selves for economic life we must needs place self-interest above other considerations. When we carried our own weapons and maintained our physical lives by our own efforts we were unable even to visualize a life of peace and protection guaranteed by the whole of society.

Now consider the different atmosphere surrounding the child who should grow up in a family where both mother and father were employed by the community in the work they preferred, a picture as simple as if he were a postman and she a public school teacher, but extended to include all kinds of socially useful work.

Both at home and in the families of his friends would be a comfortable sense of continuous employment, sufficient payment and ultimate provision for old age. Also for illness and accident. Work to do, for life, but work one chose for oneself; and *no* worry. Interest in the improvement of the work with improvement in the pay, ambition in plenty, preferment and honor for added efficiency; but no driving terror, no gringing [sic] care that carves the faces of the poor in deep and bitter lines.

There is no more merit in "the wolf at the door" as an incentive than there was in the wolves at the door in earlier times.

The child of this period of socialized industry would be watched through all his years of careful education for such special qualities as would fit him best for special work; and that education would include such wide knowledge, in picture and story and direct study, of the main branches of social service that he would know what he was choosing and why.

The story of plumbing, for instance, would go back to ancient Crete, would include the Oriental developments, the Roman Cloaca Maxima [great sewer], the great sewers of Paris. The vital place of this social necessity would be made clear, as with all the other trades. We may assume eager debates in high school as to the relative social value of the carpenter and the mason, of glass and steel.

To be sure of a living because you belong to a civilized society, to understand and honor the work you do and chose the kind you like best, to have freedom to rise as far as you are able, but no freedom to fall—that will provide a better foundation for progress.

And not to have, always lurking in the back of your mind, the dreadful consciousness of other people's poverty, of the ghastly mill grinding out its product of incapables, defectives, degenerates, its swelling stream of disease and crime.

Comfort and security, peace and efficiency, hope and power, freedom and all legitimate ambition, these are before us in due course as we gradually socialize industry.

Notes

Abbreviations

CAP = Charlotte Anna Perkins (1860–1884)

CPG = Charlotte Perkins Gilman (1900–1935)

CPS = Charlotte Perkins Stetson (1884–1900)

Diary = Journals and engagement books, The Arthur and Elizabeth Schlesinger Library on the History of Women in America, Radcliffe College, Cambridge, Mass. (folders 339–342). Charlotte kept a diary or journal relatively regularly, from 1876 to May 1903. From that point, she began to note only engagements and appointments.

GEC = Grace Ellery Channing (1884–1894)

GECS = Grace Ellery Channing Stetson (1894–1935)

GHG = George Houghton Gilman

Gilman papers = Manuscript collection at the Schlesinger Library.

Schlesinger Library = The Arthur and Elizabeth Schlesinger Library on the History of Women in America.

The Living = Charlotte Perkins Gilman, The Living of Charlotte Perkins Gilman New York: Appleton-Century, 1935; New York: Arno, 1972.

• • • • •

Preface

1. Carl N. Degler, "Charlotte Perkins Gilman on the Theory and Practice of Feminism," American Quarterly, 8 (Spring 1956), p. 21.

Introduction

1. William Leach, True Love and Perfect Union: The Feminist Reform of Sex and Society (New York: Basic, 1980), p. 134.
2. Quoted in New York Times, August 20, 1935, p. 44.

3. Quoted in Ann J. Lane, To "Herland" and Beyond: The Life and Work of Charlotte Perkins Gilman (New York: Pantheon, 1990), p. 7.

4. Amy Wellington, Women Have Told: Studies in the Feminist Tradition (Boston: Little, Brown, 1930), p. 129.

5. Edith Houghton Hooker, "Charlotte Perkins Gilman," Equal Rights Independent Feminist Weekly, 1 (August 31, 1935), p. 202.

6. Quoted in Lane, To "Herland," p. 7.

7. Edward Alsworth Ross, Seventy Years of It: An Autobiography (New York: Appleton-Century, 1936), p. 60.

8. Charles F. Lummis to Charlotte Perkins Gilman, November 6, 1909, Huntington Library, HM 44897.

9. William Dean Howells, "The New Poetry," The North American Review, 168 (May 1989), pp. 589–590; Floyd Dell, Women as World Builders: Studies in Modern Feminism (Chicago: Forbes, 1913; Westport, Conn.: Hyperion, 1976), pp. 24–25; Upton Sinclair, ed., The Cry for Justice: An Anthology of the Literature of Social Protest (Philadelphia: Winston, 1915), p. 200.

10. George Middleton, These Things Are Mine: The Autobiography of a Journeyman Playwright (New York: Macmillan, 1947), p. 128

11. Harriet Howe, "Charlotte Perkins Gilman—As I Knew Her," Equal Rights, 2 (September 5, 1936), p. 212.

12. Alexander Black, "The Woman Who Saw It First," The Century, 107 (November 1923), pp. 34–35.

13. Zona Gale, "Foreword" to The Living, pp. xxviii and xxix; and Zona Gale, "Charlotte Perkins Gilman," The Nation, 141 (September 25, 1935), p. 351.

14. Carl N. Degler, "Charlotte Perkins Gilman on the Theory and Practice of Feminism," American Quarterly, 8 (Spring 1956), pp. 21–39.

15. Eleanor Flexner, Century of Struggle: The Woman's Rights Movement in the United States (Cambridge, Mass.: Belknap, 1959; New York: Atheneum, 1972), p. 252.

16. William Theodore Doyle, "Charlotte Perkins Gilman and the Cycle of Feminist Reform," (Ph.D. dissertation, University of California, 1960), pp. iv, v, 161, 175, and 211–212.

17. See Robert E. Riegel, American Feminists (Lawrence: University of Kansas Press, 1963), pp. 163–173; Aileen S. Kraditor, The Ideas of the Woman Suffrage Movement, 1890–1929 (Garden City, N.Y.: Anchor, 1971), pp. 82–83 (originally published by Columbia University Press, 1965.); Up from the Pedestal: Selected Writings in the History of American Feminism (Chicago: Quadrangle, 1968), pp. 175–178 and 325–331; William L. O'Neill, Divorce in the Progressive Era (New Haven: Yale University Press, 1967), p. 127, Everyone Was Brave: The Rise and Fall of Feminism in America (Chicago: Quadrangle, 1969), pp. 130–133, and his introduction to Charlotte Perkins Gilman, The Home: Its Work and Influence (Urbana: University of Illinois Press, 1972); and Page Smith, Daughters of the Promised Land: Women in American History (Boston: Little, Brown, 1970), p. 245.

18. Charlotte Perkins Gilman, Women and Economics: A Study of the Economic Relation Between Men and Women as a Factor in Social Evolution, foreword by Carl N. Degler (New York: Harper and Row, 1966); The Forerunner (Westport, Conn.: Greenwood, 1966); The Home: Its Work and Influence (New York: Source Book Press, 1970; Urbana: University of Illinois Press, 1972); The Man-Made World: Our

Androcentric Culture (Minneapolis: University of Minnesota Series in American Studies, 1971); *The Living of Charlotte Perkins Gilman* (New York: Arno, 1972); Charlotte Perkins Gilman, *The Yellow Wallpaper* (New York: Feminist Press, 1973); *In This Our World* (New York: Arno, 1974); *His Religion and Hers: A Study of the Faith of Our Fathers and the Work of Our Mothers* (Westport, Conn.: Hyperion, 1976).

19. Patricia Meyer Spacks, *The Female Imagination* (New York: Knopf, 1975), pp. 208–217; Carol Ruth Berkin, "Private Woman, Public Woman: The Contradictions of Charlotte Perkins Gilman," in Carol Ruth Berkin and Mary Beth Norton, eds., *Women of America: A History* (Boston: Houghton Mifflin, 1979), pp. 150–173.

20. Mary A. Hill, "Charlotte Perkins Gilman: A Feminist's Struggle with Womanhood," *The Massachusetts Review,* 21 (Fall 1980), pp. 503–526; and *Charlotte Perkins Gilman: The Making of a Radical Feminist, 1860–1896* (Philadelphia: Temple University Press, 1980). She also edited the diaries of Charlotte's first husband: Charles Walter Stetson, *Endure: The Diaries of Charles Walter Stetson,* Mary Armfield Hill, ed. (Philadelphia: Temple University Press, 1985).

21. Charlotte Perkins Gilman, *Herland,* Ann J. Lane, ed. (New York: Pantheon, 1979); Charlotte Perkins Gilman, *Charlotte Perkins Gilman Reader: "The Yellow Wallpaper" and Other Fiction,* Ann J. Lane, ed. (New York: Pantheon, 1980). See also Ann J. Lane, "Charlotte Perkins Gilman: The Personal Is Political (1860–1935)," in *Feminist Theorists: Three Centuries of Key Women Thinkers,* Dale Spender, ed. (New York: Pantheon, 1983), pp. 203–217.

22. Lane, *To "Herland".*

23. Gary Scharnhorst, *Charlotte Perkins Gilman: A Bibliography* (Metuchen, N.J.: Scarecrow Press, 1985); *Charlotte Perkins Gilman* (Boston: Twayne, 1985); and "Making Her Fame: Charlotte Perkins Gilman in California," *California History,* 64 (Summer 1985), pp. 192–201.

24. Dolores Hayden, "Charlotte Perkins Gilman and the Kitchenless House," *Radical History Review,* 21 (Fall 1979), pp. 225–247, and *The Grand Domestic Revolution: A History of Feminist Designs for American Homes, Neighborhoods, and Cities* (Cambridge: MIT Press, 1981), pp. 182–265; Polly Wynne Allen, *Building Domestic Liberty: Charlotte Perkins Gilman's Architectural Feminism* (Amherst: University of Massachusetts Press, 1988).

25. *The Living,* p. xviii.

26. *Ibid.,* pp. 97–104.

27. CPS to GHG, November 3, 1897, Gilman papers, folder 47.

28. *Ibid.*

29. *Ibid.,* October 12, 1897, folder 46.

30. *The Living,* pp. 102–103.

31. CPS to GHG, September 11, 1897, Gilman papers, folder 45.

32. *The Living,* p. 103.

33. See Thomas F. Gossett, *Race: The History of an Idea* (Dallas: Southern Methodist University Press, 1963), pp. 160–172.

34. CPS to GHG, May 11, 1897, Gilman papers, folder 41.

35. *Ibid.,* May 22, 1898, folder 51.

36. CPG to Caroline Hill, December 4, 1921, Gilman papers, file 143. Hill reprinted five of Charlotte's poems.

37. CPS to GHG, May 22, 1898, Gilman papers, folder 51.
38. CPG to GECS, August 21, 1929, Schlesinger Library, MF-6.
39. CPS to GHG, November 7, 1897, Gilman papers, folder 47.

1. The Early Years

1. *The Living*, p. 5.
2. Mary A. Hill, *Charlotte Perkins Gilman: The Making of a Radical Feminist* (Philadelphia: Temple University Press, 1980), pp. 18–21.
3. *The Living*, p. 5.
4. CPS to GHG, February 1, 1899, Gilman papers, folder 64.
5. Hill, *Charlotte Perkins Gilman*, p. 22.
6. *The Living*, pp. 8–9.
7. *Ibid.*, pp. 6, 10, and 23.
8. Ann J. Lane, *To "Herland" and Beyond: The Life and Work of Charlotte Perkins Gilman* (New York: Pantheon, 1990), pp. 46–49.
9. *The Living*, pp. 23–24.
10. *Ibid.*, pp. 27 and 28.
11. *Ibid.*. pp. 28–29.
12. Diary, entry of October 7, 1878.
13. *The Living*, p. 34.
14. *Ibid.*, p. 36.
15. *Ibid.*, p. 37.
16. *Ibid.*
17. *Ibid.*, pp. 37–43.
18. Hill, *Charlotte Perkins Gilman*, p. 55.
19. *The Living*, pp. 49 and 61.
20. Diary, entry of February 18, 1878.
21. Diary, entry of March 3, 1879.
22. *The Living*, pp. 69, 70, and 74.
23. *Ibid.*, p. 48.
24. Hill, *Charlotte Perkins Gilman*, p. 74.
25. *Ibid.*, pp. 83–84.
26. Diary, entry of December 31, 1881.
27. *The Living*, pp. 78 and 80.
28. Diary, 1882.
29. Charles C. Eldredge, *Charles Walter Stetson: Color and Fantasy* (Spencer Museum of Art, the University of Kansas, Lawrence, 1982).
30. *The Living*, pp. 82–83.
31. Charles Walter Stetson, *Endure: The Diaries of Charles Walter Stetson,* Mary Armfield Hill, ed. (Philadelphia: Temple University Press, 1985), entries of January 14 and 26, 1882, pp. 25 and 27.
32. *Ibid.*, entries of March 19 and 22, 1883, pp. 143–145.
33. CAP to GEC, February 28, 1884, Schlesinger Library, MF-6.
34. Diary, entries of May 24, June 15 and 26, and August 11, 1884.
35. Stetson, *Endure*, entry of September 15, 1884, p. 264.
36. Diary, entry of January 1, 1885.
37. *The Living*, pp. 88–89.
38. *Ibid.*, p. 91.

39. Diary, entry of August 5, 1885.
40. Stetson, *Endure,* entries of August 27, September 11 and October 9, 1885, pp. 282, 290 and 297.
41. Hill, *Charlotte Perkins Gilman,* pp. 134–135.
42. Stetson, *Endure,* entries of April 27, May 5, and June 2, 1886, pp. 303, 304, and 308.
43. *Woman's Journal,* October 2, 1886, p. 313; reprinted in Charlotte Perkins Stetson, *In This Our World,* 2d ed. (Oakland, Calif.: Barry & Marble), 1895), p. 17.
44. Hill, *Charlotte Perkins Gilman,* pp. 137–139.
45. *Woman's Journal,* February 26, 1887, p. 66, and March 12, 1887, p. 88.
46. Diary, entry of April 4, 1887.
47. *The Living,* pp. 95–96.
48. *Ibid.,* p. 96; Stetson, *Endure,* entries of June 21 and 26, and August 6, 1887, pp. 341, 342, and 348.
49. CPS to GEC, November 21, 1887, Schlesinger Library, MF-6.
50. Stetson, *Endure,* entry of June 15, 1888, pp. 363–364.

2. The Club and Lecture Years

1. Morton White, *Social Thought in America: The Revolt Against Formalism* (Boston: Beacon paperback, 1957), p. 6.
2. Richard Hofstadter, *Social Darwinism in American Thought* (Philadelphia: University of Pennsylvania Press, 1945), p. 20.
3. *The Living,* p. 154.
4. Robert C. Bannister, *Social Darwinism: Science and Myth in Anglo-American Thought* (Philadelphia: Temple University Press, 1979), pp. 114–136.
5. There is no full-scale, critical biography of Ward. Emily Cape, who assisted him in compiling his articles for publication in book form, wrote an appreciative memoir and an uncritical overview of his philosophy: *Lester F. Ward: A Personal Sketch* (New York: Putnam's, 1922). Samuel Chugerman's *Lester Ward: The American Aristotle — A Summary and Interpretation of His Sociology* (Durham, N.C.: Duke University Press, 1939) is an unblushing panegyric, but it provides a thorough and systematic overview of Ward's work. Clifford H. Scott's *Lester Frank Ward* (Boston: Twayne, 1976) is a much shorter, drier analysis. John C. Burnham's *Lester Frank Ward in American Thought* (Washington, D.C.: Public Affairs Press, 1956) is devoted to demonstrating why Ward cannot be considered a major figure in American intellectual history. A much shorter, more favorable overview is that of Bernhard J. Stern, "The Liberal Views of Lester F. Ward," *Scientific Monthly,* 71 (August 1950), pp. 102–104. For exegeses of Ward's work in its historical context see David W. Marcell, *Progress and Pragmatism: James, Dewey, Beard, and the American Idea of Progress* (Westport, Conn.: Greenwood, 1974), pp. 129–143; Henry Steele Commager's introduction to *Lester Ward and the Welfare State* (Indianapolis: Bobbs-Merrill, 1967) and *The American Mind: An Interpretation of American Thought and Character Since the 1880's* (New Haven: Yale University Press paperback, 1971), pp. 204–216; Ellsworth H. Fuhrman, *The Sociology of Knowledge in America, 1883–1915* (Charlottesville: University Press of Virginia, 1980), pp. 75–99; Paul J. Boller, Jr., *American Thought in Transition: The Impact of Evolutionary Naturalism, 1865–1900* (Chicago: Rand McNally, 1969), pp. 64–69; Hofstadter, *Social Darwinism,* pp. 52–67; Cynthia Eagle Russett, *Darwin in America: The Intellec-*

tual Response, 1865–1912 (San Francisco: Freeman, 1976), pp. 102–111; Ralph Henry Gabriel, *The Course of American Democratic Thought,* 2d ed. (New York: Ronald, 1956), pp. 215–220; Sidney Fine, *Laissez Faire and the General Welfare State: A Study of Conflict in American Thought, 1865–1901* (Ann Arbor: University of Michigan Press, 1956), pp. 253–264; and Charles H. Page, *Class and American Sociology: From Ward to Ross* (New York: Schocken, 1969), pp. 29–69.

6. Marcell, *Progress and Pragmatism,* pp. 102–103, 124–126, and 132–133.

7. Page, *Class and American Sociology,* pp. 56 and 58.

8. Lester F. Ward, *Dynamic Sociology, or Applied Social Science, As Based Upon Statistical Sociology and the Less Complex Sciences* (New York: Appleton, 1883), 1:647, 650–651, 657, and 658–659.

9. For an explication of the genesis of the speech and article see Lester F. Ward, *Pure Sociology: A Treatise on the Origin and Spontaneous Development of Society,* 2d ed. (New York: Macmillan, 1925), pp, 297–298. See also Lester F. Ward, *Glimpses of the Cosmos* (New York: Putnam's, 1915), 4:127–131.

10. Lester F. Ward, "Our Better Halves," *Forum,* 6 (November 1888), pp. 274–275; see also his "Genius and Women's Intuition," *Forum,* 9 (June 1890), pp, 401–408; *The Psychic Factors of Civilization* (Boston: Ginn, 1893), p. 87; "The Exemption of Women from Labor," *The Monist,* 4 (April 1894), pp. 385–395, reprinted in Ward, *Glimpses of the Cosmos,* 5:108; *Pure Sociology,* pp. 296–297.

11. Hal D. Sears, *The Sex Radicals: Free Love in High Victorian America* (Lawrence: Regents Press of Kansas, 1977), p. 222; Mary Jo Buhle, *Women and American Socialism, 1870–1920* (Urbana: University of Illinois Press, 1981), pp. 156–157.

12. Ward, *Glimpses of the Cosmos,* 3:30 and 4:131.

13. *Woman's Journal,* April 16, 1904, p. 122; *The Forerunner,* 1 (October 1910), p. 26; her dedication of *The Man-Made World; or, Our Androcentric Culture* (New York: Charlton, 1911), p. 3; *The Forerunner,* 3 (June 1913), p. 166; *His Religion and Hers: A Study of the Faith of Our Fathers and the Work of Our Mothers* (New York: Century, 1923; Westport, Conn.: Hyperion, 1976), p. 57; and "Feminism and Social Progress," in *Problems of Civilization,* Ellsworth Huntington et al., eds. (New York: Van Nostrand, 1929), p. 120.

14. See her letters to George Houghton Gilman, June 5 and July 22, 1897, Gilman papers, folders 42 and 43; and "Notes, The Epic [an epic poem on womanhood]," March 4, 1908, Gilman papers, folder 336, v. 24.

15. Lester F. Ward, "Collective Telesis: Contributions to Social Philosophy," *American Journal of Sociology,* 2 (March 1897), p. 815, n. 1; Ward to CPG, February 9, 1907 and February 11, 1911, Gilman papers, folder 124. Edward A. Ross was also stingy with his public acknowledgements of Charlotte's work. Though her *The Man-Made World* inspired a chapter—"Women in a Man-Made World"—in his *The Social Trend* (1922), he did not mention nor cite her book. His explanation is in *The Living,* p. xvii.

16. William Leach, *True Love and Perfect Union: The Feminist Reform of Sex and Society* (New York: Basic, 1980), pp. 23–24, 34, and 50; Barbara Miller Solomon, *In the Company of Educated Women: A History of Women and Higher Education in America* (New Haven: Yale University Press, 1985), p. 82; Jacqueline Van Voris, *Carrie Chapman Catt: A Public Life* (New York: Feminist Press, 1987), p. 9; Karen J. Blair, *The Clubwoman as Feminist: True Womanhood Redefined* (New York: Holmes and

Meier, 1980) and Theodora Penny Martin, *The Sound of Our Own Voices: Women's Study Clubs, 1860–1910* (Boston: Beacon, 1987).

17. Leach, *True Love*, pp. 143–152; Florence Kelley, "The Need of Theoretical Preparation for Philanthropic Work," written in 1887 and reprinted in *Notes of Sixty Years: The Autobiography of Florence Kelley* (Chicago: Kerr, 1986), p. 102.

18. For her comments on George see Charlotte Perkins Stetson, "The Land Question: A Woman's Symposium—Land Must Be Free That We May Live," *The Arena,* 10 (October 1894), p. 641; "Representative Women on Vital Social Problems (Part III)—The Solution to the Labor Question," *The Arena,* 14 (October 1895), p. 273; and diary, entry of February 14, 1896. For Gronlund, see CPS to GHG, October 13, 1898, Gilman papers, folder 56; *The Impress,* January 19, 1895, p. 2, and January 26, p. 12. For Lloyd, see *The Impress,* October 13, 1894, p. 11; *The Forerunner,* 3 (June 1912), p. 167.

19. *The Impress,* September 1894, p. 6; CPG to GHG, August 1 and 29, 1897, folder 44; September 1 and 8, 1897, folder 45.

20. Edward Bellamy, *Looking Backward: 2000–1887* (New York: Signet Classic, 1960), p. 176.

21. *The New Nation,* March 5, 1892, p. 145.

22. CPS to GHG, July 22 and August 1, 1897, Gilman papers, folders 43 and 44.

23. Nancy Woloch, *Women and the American Experience* (New York: Knopf, 1984), p. 269; see also Carrol Smith-Rosenberg, "The New Woman as Androgyne: Social Disorder and Gender Crisis, 1870–1936," in her *Disorderly Conduct: Visions of Gender in Victorian America* (New York: Knopf: 1985), pp. 245 and 247. Neither author mentions Charlotte as an example of the "new woman."

24. Leach, *True Love*, pp. 297 and 316.

25. Jane C. Croly, *The History of the Woman's Club Movement In America* (New York: Allen, 1898), pp. 15 and 16.

26. *The Mother of Clubs: Carolina M. Seymour Severance. An Estimate and an Appreciation,* Ella Giles Ruddy, ed. (Los Angeles: Baumgardt, 1906), p. 24.

27. Charlotte Perkins Stetson, "Mrs. Cooper in St. Louis," *The Impress,* October 6, 1894, p. 12.

28. Harold D. Carew, *History of Pasadena and the San Gabriel Valley* (Chicago: Clarke, 1930), 1:482 and 505–506; Glenn S. Dumke, *The Boom of the Eighties in Southern California* (San Marino, Calif.: Huntington Library, 1966), pp. 259–261; Carey McWilliams, *Southern California Country: An Island on the Land* (New York: Duell, Sloan and Pearce, 1946), pp. 118–122 and 251; Kevin Starr, *Inventing the Dream: California Through the Progressive Era* (New York: Oxford University Press, 1985), pp. 95–96; Joan M. Jensen, "Carolina Maria Seymour Severance," in *Notable American Women, 1607–1950: A Biographical Dictionary,* Edward T. James, ed. (Cambridge, Mass.: Belknap, 1971), 3:265–268.

29. *The New Nation,* February 14, 1891, p. 51; F. J. Vassault, "Nationalism in California," *The Overland Monthly,* 15, second series (June 1890), pp. 659–661; Howard H. Quint, "Gaylord Wilshire and Socialism's First Congressional Campaign," *Pacific Historical Review,* 26 (November 1957), pp. 328–339; Grace Heilman Stimson, *Rise of the Labor Movement in Los Angeles* (Berkeley: University of California Press, 1955), pp. 98–101; Starr, *Inventing the Dream,* pp. 207–211.

30. *The Living,* p. 110.
31. "Thoughts and Figgerings," entry of August 2, 1889, Gilman papers, folder 16.
32. Mary A. Hill, *Charlotte Perkins Gilman: The Making of a Radical Feminist, 1860–1896* (Philadelphia: Temple University Press, 1980), p. 160.
33. *The Living,* p. 111.
34. "Nationalism and the Virtues," lecture presented December 20, 1890, Gilman papers, folder 163, pp. 21–23.
35. "Nationalism and Religion," lecture delivered January 3, 1891, Gilman papers, folder 164, p. 31.
36. "What Is Nationalism?" lecture presented January 14, 1892, Gilman papers, folder 168, p. 23.
37. Hill, *Charlotte Perkins Gilman,,* p. 182.
38. *The Nationalist,* 2 (April 1890), pp. 165–166; *In This Our World,* pp. 72–76.
39. Diary, entries of June 15 and December 28, 1890.
40. Harriet Howe, "Charlotte Perkins Gilman—As I Knew Her," *Equal Rights,* 2 (September 5, 1936), p. 211.
41. *Ibid.,* pp. 211–212.
42. Charlotte Perkins Gilman, "Why I Wrote The Yellow Wallpaper?" *The Forerunner,* 4 (October 1913), p. 271.
43. Diary, entry of December 31, 1890.
44. CPS to GEC, December 3, 1890, Schlesinger Library, MF-6.
45. Diary, entry of March 6, 1891.
46. Sarah E. Reamer, "Notes by the Historian," in Abbie E. Krebs, ed., *La Copa de Oro (The Cup of Gold): A Collection of California Poems, Sketches and Stories by the Members of the Pacific Coast Women's Press Association,* (San Francisco: by the Association, 1905), p. 113; Emilie Tracy Y. Parkhurst, "Pacific Coast Women's Press Association," *The Californian Illustrated Magazine,* 4 (September 1893), pp. 526–534.
47. *The New Nation,* April 18, 1891, p. 195; April 25, 1891, p. 211.
48. Diary, entries of May 11, 21, and 23, and June 1, 7, and 11, 1891.
49. *The Living,* p. 132.
50. *The New Nation,* September 10, 1892, p. 574. For information on political activity in the Bay Area see: Howard H. Quint, *The Forging of American Socialism: Origins of the Modern Movement* (Columbia: University of South Carolina Press, 1953), pp. 85, 101, and 218; Ira B. Cross, *A History of the Labor Movement in California* (Berkeley: University of California Press, 1935), pp. 162–165; Chester McArthur Destler, *American Radicalism, 1865–1901: Essays and Documents* (New York: Octagon, 1963); Michael Kazin, *Barons of Labor: The San Francisco Building Trades and Union Power in the Progressive Era* (Urbana: University of Illinois Press, 1987), p. 38; Alexander Saxton, *The Indispensable Enemy: Labor and the Anti-Chinese Movement in California* (Berkeley: University of California Press, 1971), p. 237.
51. Reda Davis, *California Women: A Guide to Their Politics, 1885–1911* (San Francisco, 1967), pp. 5, 36, 43, 44, 60, and 66.
52. *The Living,* p. 131.
53. Handbill, folder 10, Gilman papers.
54. Charlotte Perkins Stetson, *Women and Economics: A Study of the Economic Relation*

Between Men and Women as a Factor in Social Evolution (Boston: Small, Maynard, 1898; New York: Harper & Row, 1966), p. 164.

55. *The Living,* pp. 168–169.
56. Howe, "Charlotte Perkins Gilman," p. 214.
57. Diary, entries of March 16 and 19, and April 17, 1894.
58. Diary, entry of December 31, 1891.
59. CPS to GEC, January 23, 1893, Schlesinger Library, MF-6.
60. CPS to GHG, May 18, 1897, Gilman papers, folder 41.
61. Diary, entry, January 31, 1894.
62. "Thoughts and Figgerings," May 9, 1894, Gilman papers, folder 16.
63. *The Impress,* September 1894, p. 3.
64. *The Living,* p. 173.
65. "Thoughts and Figgerings," November 30, 1894, Gilman papers, folder 16; CPS to GECS, January 9, 1895.
66. CPS to GECS, June 15, 1895, Schlesinger Library, MF-6.
67. *Ibid.,* June 26, 1895, Schlesinger Library, MF-6.
68. "Thoughts and Figgerings," January 1, 1896, Gilman papers, folder 16.
69. Diary, entry of March 16, 1896; CPS to GECS, May 3, 1896, Schlesinger Library, MF-6.
70. Dolores Hayden, *The Grand Domestic Revolution: A History of Feminist Designs for American Homes, Neighborhoods, and Cities* (Cambridge: MIT Press, 1981), pp. 186–187.
71. CPS to GECS, May 3 and June 8, 1896, Schlesinger Library, MF-6.
72. *The Living,* pp. 186–187.
73. See "Women Teachers, Married and Unmarried," *The Forerunner,* 1 (November 1910), pp. 8–10, and "Difficulties of Organizing Saleswomen," *The Forerunner,* 5 (February 1914), pp. 46–47.
74. *The Living,* p. 198.
75. "Charlotte Perkins Stetson: A Daring Humorist of Reform," *The American Fabian,* January 1897, pp. 1–3.
76. Diary, entry of July 1, 1897.

3. The Book Years

1. Samuel P. Hays, *The Response to Industrialism, 1885–1914* (Chicago: University of Chicago Press, 1957), pp. 76–77, 79, and 82.
2. Rosalind Rosenberg, "In Search of Woman's Nature, 1850–1920," *Feminist Studies,* 3 (Fall 1975), p. 152; see also her *Beyond Separate Spheres: Intellectual Roots of Modern Feminism* (New Haven: Yale University Press, 1982).
3. Hamilton Cravens, *The Triumph of Evolution: American Scientists and the Hereditary-Environment Controversy, 1900–1941* (Philadelphia: University of Pennsylvania Press, 1978), pp. 37–39; Robert C. Bannister, *Social Darwinism: Science and Myth in Anglo-American Thought* (Philadelphia: Temple University Press, 1979), p. 138; Loren Eiseley, *Darwin's Century: Evolution and the Men Who Discovered It* (Garden City, N.Y.: Anchor, 1961), pp. 216–219.
4. See Lester F. Ward, *Glimpses of the Cosmos* (New York: Putnam's, 1915), 4:253–295, 327–328, and 385–388; Charlotte's comment in *The Impress,* June 1894, p. 1;

Helen Campbell, *Household Economics; a Course of Lectures in the School of Economics of the University of Wisconsin*, rev. ed. (New York: Putnam's, 1907) p. 11. (Originally published in 1896.)

5. CPG to Carolina Severance, January 25, 1904, Severance Collection, Box 17, Huntington Library.

6. Bruce Dancis, "Socialism and Women in the United States, 1900–1917," *Socialist Revolution*, 6 (January-March 1976), p. 91.

7. Nancy Schrom Dye, *As Equals and Sisters: Feminism, the Labor Movement, and the WTUL of New York* (Columbia: University of Missouri Press, 1980), p. 74.

8. CPG to Carolina Severance, January 25, 1904, Severance Collection, Box 17, Huntington Library.

9. *The Living*, p. 303.

10. Joseph J. Spengler, "Economics: Its Direct and Indirect Impact in America, 1776–1976," in Charles M. Bonjean et al., *Social Science in America: The First Two Hundred Years* (Austin: University of Texas Press, 1976), pp. 58–59.

11. Mabel Newcomer, *A Century of Higher Education for Women* (New York: Harper, 1959), pp. 79–81; John P. Rousmanière, "Cultural Hybrid in the Slums: The College Woman and the Settlement House, 1889–94," in *Education in American History: Readings on the Social Issues*, Michael B. Katz, ed. (New York: Praeger, 1973), pp. 122–138; Katherine Coman, "Preparation for Citizenship, V. At Wellesley College," *Education*, 10 (February 1890), pp. 341–347; *The Wellesley College News*, 23 (April 1915); J. B. Clark, "Preparation for Citizenship, III. At Smith College," *Education*, 9 (February 1889), pp. 403–406; Walter Crosby Eells, "Earned Doctorates for Women in the Nineteenth Century," *American Association of University Professors Bulletin*, 42 (Winter 1956), pp. 649–651; American Economic Association, *Supplement to Economic Studies*, 3 (February 1898), *Handbook of the American Economic Association, 1898, together with report of the tenth annual meeting . . .* , (New York: AEA, 1898), pp. 20–38; Ellen Fitzpatrick, *Endless Crusade: Women Social Scientists and Progressive Reform* (New York: Oxford University Press, 1990), pp. 75–76 and 82–89.

12. "Thoughts and Figgerings," May 11, 1890, Gilman papers, folder 16.

13. CPS to GHG, May 11, 1897, Gilman papers, folder 41; and July 22, 1897, folder 43.

14. *The Living*, p. 259.

15. CPS to GHG, May 1, July 10, and July 27, 1897, Gilman papers, folders 41 and 43.

16. Diary entries August-November 1897; CPS to GHG, Gilman papers, September 1 and November 10, 1897, folders 45 and 47.

17. *The Living*, pp. 284–285.

18. Diary, entry of July 19, 1897; Kelley to CPS, July 26, 1898, Gilman papers, folder 137; Inez Haynes Irwin, *Angels and Amazons: A Hundred Years of American Women* (Garden City, N.Y.: Doubleday, Doran, 1933), p. 267; Edith Houghton Hooker, "Charlotte Perkins Gilman," *Equal Rights Independent Feminist Weekly*, 1 (August 31, 1935), p. 202.

19. George E. Howard, *A History of Matrimonial Institutions: Chiefly in England and the United States with an Introductory Analysis of the Literature and the Theories of Primitive*

Marriage and the Family, 3 vols. (Chicago: University of Chicago Press, 1904), 3:249, n.

20. CPS to GHG, October 16, 1898, Gilman papers, folder 56.
21. Charlotte Perkins Gilman, *Women and Economics: A Study of the Economic Relations Between Men and Women as a Factor in Social Evolution* (New York: Harper and Row, 1966), p. xiii.
22. CPS to GHG, April 28 and May 18, 1897, folder 41; CPS to GECS, May 1, 1897, Schlesinger Library, MF-6.
23. Charlotte Perkins Stetson, "The Woman's Congress of 1899," *The Arena,* 22 (September 1899), p. 350.
24. Charlotte Perkins Gilman, *Concerning Children* (Boston: Small, Maynard, 1900), pp. 3–4 and 18.
25. *The Living,* p. 284.
26. Diary, entry of June 20, 1900.
27. CPS to GHG, October 17, 1898, Gilman papers, folder 57.
28. *The Living,* p. 286; Charlotte Perkins Gilman, *The Home: Its Work and Influence* (New York: McClure, Phillips, 1903).
29. *Current Literature,* 36 (May 1904), p. 511.
30. *The Living,* p. 275; *The Forerunner,* 4 (January 1913), p. 20.
31. Charlotte Perkins Gilman, *Human Work* (New York: McClure, Phillips, 1904), pp. 14, 16, 117, 119, and 182.
32. *The Living,* p. 286.
33. Harriot Stanton Blatch and Alma Lutz, *The Challenging Years: The Memoirs of Harriot Stanton Blatch* (New York: Putnam's, 1940), p. 108.
34. "Thoughts and Figgerings," June 28, 1908, Gilman papers, folder 16.

4. The Forerunner Years

1. *The Living,* pp. 303–304.
2. Charlotte Perkins Gilman, "A Summary of Purpose," *The Forerunner,* 7 (November 1916), p. 287.
3. *Putnam's Magazine,* 7 (January 1910), pp. 501–502.
4. Mary Austin, *Earth Horizon: Autobiography* (New York: Literary Guild, 1932), p. 326.
5. Charlotte Perkins Gilman, "The Dress of Women," *The Forerunner,* 5 (December 1915), p. 333.
6. *The Living,* p. 305; CPG to Katharine Stetson Chamberlin, March 24 and June 26, 1920, Gilman papers, folder 91.
7. Louise Nyström-Hamilton, *Ellen Key—Her Life and Her Work,* A. E. B. Fries, trans. (New York: Putnam's, 1913), p. 110. This book, written in 1904, is outdated and uncritical. At present, Key lacks a comprehensive, critical biography in English.
8. Cheri Register, "Motherhood at Center: Ellen Key's Social Vision," *Women's Studies International Forum,* 5 (1982), pp. 600–601; Kay Goodman, "Motherhood and Work: The Concept of the Misuse of Women's Energy, 1895–1905," in *German Women in the Eighteenth and Nineteenth Centuries: A Social and Literary History,* Ruth-Ellen B. Joeres and Mary Jo Maynes, eds. (Bloomington: Indiana University

Press, 1986), p. 113; see also Torborg Lundell, "Ellen Key and Swedish Feminist Views on Motherhood," *Scandinavian Studies* 56 (Autumn 1984), pp. 351–369.

9. "Ellen Key, The Inspired Swedish Enthusiast," *Review of Reviews*, 32 (November 1905), p. 609.

10. Ellen Key, "The Woman of the Future," *The Independent*, 63 (October 31, 1907), pp. 1043–1045.

11. Rheta Childe Dorr, *A Woman of Fifty*, 2d ed. (New York: Funk and Wagnalls, 1924), pp. 224 and 230.

12. Ellen Key, *Century of the Child* (New York: Putnam's, 1909), reviewed in *The Forerunner*, 1 (December 1910), pp. 25–26, and commented on in the same issue, "The New Motherhood," pp. 17–18; Ellen Key, *Love and Marriage* (New York: Putnam's, 1911), reviewed in *The Forerunner*, 2 (October 1911, pp. 280–282.

13. Jessie Taft, *The Woman Movement from the Point of View of Social Consciousness* (Chicago: University of Chicago Press, 1916), pp. 20–22. Taft also briefly examined the thinking of Olive Schreiner and Ida Tarbell.

14. "The Conflict Between 'Human' and 'Female' Feminism," *Current Opinion*, 56 (April 1914), p. 291; see also "Ellen Key's Attack on 'Amaternal' Feminism" and "Charlotte Gilman's Reply to Ellen Key," 54 (February 1913), pp. 138–139 and (March 1913), pp. 220–221.

15. *The American Magazine*, 73 (January 1912), pp. 259–262; (February 1912), pp. 427–430; (March 1912), pp. 563–568; (April 1912), pp. 689–693; 74 (May 1912), pp. 49–53; 74 (June 1912), pp. 217–220. They were reprinted in *The Business of Being A Woman* (New York: Macmillan, 1921), pp. 1–83 and 142–215.

16. Tarbell, *The Business of Being A Woman*, pp. 5 and 42–43.

17. "Miss Tarbell's Third Paper," *The Forerunner*, 3 (April 1912), pp. 92 and 95.

18. "Ida Tarbell Answered," *The Woman Voter*, 3 (June 1912), pp. 7–13.

19. *The Progressive Woman*, 5 (March 1912), p. 8; Charlotte Perkins Gilman, "The Progressive Woman Off the Track," *The Forerunner*, 3 (April 1912), pp. 111–112; Josephine Conger-Kaneko, "The Progressive Woman Off the Track," *The Progressive Woman*, 5 (May 1912), pp. 11–12.

20. George Middleton, *These Things Are Mine: The Autobiography of a Journeyman Playwright* (New York: Macmillan, 1947), p. 128.

21. Charlotte Perkins Gilman, "World Peace and Sex Combat," *Woman's Journal*, October 8, 1904, p. 322; Charlotte Perkins Stetson, "Does the War Postpone Social Reform?" *The American Fabian*, 4 (August 1898), p. 6; and Gilman, "Japan's Reserve," *Woman's Journal*, December 19, 1904, p. 370.

22. *New York Times*, April 24, 1914, p. 6.

23. Charlotte Perkins Gilman, letter to *New York Times*, August 28, 1914, p. 8.

24. Harriot Stanton Blatch and Alma Lutz, *The Challenging Years: The Memoirs of Harriot Stanton Blatch* (New York: Putnam's, 1940), p. 252; *New York Times*, December 18, 1914, p. 15; January 6, 1915, p. 15; February 20, 1915, p. 7; and June 16, 1915, p. 4. See also C. Roland Marchand, *The American Peace Movement and Social Reform, 1898–1918* (Princeton, N.J.: Princeton University Press, 1972), pp. 204 and 207.

25. Charlotte Perkins Gilman, "The Balkan War and Universal Peace," *The Forerunner*, 4 (August 1913), p. 213.

26. Charlotte Perkins Gilman, "Feminism or Polygamy," *The Forerunner*, 5 (October 1914), p. 261.

27. Charlotte Perkins Gilman, "War-Maids and War-Widows," *The Forerunner*, 6 (March 1915), pp. 63–64.

28. Charlotte Perkins Gilman, "As to World Federation," *The Forerunner*, 5 (December 1914), p. 310.

29. *The Forerunner*, 7 (January 1916), p. 27; "Studies in Social Pathology. II," *The Forerunner*, 7 (May 1916), p. 120.

30. *The Living*, p. xxxi.

31. Middleton, *These Things Are Mine*, p. 128.

32. CPG to Katharine Stetson Chamberlin, April 21, 1921, Gilman papers, folder 92.

33. *The Living*, pp. 309–310.

5. The Last Years

1. J. Stanley Lemons, *The Woman Citizen: Social Feminism in the 1920s* (Urbana: University of Illinois Press, 1973), p. 181.

2. *The Living*, p. 317.

3. *Ibid.*, p. 320.

4. CPG to William English Walling, July 28, 1925, Huntington Library, AW Box 2.

5. Charlotte Perkins Gilman, "The Making of Americans," *Woman's Journal*, August 13, 1904, p. 258; "Malthusianism and Race Suicide," *Woman's Journal*, September 3, 1904, p. 282.

6. *The Living*, pp. 284, 329, and 330.

7. *Ibid.*, p. 310.

8. *Ibid.*, p. 311.

9. Christine A. Lunardini, *From Equal Suffrage to Equal Rights: Alice Paul and the National Woman's Party, 1910–1925* (New York: New York University Press, 1986), p. 153; Nancy F. Cott, *The Grounding of Modern Feminism* (New Haven: Yale University Press, 1987), p. 66.

10. Cott, *The Grounding*, pp. 251–253.

11. Charlotte Perkins Gilman, "Woman's Achievement Since the Franchise," *Current History*, 27 (October 1927), pp. 7–8.

12. CPS to GHG, October 18, 1898, Gilman papers, folder 57.

13. Charlotte Perkins Gilman, *His Religion and Hers: A Study of the Faith of Our Fathers and the Work of Our Mothers* (New York: Century, 1923), pp. 11–13.

14. Charlotte Perkins Gilman, "Parasitism and Civilised Vice," in *Woman's Coming of Age: A Symposium*, Samuel D. Schmalhausen and V. F. Calverton, eds. (New York: Liveright, 1931), p. 123.

15. Charlotte Perkins Gilman, "Vanguard, Rear-Guard, and Mud-Guard," *The Century Magazine*, 104 (July 1922), pp. 349–350 and 353.

16. Charlotte Perkins Gilman, "Progress Through Birth Control," *North American Review*, 224 (December 1927), p. 624.

17. United States Congress, House of Representatives, Committee on Ways and Means, *Birth Control, Hearings on House Resolution 11082, May 19 and 20, 1932*, 72nd Congress, 1st session (Washington, D.C.: GPO, 1932), p. 55.

18. "Thoughts and Figgerings," May 7, 1924, Gilman papers, folder 17.

19. CPG to GECS, July 6, 1929, Schlesinger Library, MF-6.

20. Gary Scharnhorst, *Charlotte Perkins Gilman* (Boston: Twayne, 1985), pp. 116–117.

21. Letter from Rosika Schwimmer to *New York Times Book Review,* September 3, 1933, p. 13.

22. Charlotte Perkins Gilman, "Euthanasia Again," *The Forerunner,* 3 (October 1912), pp. 262–263; see also, "Good and Bad Taste in Suicide," *The Forerunner,* 3 (May 1912), p. 130.

23. Edward A. Ross, *Seventy Years of It: An Autobiography* (New York: Appleton-Century, 1936), p. 244.

24. "Dies to Avoid Pain," *New York Times,* August 20, 1935, p. 44; she had also written an article defending "mercy deaths," which she placed with her literary agent, requesting that it be submitted for publication after her death. It was published as "The Right to Die," *Forum and Century,* 94 (November 1935), pp. 297–300.

25. *New York Times,* August 21, 1935, p. 21.

26. *Ibid., Book Review,* June 28, 1936, p. 15.

Bibliography:
Books and Articles Consulted
but Not Cited in Notes

Introduction

Cooper, James L. and Sheila McIsaac Cooper, eds. *The Roots of American Feminist Thought,* pp. 177–192. Boston: Allyn and Bacon, 1973.

Hobbs, Margaret. "The Perils of 'Unbridled Masculinity': Pacifist Elements in the Feminist and Socialist Thought of Charlotte Perkins Gilman." In Ruth Roach Peirson, ed., *Women and Peace: Theoretical, Historical and Practical Perspectives,* pp. 149–169. London: Croom Helm, 1987.

Howe, Harriet. "A Tribute to Charlotte Perkins Gilman." *Equal Rights,* July 1, 1938, p. 286.

Jordan, David Starr. *The Days of a Man: Being Memories of a Naturalist, Teacher and Minor Prophet of Democracy.* Yonkers-on-Hudson, N.Y.: World Book, 1922.

Karpinski, Joanne B. "When the Marriage of True Minds Admits Impediments: Charlotte Perkins Gilman and William Dean Howells." In Shirely Marchalonis, ed., *Patrons and Protegees: Gender, Friendship, and Writing in Nineteenth-Century America,* pp. 212–234. New Brunswick, N.J.: Rutgers University Press, 1988.

Martin, Jane Roland. *Reclaiming a Conversation: The Ideal of the Educated Woman,* pp. 139–170. New Haven: Yale University Press, 1985.

Meyering, Sheryl L., ed. *Charlotte Perkins Gilman: The Woman and Her Work.* Ann Arbor, Mich.: UMI Research Press, 1989.

Nies, Judith. *Seven Women: Portraits from the American Radical Tradition,* pp. 127–145. New York: Viking, 1977.

Sachs, Carolyn, Sally Ward, and S. Randi Randolph. "Sexuality, the Home and Class." *Midwest Feminist Papers,* 2 (1981), pp. 31–44.

Winkler, Barbara Scott. *Victorian Daughters: The Lives and Feminism of Charlotte Perkins Gilman and Olive Schreiner.* Occasional Paper in Women's Studies, no. 13, American Culture Program. Ann Arbor: University of Michigan, 1980.

1. The Early Years

Bassuk, Ellen L. "The Rest Cure: Repetition or Resolution of Victorian Women's Conflicts?" In Susan Rubin Suleiman, ed., *The Female Body in Western Culture: Contemporary Perspectives*, pp. 139–151. Cambridge: Harvard University Press, 1986.

Boydston, Jeanne, Mary Kelley, and Anne Margolis. *The Limits of Sisterhood: The Beecher Sisters on Women's Rights and Woman's Sphere.* Chapel Hill: University of North Carolina Press, 1988.

Burr, Anna Robeson. *Weir Mitchell: His Life and Letters.* New York: Duffield, 1929.

DuBois, Ellen Carol. *Feminism and Suffrage: The Emergence of an Independent Women's Movement in America, 1848–1869.* Ithaca, N.Y.: Cornell University Press, 1978.

Earnest, Ernest. S. *Weir Mitchell: Novelist and Physician.* Philadelphia: University of Pennsylvania Press, 1950.

Ehrenreich, Barbara and Deirdre English. *For Her Own Good: 150 Years of the Experts' Advice to Women.* Garden City, N.Y.: Anchor Press/Doubleday, 1978.

Morantz, Regina. "The Lady and Her Physician." In Mary S. Hartman and Lois Banner, eds., *Clio's Consciousness Raised: New Perspectives on the History of Women*, pp. 38–53. New York: Harper Torchbook, 1974.

Rugoff, Milton. *The Beechers: An American Family in the Nineteenth Century.* New York: Harper and Row, 1981.

Wood, Ann Douglas. " 'The Fashionable Diseases': Women's Complaints and Their Treatment in Nineteen-Century America." In Mary S. Hartman and Lois Banner, eds., *Clio's Consciousness Raised: New Perspectives on the History of Women*, pp. 1–22. New York: Harper Torchbook, 1974.

2. The Club and Lecture Years

Anthony, Susan B. and Ida Husted Harper, eds. *The History of Woman Suffrage*, vol. 4, *1883–1900.* Indianapolis: Hollenbeck, 1902; Salem, N.H.: Ayer, 1985.

Antler, Joyce. *Lucy Sprague Mitchell: The Making of a Modern Woman.* New Haven: Yale University Press, 1987.

Barker, Charles Albro. *Henry George.* New York: Oxford University Press, 1955.

Barry, Kathleen. *Susan B. Anthony: A Biography of a Singular Feminist.* New York: New York University Press, 1988.

Berkman, Joyce Avrech. *Feminism on the Frontier.* Montreal: Eden, 1979.

—— *The Healing Imagination of Olive Schreiner: Beyond South African Colonialism.* Amherst: University of Massachusetts Press, 1989.

Blocker, Jack S., Jr. *American Temperance Movements: Cycles of Reform.* Boston: Twayne, 1989.

Blumberg, Dorothy Rose. *Florence Kelley: The Making of a Social Pioneer.* New York: Kelley, 1966.

Bordin, Ruth. *Woman and Temperance: The Quest for Power and Liberty, 1873–1900.* Philadelphia: Temple University Press, 1981.

Bowman, Sylvia E. *The Year 2000: A Critical Biography of Edward Bellamy.* New York: Bookman, 1958.

Brandt, Allan M. *No Magic Bullet: A Social History of Venereal Disease in the United States Since 1880.* New York: Oxford University Press, 1985.

Bremner, Robert H. *The Public Good: Philanthropy and Welfare in the Civil War Era.* New York: Knopf, 1980.

Campbell, Helen."Famous Persons at Home—Charlotte Perkins Gilman." *The Bookman,* 12 (November 1900), pp. 205–206.

—— "Household Furnishings." *Architectural Record,* 6 (October-December 1896), pp. 97–104.

Cole, Margaret. *The Story of Fabian Socialism.* London: Heinemann, 1962.

Conway, Jill. "Stereotypes of Femininity in a Theory of Sexual Evolution." In Martha Vicinus, ed., *Suffer and Be Still: Women in the Victorian Age,* pp. 140–154. Bloomington: Indiana University Press, 1972.

Davis, Allen F. *Spearheads for Reform: The Social Settlements and the Progressive Movement, 1890–1914.* New York: Oxford University Press, 1967.

Debs, Eugene V. *Writings and Speeches of Eugene V. Debs.* New York: Hermitage, 1948.

Deegan, Mary Jo. *Jane Addams and the Men of the Chicago School, 1892–1918.* New Brunswick, N.J.: Transaction, 1988.

D'Emilio, John D. and Estelle B. Friedman. *Intimate Matters: A History of Sexuality in America.* New York: Harper and Row, 1988.

Dombrowski, James. *The Early Days of Christian Socialism in America.* New York: Columbia University Press, 1936; New York: Octagon, 1966.

Epstein, Barbara Leslie. *The Politics of Domesticity: Women, Evangelism, and Temperance in Nineteenth-Century America.* Middletown, Conn.: Wesleyan University Press, 1981.

Filler, Louis, *The Unknown Edwin Markham: His Mystery and Its Significance.* Yellow Springs, Ohio: Antioch Press, 1966.

Foner, Philip S. *Women and the American Labor Movement: From Colonial Times to the Eve of World War I.* New York: Free Press, 1979.

Goldmark, Josephine. *Impatient Crusader* [A biography of Florence Kelley]. Urbana: University of Illinois Press, 1953; Westport, Conn.: Greenwood, 1976.

Gordon, Linda. *Woman's Body, Woman's Right: A Social History of Birth Control in America.* New York: Grossman, 1976.

Gould, Stephen Jay. *Ontogeny and Phylology.* Cambridge, Mass.: Belknap, 1977.

Grier, Katherine C. *Culture and Comfort: People, Parlors, and Upholstery, 1850–1930.* Rochester, N.Y.: The Strong Museum, 1988; distributed by University of Massachusetts Press, Amherst.

Herreshoff, David. *American Disciples of Marx: From the Age of Jackson to the Progressive Era.* Detroit: Wayne State University Press, 1967.

Hine, Robert V. *California's Utopian Colonies.* San Marino, Calif.: Huntington Library, 1953.

Hobsbawm, E. J. "The Fabians Reconsidered." In his *Labouring Men: Studies in the History of Labour,* pp. 250–271. New York: Basic, 1964.

Holroyd, Michael. *Bernard Shaw: The Search for Love.* New York: Random House, 1988.

Jenkins, Thomas P. "The American Fabian Movement." *Western Political Quarterly,* 1 (June 1948), pp. 113–123.

Kessler-Harris, Alice. *Out of Work: A History of Wage-Earning Women in the United States.* New York: Oxford University Press, 1982.

Lane, Ann J. "Women in Society: A Critique of Frederick Engels." In Berenice A. Carroll, ed., *Liberating Women's History: Theoretical and Critical Essays,* pp. 4–25. (Urbana: University of Illinois Press, 1976).

Leaf, Murray J. *Man, Mind, and Science: A History of Anthropology.* New York: Columbia University Press, 1979.

Lerner, Gerda. *The Woman in American History.* Menlo Park, Calif.: Addison-Wesley, 1971.

Levy, David W. *Herbert Croly of The New Republic: The Life and Thought of an American Progressive.* Princeton: Princeton University Press, 1985.

Lipow, Arthur. *Authoritarian Socialism in America: Edward Bellamy and the Nationalist Movement.* Berkeley: University of California Press, 1982.

McBriar, A. M. *Fabian Socialism and English Politics, 1884–1918.* Cambridge: Cambridge University Press, 1962.

May, Henry F. *Protestant Churches and Industrial America.* New York: Octagon, 1963.

Morgan, Arthur E. *Edward Bellamy.* New York: Columbia University Press, 1944.

Morgan, Lewis H. *Ancient Society, or Researches in the Lines of Human Progress from Savagery Through Barbarism to Civilization.* New York: Holt, 1878.

Newton, Bernard. *The Economics of Francis Amasa Walker: American Economics in Transition.* New York: Kelley, 1968.

Payne, Elizabeth Anne. *Reform, Labor, and Feminism: Margaret Dreier Robins and the Women's Trade Union League.* Urbana: University of Illinois Press, 1988.

Persons, Stow. *American Minds: A History of Ideas.* New York: Holt, 1958.

Persons, Stow, ed. *Evolutionary Thought in America.* New Haven: Yale University Press, 1950; New York: Braziller, 1956.

Pleck, Elizabeth. *Domestic Tyranny: The Making of Social Policy Against Family Violence from Colonial Times to the Present.* New York: Oxford University Press, 1987.

Resek, Carl. *Lewis Henry Morgan: American Scholar.* Chicago: University of Chicago Press, 1960.

Rhodehamel, Josephine De Witt and Raymond Francis Wood. *Ina Coolbrith: Librarian and Laureate of California.* Provo, Utah: Brigham Young University Press, 1973.

Riesman, David. *Thorstein Veblen: A Critical Interpretation.* New York: Seabury, 1960.

Robertson, J. M. *A History of Free Thought in the Nineteenth Century.* London: Watts, 1929; London: Dawsons, 1969.

Russett, Cynthia Eagle. *Sexual Science: The Victorian Construction of Womanhood.* Cambridge: Harvard University Press, 1989.

Schlesinger, Elizabeth Bancroft. "The Nineteenth-Century Woman's Dilemma and Jennie June." *New York History,* 42 (October 1961), pp. 365–379.

Seretan, L. Glen. *Daniel DeLeon: The Odyssey of an American Marxist.* Cambridge: Harvard University Press, 1979.

Singer, Charles. *A History of Biology: A General Introduction to the Study of Living Things,* rev. ed. New York: Schuman, 1950.

Spann, Edward K. *Brotherly Tomorrows: Movements for a Cooperative Society in America, 1820–1920.* New York: Columbia University Press, 1989.

Stansell, Christine. *City of Women: Sex and Class in New York, 1789–1860.* New York: Knopf, 1986.

Stanton, Elizabeth Cady. *Eighty Years and More: Reminiscences, 1815–1897.* New York: Unwin, 1898; New York: Schocken, 1971.

Stineman, Esther Lanigan. *Mary Austin: Song of a Maverick.* New Haven: Yale University Press, 1989.

Stubbe, Hans. *History of Genetics: From Prehistoric Times to the Rediscovery of Mendel's Laws,* T. R. W. Waters, trans. Cambridge: MIT Press, 1972.

Talbot, Marion and Lois K. M. Rosenberry. *The History of the American Association of University Women, 1881–1931.* Boston: Houghton Mifflin, 1931.

Thomas, John L. *Alternative America: Henry George, Edward Bellamy, Henry Demarest Lloyd and the Adversary Tradition.* Cambridge, Mass.: Belknap, 1983.

Weinberg, Julius. *Edward Alsworth Ross and the Sociology of Progressivism.* Madison: The State Historical Society of Wisconsin, 1972.

Wells, Ida B. *Crusade for Justice: The Autobiography of Ida B. Wells.* Alfreda M. Duster, ed. Chicago: University of Chicago Press, 1970.

Wiener, Philip P. *Evolution and the Founders of Pragmatism.* Cambridge: Harvard University Press, 1949.

Wilson, R. Jackson, ed. *Darwinism and the American Intellectual: A Book of Readings.* Homewood, Ill.: Dorsey, 1967.

Wilson, R. Jackson. *In Quest of Community: Social Philosophy in the United States, 1860–1920.* New York: Wiley, 1968.

Wright, Gwendolyn. *Moralism and the Model Home: Domestic Architecture and Cultural Conflict in Chicago, 1873–1913.* Chicago: University of Chicago Press, 1980.

3. The Book Years

Bliss, William D. P. and Rudolph M. Binder, eds. *The New Encyclopedia of Social Reform* . . . . Enlarged and revised edition. London and New York: Funk and Wagnalls, 1908.

Boardman, Philip. *Patrick Geddes: Maker of the Future.* Chapel Hill: University of North Carolina Press, 1944.

Cantor, Milton and Bruce Laurie, eds. *Class, Sex, and the Woman Worker.* Westport, Conn.: Greenwood, 1977.

Dall, Caroline H. *The College, the Market, and the Court; or, Woman's Relation to Education, Labor, and Law.* Boston: Lee and Shepard, 1867.

Dorfman, Joseph. *The Economic Mind in American Civilization,* vol. 3, *1865–1918.* New York: Viking, 1949.

—— *Thorstein Veblen and His America.* New York: Viking, 1934.

Dorr, Rheta Childe. *What Eight Million Women Want.* Boston: Small, Maynard, 1910.

DuBois, Ellen Carol. "Working Women, Class Relations, and Suffrage Militance: Harriot Stanton Blatch and the New York Woman Suffrage Movement." *Journal of American History,* 74 (June 1987), pp. 34–58.

Easton, Barbara. "Feminism and the Contemporary Family." In Nancy F. Cott and Elizabeth H. Pleck, eds., *A Heritage of Her Own: Toward a New Social History of American Women,* pp. 555–577. New York: Simon and Schuster, 1979.

Ekirch, Arthur A., Jr. *Progressivism in America: A Study of the Era from Theodore Roosevelt to Woodrow Wilson.* New York: New Viewpoints, 1974.

Gould, Lewis L., ed. *The Progressive Era.* Syracuse, N.Y.: Syracuse University Press, 1974.

Irwin, Inez Haynes. *The Story of the Woman's Party.* New York: Harcourt, Brace, 1921.

Lippmann, Walter. *Drift and Mastery: An Attempt to Diagnose the Current Unrest.* New York: Kennerley, 1914; Englewood Cliffs, N.J.: Prentice-Hall, 1961.

Lowie, Robert H. and Leta Stetter Hollingsworth. "Science and Feminism." *The Scientific Monthly,* 3 (September 1916), pp. 277–284.

Mairet, Philip. *Pioneer of Sociology: The Life and Letters of Patrick Geddes.* London: Humphries, 1957.

Marsh, Margaret S. *Anarchist Women, 1870–1920.* Philadelphia: Temple University Press, 1981.

Parsons, Elsie Clews. *Family: An Ethnographical and Historical Outline with Descriptive Notes, Planned as a Text-book for the Use of College Lectures and of Directors for Home-reading Clubs.* New York: Putnam's, 1906.

Rader, Benjamin G. *The Academic Mind and Reform: The Influence of Richard T. Ely in American Life.* Lexington: University of Kentucky Press, 1966.

Rossiter, Margaret W. *Women Scientists in America: Struggles and Strategies to 1940.* Baltimore: Johns Hopkins University Press, 1982.

Schneider, Herbert W. *A History of American Philosophy.* New York: Columbia University Press, 1946.

Stocking, George W., Jr. *Race, Culture, And Evolution: Essays in the History of Anthropology.* New York: Free Press, 1968.

Thelen, David P. "Social Tensions and the Origins of Progressivism." In Gerald N. Grob and George A. Billias, eds., *Interpretations of American History: Patterns and Perspectives,* vol. 2, 3d ed., pp. 232–246. New York: Free Press, 1978.

Wishy, Bernard. *The Child and the Republic: The Dawn of Modern American Child Nurture.* Philadelphia: University of Pennsylvania Press, 1968.

4. The Forerunner Years

Brady, Kathleen. *Ida Tarbell: Portrait of a Muckraker.* New York: Seaview/Putnam, 1984.

Conlin, Joseph R., ed. *The American Radical Press, 1880–1960,* 2 vols. Westport, Conn.: Greenwood, 1974.

Conway, Jill. "The Woman's Peace Party and the First World War." In J. L. Granatstein and R. D. Cuff, eds., *War and Society in North America,* pp. 52–65. Toronto: Nelson, 1971.

Degen, Mary Louise. *The History of the Woman's Peace Party.* Baltimore: Johns Hopkins University Press, 1939.

Fishbein, Leslie. *Rebels in Bohemia: The Radicals of The Masses, 1911–1917.* Chapel Hill: University of North Carolina Press, 1982.

Schwarz, Judith. *Radical Feminists of Heterodoxy: Greenwich Village, 1912–1940.* Lebanon, N.H.: New Victoria, 1982.

Schwarz, Judith, Kathy Peiss, and Christina Simmons. " 'We Were a Little Band of Willful Women': The Heterodoxy Club of Greenwich Village." In Kathy Peiss and Christina Simmons, eds., *Passion and Power: Sexuality in History,* pp. 118–137. Philadelphia: Temple University Press, 1989.

Sochen, June. *Movers and Shakers: American Women Thinkers and Activists, 1900–1970.* New York: Quadrangle, 1973.

—— *The New Woman: Feminism in Greenwich Village, 1910–1920.* New York: Quadrangle, 1972.

Trimberger, Ellen Kay. "Feminism, Men, and Modern Love: Greenwich Village, 1900–1925." In Ann Snitow, Christine Stansell, and Sharon Thompson, eds., *Powers of Desire: The Politics of Sexuality,* pp. 131–152. New York: Monthly Review Press, 1983.

5. The Last Years

Becker, Susan D. *The Origins of the Equal Rights Amendment: American Feminism Between the Wars.* Westport, Conn.: Greenwood, 1981.

Brown, Dorothy M. *Setting a Course: American Women in the 1920s.* Boston: Twayne, 1987.

Kennedy, David M. *Birth Control in America.* New Haven: Yale University Press, 1970.

Ware, Susan. *Holding Their Own: American Women in the 1930s.* Boston: Twayne, 1982.

Index